Romania in Turmoil

Romania
in Turmoil

A contemporary history

MARTYN RADY

IB Tauris & Co Ltd
Publishers
London · New York

For Letty

Published in 1992 by
IB Tauris & Co Ltd
45 Bloomsbury Square
London WC1A 2HY

175 Fifth Avenue
New York
NY 10010

In the United States of America
and Canada distributed by
St Martin's Press
175 Fifth Avenue
New York
NY 10010

A CIP record for this book is available from the British Library

Library of Congress catalog card number: available
A full CIP record is available from the Library of Congress

ISBN 1-85043-500-6

Photoset in North Wales by
Derek Doyle & Associates, Mold, Clwyd.
Printed and bound in Great Britain by
WBC Print Ltd, Bridgend, Mid-Glamorgan.

CONTENTS

DIAGRAMS AND MAPS

PREFACE

This work attempts to achieve two separate but interrelated purposes: to provide an authoritative account of events in Romania during and after the 1989 revolution; and to place these developments in their broader historical context. As a 'contemporary history' it seeks therefore to unite not only the present and the past but also the different disciplines of historical writing and of contemporary political analysis.

I am particularly grateful for the help and support of colleagues and visitors to the School of Slavonic and East European Studies, and to the many people in Romania who have given me their time on the understanding that I would not needlessly cite them by name. Representatives of the NSF, NPP, NLP, *Vatra* and HDUR have all assisted in the making of this book. To Veronica I owe especial thanks both for her patience and for her observations.

Martyn Rady
June 1991

1

THE POLITICS OF ILLUSION

The Romanians are an ancient people and claim, probably with some justice, to be one of the oldest nations in Europe. As their Latin language suggests, they are descended from the Romans of antiquity. Roman legionaries and settlers were established as colonists in the Balkans and in the Carpathian province of Dacia during the first centuries of the Christian era. There they remained, enduring the passage of Goths, Slavs, and other newcomers. Doubtless, the purity of the original Roman stock was diluted by intermarriage both with later invaders as well as with the original Thracian population of the region. Nevertheless, the Romanian language still bears eloquent testimony to the ancestry of the Romanian people and to their continuous presence in the Balkan region. Speakers of French or Italian will find little difficulty in learning Romanian or, with the help of a pocket dictionary, in reading Romanian newspapers.

Romanians take considerable pride in their ancestry. There is scarcely a museum in Romania which does not include a *lapidarium* of classical headstones and foreign historians who impugn the Romanians' antiquity as a nation customarily receive short shrift. Only in recent years has an exaggerated historiography, emanating from the upper reaches of the communist government, put forward the view that the Romanians are the pure descendants of the prehistoric Thracian (or Dacian) population of the Carpathians, who acquired a Latin language from the Roman conquerors but who never interbred with them. Implausible though this theory is, it has helped to prolong the popular conviction among Romanians that they are an 'exceptional' people with a unique ancestry and special national destiny.

Although the Romanian people have a long history, the Romanian state is a new creation. In the middle ages, two shadowy Romanian principalities, Moldavia and Wallachia, survived on the edge of the

1

Carpathians. Both were overrun by the Ottoman Turks in the fourteenth and fifteenth centuries and they remained under Turkish suzerainty for almost half a millenium.

To begin with, the Ottomans were content to leave the government of the principalities in the hands of native princes, providing that these fought on the Turkish side and paid an annual tribute. In the eighteenth century, however, it became usual for the office of prince to be auctioned off by the Sultan to wealthy members of the Greek merchant community in Constantinople. The Phanariot princes (so called because many of them came from the Greek *phanar* quarter of Constantinople) recovered their costs – and more besides – by levying additional taxes on the already hard-pressed and impoverished Romanian population. Once they had enriched themselves out of the business of government, the Phanariots customarily returned to Constantinople. In the period from 1711 to 1821 Moldavia and Wallachia had altogether some 80 different rulers. It was at this time that the famous Romanian proverb was coined, 'A change of rulers is the joy of fools'.

Since Turkish rule was indirect, there were few attempts to convert the population to Islam. Thus, the orthodox faith which the Romanians had embraced in the middle ages, has continued right up to the present time to be the dominant religion. In keeping with the traditions of Balkan orthodoxy, the Romanian language was written in Cyrillic lettering until the middle years of the nineteenth century. Even today, the influence of the older script may be discerned in right-wing publications which make their appeal to national traditions and culture. Their headlines are frequently composed in a curious runic form which combines both Cyrillic and Roman elements; their contents are invariably as obscure.

Moldavia and Wallachia recovered a measure of autonomy during the first half of the nineteenth century and, with the help of the great powers, hastened towards statehood and political unity. In 1859 the two principalities were joined together under the leadership of Colonel Alexander Cuza. Seven years later, they acquired as their common ruler the German prince, Karl or Carol of Hohenzollern-Sigmaringen, whose descendant, King Michael, is the present sovereign. In 1878, Hohenzollern Romania gained full independence at the Congress of Berlin and, three years later, the status of a kingdom.

The kingdom of Romania did not include at this stage the entirety of the Romanian people. Three million Romanians were cut off from their kinsfolk in Transylvania, which comprised until 1918 a part of the Habsburg kingdom of Hungary. A further two million dwelled in Bessarabia, a slice of Moldavia which had been seized by the Russians in 1812. Smaller groups also lived in the Dobrudja, a part of Bulgaria, and in the Bukovina, which was ruled from distant Vienna. With the growth of national self-consciousness in the nineteenth century, the political demand grew for the freeing of these 'Romanian lands' from foreign oppression and for their unification with the independent kingdom of Romania.

Romania joined the First World War in 1916 on the side of the Entente powers. In the negotiations preceding her entry, Romania had been promised considerable allied military help to be followed by massive territorial rewards in Eastern Europe. Aid from the West was not, however, forthcoming. The Romanian army had therefore to face the combined assaults of the Germans, Austrians, Hungarians and Bulgarians largely unassisted. Accordingly, most of the country was rapidly occupied and the seat of government had to be transferred from Bucharest to the crowded and typhus-ridden city of Iasi. In order to protect its southern flank, the Russian high command was obliged to divert some of its own forces from the Eastern Front to the Romanian theatre. Russian frustration at the speed of Romania's defeat expressed itself in the common conviction that Romanian military regulations permitted officers to wear make-up (which they did not), and in the repetition of an old insult about Romanians: 'des hommes sans honneur, des femmes sans pudeur, des fleurs sans odeur, des titres sans valeur.'

Following the collapse of Russia in 1917, Romania was obliged to sue for peace with Germany and Austria. Nevertheless, among the western allies, Romania's reputation remained remarkably good. This was in part due to the publicity surrounding Queen Marie of the Romanians, the granddaughter of Queen Victoria. Marie's spirited defence of Romanian interests, and the international acclaim she received for her wartime activities as a nurse, ensured a flow of sympathy towards her adopted nation. On the morrow of the allied victory, George V gave her his personal commitment that 'Romania will not be forgotten'. (As befitted the theatrical Marie, the message was dropped to her by aeroplane.)

Allied support for Romania derived, however, from more than just sentimentality. The commitment of the Romanian government to resisting the spread of the Bolshevik contagion from neighbouring Russia made the kingdom seem a European necessity to the victorious powers. There were thus few allied objections when in the winter of 1918 Romanian troops entered Transylvania, claiming the territory on behalf of *Romania Mare*, the Greater Romania. Shortly afterwards, Romanian troops occupied Budapest and put to flight the Hungarian communist government of Bela Kun.

The allied negotiators at the Paris Peace Conference endorsed most of the Romanian territorial claims, seeing them as justified both strategically and by the principle of national self-determination. Transylvania, Bessarabia, the Dobrudja and the Bukovina were accordingly ceded to Romania on the grounds that the Romanians comprised the majority population in these regions. As a consequence of the peace treaties worked out in Paris, Romania more than doubled in size: from about 130,000 square kilometres and a population of just under eight million before the war, to 300,000 square kilometres and 15½ million persons in 1920. The acquisition of these new territories, although bringing a substantial minority population, ensured that for the first time in their history the Romanian people were gathered together in a national state of their own.

Nevertheless, Romania rested uncertainly in its new borders. Throughout the interwar period, Hungarian politicians continued to nurse claims on Transylvania, arguing that this territory had belonged to the Hungarian state since the tenth century, and that a historical claim outweighed the principle of national self-determination. Eventually, Hungarian diplomacy prevailed and in the Vienna Diktat of 1940 the northern part of Transylvania was returned by Hitler to Magyar rule. The restoration was accompanied by several atrocities and by the enforced deportation of many hundreds of Romanian civil servants. In the same year, Bessarabia was acquired by Soviet Russia and was, as part of Hitler's deal with Stalin, incorporated within the USSR as the Moldavian Soviet Socialist Republic. But whereas Transylvania was returned entirely to Romanian control at the end of the Second World War, Bessarabia remained both a Soviet republic and a source of intense Romanian grievance.

For much of Romanian history, therefore, nationhood and statehood have not coincided. Although Romanians comprise one of Europe's oldest nations, their state is a modern creation and is, like Yugoslavia and Czechoslovakia, essentially a product of this century's diplomacy. In a sense, the Romanian nation has been left a political orphan by the vicissitudes and experiences of the past. In their behaviour Romanians still frequently betray elements of precocity and sensitivity towards their identity as is characteristic of those who have been deprived of their parents at a formative stage. They are, thus, fiercely patriotic and reluctant to criticize their country in the presence of outsiders. They are ready to argue, against all evidence to the contrary, that their recent forbears were the inventors of the aeroplane, of the jet engine and of the laser beam. Romanian 'exceptionalism' thus retains a powerful appeal despite the country's recent descent to the condition of a third world despotism.

The border revisions of 1940, which deprived Romania of Bessarabia and of northern Transylvania, have added a sense of fragility to the Romanian state. Still today, Romanians are apt to perceive themselves as a Latin island threatened by 'a sea of Slavs' on the one side and by 'Asiatic Magyars' on the other. In this respect, they share with the Hungarians a sense of national beleaguerment and of isolation in Europe.[1] Among Romanians, popular patriotism has often broken down into outbursts of xenophobia directed against their Russian and Hungarian neighbours. Since there is also a substantial Hungarian ethnic minority in Transylvania, this group has often borne the brunt of intolerance. Even in the 1990s, otherwise intelligent Romanians hold firm to the belief that the Hungarians of Transylvania are disloyal and that the Hungarian state is plotting with their connivance to annex the western part of Romania.

Romanians' distrust of their neighbours has since the nineteenth century been accompanied by an ambivalent attitude towards western Europe. The period of national unification saw the widespread adoption in Romania of western cultural and political norms. Owing to the linguistic kinship between the French and the Romanians, as well as to the diplomatic support given by Napoleon III, France provided an important pattern. Prince Cuza, the first joint ruler of Moldavia and Wallachia, sanctioned his political actions with the Napoleonic device of the fraudulent plebiscite and modelled his own facial appearance on the French Emperor's whiskers. More lastingly, Bucharest was substantially rebuilt with the assistance of French architects and sculptors so as to form 'the Paris of the Balkans'. In imitation of the French capital, radiating boulevards were driven through the city. (It was only after the First World War, however, that Romanians felt entitled to construct their own Arc de Triomphe as the centrepiece.) In the course of the nineteenth-century development of Bucharest, the winding streets inherited from the period of Turkish rule were replaced with wide, tree-lined avenues and imposing neo-classical buildings: the Atheneum, Royal Palace, University, National Museum and the curiously conceived Palace of the Post Office. Similar transformations took place in provincial cities, most notably in Constanta and Iasi.

During the same period, French classical and modern literature was enthusiastically received and read by the educated classes. Corneille, Racine, Voltaire and Lamartine formed a staple literary diet and were consulted both in translation and in the original text. Romanian students frequently interrupted their university studies to make a pilgrimage to Paris and to bathe in the springs of French culture and learning. The visitor to modern-day Bucharest will be impressed by the wealth of nineteenth-century editions of French *belle lettres* still available for purchase on the shelves of second-hand bookshops. A sterner literature, the *Code Napoleon*, was adopted in the 1860s as the foundation of Romanian law.

Political institutions were similarly based on French, or at least on Francophone, precedents. The constitution adopted in 1866 was modelled on the Belgian Charter of 1831. It provided for trial by jury, for liberty of assembly and of the press, and for free, compulsory education. The constitution additionally imposed constraints on royal government (which were indeed upheld by a Supreme Court in several notable judgements) and allowed for two legislative houses, a Senate and a Chamber of Deputies. Political parties, a conservative 'right' and a liberal 'left', took up their place in the new parliament, following the procedures of debate commonly adhered to in western legislatures. Only rarely was the prolonged oratory of the deputies interrupted by gunfire.

The imitation of the West was, nevertheless, greeted with profound dismay even in educated circles. During the nineteenth century there emerged in Romania a powerful philosophical school which deplored the 'false orientation in our modern culture'[2] and called for the restoration of the traditional values of the Romanian peasantry. In place of economic and political modernization, the 'peasant populist school' advocated a rural democracy based on village meetings, and a rustic economy consisting of husbandry and cottage industry. The populists extolled the 'native genius' of the Romanian people, as epitomized in their customs and crafts, and sought the roots of Romanian nationhood in the ancestral soil of the countryside. They thus rejected both 'the thorny road of capitalist industrialism' and the indiscriminate adoption of West European values.

In their defence of traditional Romanian virtues, the populists inveighed against the urban classes for sustaining an artificial culture at the expense of the peasantry. As one advocate, Titu Maiorescu, put it in the 1860s:

> The culture of our higher classes is hollow and worthless, and the gap between it and that of the average people gets wider and wider. The only thing that is real in our society is the Romanian village, and its dwellers are burdened with paying for the upper classes' phantasmagoria. For it is from peasant hard work that comes the money to build and maintain the fictitious structure called Romanian culture.[3]

Peasant populism, with its stress on the uniqueness of Romanian rural culture, coincided closely with the belief in Romanian 'exceptionalism'. It thus struck a powerful chord and continued in a variety of forms to retain influence as a political and social doctrine until well into the twentieth century. On the one hand, it sustained Romanian socialism by its championship of the labouring classes and by its condemnation of the 'urban interest', which might easily be associated with capitalism. On the other, it lent to anti-Semitism since the cosmopolitan elite which most readily embraced western culture was predominantly perceived of as Jewish. The legacy of peasant populism may be felt today in the distrust of countryfolk for the town, in the mutual suspicion of the lower and the educated classes, and in the widespread repudiation of specifically 'western' forms of organization.

The success of populism as a political and social doctrine owed much to the illusory nature of Romania's westernization. As the populists were fond of pointing out, there could be few greater contrasts between what the new Romania claimed to be and what it really was. As Maiorescu explained in his powerful critique of the 'falsehood' of Romanian public life:

> Before we had enough teachers, we built elementary schools in villages ... thus falsifying public education. Before we had any culture, we created literary societies and clubs, thus cheapening the spirit of cultural association. Before we had even the shadow

of original scientific activity, we created the Romanian Academic Society with branches for linguistics, history, archaeology, natural sciences etcetera, thus falsifying the idea of academic life. Before we had any artists to speak of, we created the conservatoire; before we had even one painter of talent, we set up the Fine Arts School; and before we had even one playwright, we established the National Theatre, thus demeaning all these forms of culture.

Maiorescu's attack on the superficiality of contemporary Romanian culture was widened by Constantin Dobrogeanu-Gherea. According to this early socialist thinker, the illusory qualities of Romanian public life affected not just the cultural sphere but extended to politics and society as well. There was, thus, a disparity between what he called the *pays legal* and the *pays reel*, between the set of laws and institutions bestowed upon the country by its ruling class and the primitive conditions and scant freedoms endured by the population as a whole. Dobrogeanu-Gherea explained this phenomenon as the consequence of economic retardation and of incomplete and overhasty moderniz-ation. As he saw it, the mixture of the old and the new had led to immense distortions in the fabric of Romanian life and to a new condition of misery on the land, which he characterized as *neoiobagia* or 'neo-feudalism'.

Peasants accounted for five million of the total Romanian population of six million in 1900 and Dobrogeanu-Gherea's concern for their plight may be easily understood. The peasantry had been freed from the worst excesses of manorial serfdom in the late eighteenth century, after which time bondage and the *ius primae noctis* only applied to a few categories of Gypsy.[4] Nevertheless, conditions on the land remained grim, particularly since landowners extracted arduous labour services from the peasants in return for granting them tenancies. Among the worst off were the Moldavian peasants. In a vivid account, Constantin Golescu (1777–1828), a Wallachian nobleman, described the condition of the 'troglodytes' of the eastern plains:

These unrighteous practices [i.e. treatment of villagers], unheard of elsewhere in the world, have brought the unhappy inhabitants to such a state, that anyone who enters the so-called villages will see neither church nor house nor fence around the house, nor cart, nor ox, nor cow, nor fowl, nor patch sown for the family's food – in a word nothing; only some rooms in the earth ... Anyone who goes in sees nothing but a hole in the earth, which will hold a man with his wife and children around the hearth, and a chimney of basketwork plastered with dung, protruding from the surface of the ground. Behind the stove is another hole, through which he must escape in haste when he perceives that someone has come to his door; for he knows that it can only be sent to demand payment.

In similar vein, a French diplomat described the Moldavian peasantry in the 1830s as being, 'thin and emaciated, humble, submissive and ready to endure anything. Their hollow eyes, which they dare not raise, proclaim their slavery and absence of well-being'.[5]

Only in the mid-1860s – several years after Tsarist Russia – were labour obligations removed in their entirety and a start made at the distribution of rural land to the peasants. Nevertheless, the process of agrarian reform had the consequence of actually worsening conditions. Although landowners were compensated for losses, they were not obliged to surrender more than a portion of their estates. Invariably they selected for the peasantry the worst properties. Once the peasants had obtained freehold land of their own, they began to apply the tradition of partible inheritance which their previous tenancy agreements had disallowed. Plots were thus divided and subdivided up among children and grandchildren with the result that they rapidly became too small to sustain a livelihood. In order to survive, peasants often had to lease additional land from wealthy proprietors. The contracts which peasants entered into frequently obliged them to perform services for the landowner and to put up with the indignity of corporal punishment for misdemeanours.

Peasant exasperation was usually confined to rick-burning and the trampling of fences. Only rarely did it spill over into revolt. However, a serious uprising took place in 1907 and eventually claimed some 10,000 lives. Armed mobs of peasant rioters engaged in violent demonstrations for land, attacked manor houses, and vented their fury on such Jews as they could find. The revolt was suppressed with great brutality, but not before it had brought about the fall of the government, a near mutiny in the army, and strongly-worded protests in the international press. The 1907 uprising was Europe's last peasant *jacquerie* and, until 1989, the only spontaneous insurrection in recent Romanian history.

The impoverishment of the Romanian countryside was matched by a lack of industrial development and by the virtual absence of a Romanian commercial class. At the turn of the century, the industrial workforce in Romania numbered less than 200,000 persons, the majority of whom were employed in small workshops rather than in factories. Attempts by the government to build a modern manufacturing economy through the provision of credit and by protectionist measures failed to stimulate growth. State funds intended for industry were frequently diverted to companies which had previously bought the services of the ministry, or were siphoned off to financial institutions which, like the National Bank of Romania, were owned by the country's leading politicians.

As is common in underdeveloped countries, the most modern sectors of the Romanian economy – the railway service and the oil industry – were owned either by the government or by foreign investors. In 1914, therefore, native shareholding amounted to only one percent of the total capital in the Romanian oil business. The bulk of the remainder was provided by enterprises such as Standard Oil, Royal Dutch and Petrofina. Even so, Romanian oil output accounted in 1910 for less than 3 per cent of the world total. In contrast, railway construction showed some advance, amounting to 3000 kilometres of line by 1900. As today, however, most of this consisted of single track and it might take an oil cargo two weeks to travel the 200 kilometres from the refineries at Ploesti to the terminal at Constanta. It is salutary also to reflect that the current Romanian timetable is based on one originally devised at the end of last century, and that the present arcane system of ticket purchase has procedural precedents of similar antiquity.

Throughout the nineteenth century, the urban middle class consisted of largely the same elements as had been commercially active during the period of Turkish rule: Greeks, Germans, Armenians and Jews. These made up the class of shopkeepers, small traders, financiers and shipping brokers. Around 1900, these groups comprised up to a half of the total population of Bucharest. In some Moldavian towns, the Jewish commercial class was so numerous that signposts were written in Hebrew letters. The preponderant role of the Jews in money-lending, tavern-keeping and estate-stewardship led to frequent outbursts of anti-Semitism. As in 1907, peasants on the rampage were only too ready to vent out their personal frustrations on members of the Jewish community.

In the capital itself, the principal bourgeois employment among Romanians was the state bureaucracy. The mushroom growth of office-holding during the late nineteenth century owed much to political patronage and to the government's need to cultivate a reliable bank of supporters. As one leading commentator on this subject has suggested, the cooption of the educated classes into government service may well explain the tendency towards political conformity and dissimulation still evident among the Romanian bourgeoisie and professional classes. After all, when one's employment is dependent upon political preferment, it makes little sense to adopt an overtly critical position on aspects of public policy.[6]

The corruption of the bureaucracy represented only one aspect of the debasement of civil life in Romania. Although the country had a liberal constitution and an elected parliament, political power was both won and exercised in an arbitrary fashion. Typically, the king would choose the government. Once in power, the new ministry would hold or, in the expressive Romanian idiom, 'make' elections, which invariably recorded a vote in its favour. The politicians and party excluded from power by this arrangement would wait upon the government's fall from royal favour, while intriguing against it and organizing street demonstrations as evidence of their own support. The collapse of the incumbent ministry would invariably be followed by the promotion of the opposition to power and by the 'making' of fresh elections.

The electoral law which proved so easy to manipulate, had been passed in 1884. On paper at least, it was one of the most liberal in Europe, for it extended the franchise to over a million taxpayers: about a half of the active male population. However, a complex method of dividing the electorate into three 'houses' on the basis of taxation, deprived the majority of influence and worked to the advantage of the wealthy. It has been calculated that in the elections of 1911 the top landowners, 0,2 per cent of the population, controlled 41 per cent of the seats in the legislature. Under these circumstances, the ballot could be determined by the government in power simply by promising financial rewards and political advancement to a few thousand voters. Any shortfall in votes could usually be made up for by surgical police actions aimed against the opposition's supporters.

During the nineteenth century, two separate political groupings emerged in Romania, the Conservatives and the National Liberals. Very broadly, the former was the party of the large landowners, and the latter was the party of the 'squirearchy', of the civil service and of the urban middle class. Thus, the Conservatives shied away from agrarian reform; the National Liberals pressed for further concessions to the peasantry and for increased state investment in business. The Liberals retained a more nationalist approach to politics and the economy, as epitomized in their slogan 'By ourselves, alone', and they were strongly opposed to foreign investment in the country's fledgling industry.

The electoral system upset the development of these two political parties and hindered the emergence of a parliamentary system of government. The key to success at the polls was evidently not the presentation of attractive policies before the electorate, but the favour of the king and the dispensing of electoral bribes. Under these conditions, personal contacts and patronage mattered more than party programmes and political reputation. Accordingly, both Conservatives and National Liberals sought to construct their own networks of clients within the state bureaucracy, handing out jobs in return for support. Leading politicians frequently built up personal followings of their own, which like the political machine run by the Bratianu family might be passed on through several generations. The permeation of party politics by individual loyalties led to a relentless process of fragmentation which made every government a fragile coalition of separate personal interests. Since the influence of the crown benefited from the weaknesses of the political parties, King Carol I kept the political 'merry-go-round' in constant circulation. Between 1901 and 1914 he appointed altogether six separate governments, alternating the party in power as many times.[7]

Students of Romanian public life discerned in its political institutions - the most extreme example of the tendency towards falsehood and illusion. The failure of the country to adopt European norms and its only superficial adherence to constitutional principles stood no more starkly revealed than in the practice of its domestic politics. As one early twentieth-century commentator put it:

> Unfortunately, our glorious urban institutions, for all their liberal-democratic techniques, are pure sham ... We have introduced democracy but with ballot-stuffing ... We have encouraged national industry, but not for the benefit of the rural population, as would have been right since they made the sacrifices, but for the benefit of politicians who are the pensioners of this national industry. We have put the

administration of the country not in the hands of a trained bureaucracy, but in the hands of the party and its partisans. In a word, we have aped the European bourgeoisie in form, but at bottom we have persisted in the sycophantic habits of the past. In this way we have transformed political life into a hopeless turmoil.[8]

It was in this condition of social and economic backwardness, ill concealed behind a veneer of political sophistication, that Romania entered upon its inheritance as a nation-state in 1918.

NOTES

1. This resemblance was noted by Miklos Kallay, a former prime minister of Hungary, in his autobiographical *Hungarian Premier* (Oxford: Oxford University Press, 1954), pp. 56–7.
2. Cited by Henry Roberts, *Rumania: Political Problems of an Agrarian State* (New Haven and London: Yale University Press and Oxford University Press, 1951), p. 144.
3. Titu Maiorescu, 'Against some Tendencies in Romanian Culture', *Romanian Sources*, vol. 3, part 1 (1977), p. 7.
4. Gypsy slavery was finally abolished in 1851.
5. Doreen Warriner, *Contrasts in Emerging Societies*, (Bloomington: Indiana University Press, 1965), pp. 144–5.
6. Michael Shafir, *Romania. Politics, Economics and Society* (London: Frances Pinter (Publishers), 1985), p. 147.
7. This figure includes the 'reconstructed' conservative ministry appointed in April 1912.
8. C. Radulescu-Motru, cited in Henry L. Roberts, *Rumania. Political Problems of an Agrarian State* (New Haven, Conn: Yale University Press, 1951), pp. 115–16. Radulescu-Motru was writing in 1924 after the introduction of full manhood suffrage.

2

THE CULTURE
OF VIOLENCE

In 1918 Europe's old empires fell apart and were replaced by a constellation of independent nation-states. In each of the new states, liberal constitutions were drawn up which allowed for parliamentary government, for multiparty politics, and for free elections based on the principle of full adult suffrage. Democratic politicians took their place at the forefront of public life and pledged themselves to removing both social injustice and the corruption of public life. Yet within the space of a few years, the new leaders were either discarded or 'transformed'. During the 1920s, authoritarian trends inherited from the previous century were resumed in much of Eastern Europe and political violence squeezed out parliamentary government. It only required the depression and the rise of the fascist alternative to democracy to set the region irretrievably in the direction of dictatorship.

Romania was one of the principal beneficiaries of the peace settlement which concluded the First World War. Her territory and population were doubled and she became a nation-state for the first time in her history. Romania did not, however, escape the general ruin. Despite the promise of the first years, the country rapidly returned to governmental corruption, to electoral malpractice and to sham constitutionalism. These features of interwar politics were compounded by a ferocious anti-Semitism and by a debased form of peasant populism. During the 1930s, democracy was completely abandoned in Romania and the country languished under the royal absolutism of Carol II. Carol's eventual failure admitted to power one of Europe's most unpleasant and least successful fascist dictatorships: the 'national legionary' government of the Iron Guard.

One of the principal difficulties attending interwar Romania was the national composition of the state. The boundaries of Romania had been substantially extended after 1918 to include Bessarabia, the

Bukovina, Transylvania and the Dobrudja, for each of these regions contained a predominantly Romanian population. However, substantial minority groups were also enclosed within the annexed areas. Bukovina and Bessarabia thus contained a sizeable number of Jews, Russians and Ukrainians. For its part, Transylvania had almost a million and a half Hungarians as well as some 500,000 Germans. Both of these groups had been settled in the region since the middle ages. So, although the kingdom of Romania had been reasonably homogeneous in its ethnic composition before the war, the new nation-state was notably diverse on account of the territories recently added to it. Altogether 30 per cent of the population of Greater Romania belonged to national minorities.

The response of the interwar Romanian governments to the challenge of ethnic diversity was to pretend on paper that a single national state existed while in practice doing all they could to assert Romanian national supremacy over the minorities. The constitution of 1923 thus included no safeguards for the non-Romanian communities and proclaimed in its first article that the state was 'unitary, national and Romanian'. In accordance with this principle, the provincial administration was heavily centralized and government nominees were appointed as prefects and mayors without any reference to the ethnic composition of the areas in which they served. No rights of local autonomy, through which minority groups might organize and advance themselves politically, were permitted. Public employment was likewise made dependent upon passing a qualification in the Romanian language and official attempts were even made to 'Romanize' surnames. The fiction was thus perpetrated that Romania was a nation-state akin to France, whereas a fairer analogy might have been to Belgium or to Switzerland.

Behind the scenes concerted attempts were put in train to disadvantage the minorities and force them into submission. As one leading politician put it in 1919, the intention was to secure for the Romanian element a position of unquestioned superiority.[1] In accordance with this aim, state funding was withdrawn from minority schools, businesses and properties owned by non-Romanians were frequently expropriated and non-Romanian civil servants were dismissed from their posts. Absurd discriminatory provisions were applied, such as the tax on shop signs not written in Romanian, the surcharge on accounts composed other than in the language of the state, and the obligation on non-Romanian children to attend Sunday morning classes in gymnastics.

The three groups which suffered the harshest discrimination were the Jews, the Hungarians, and the Germans. The Jews suffered severe disabilities, not least because the government practised a policy of refusing citizenship to Jewish residents and then sequestrating their assets on the grounds that they were aliens. Immediately after the war, local administrations connived in Jew-baiting and in the 1930s pogroms were organized with the assistance of the government and police. The deplorable anti-Semitism of these years had its roots in the populist philosophy of the nineteenth century and in the widespread resentment of Jewish 'vagabond capitalism' and 'cosmopolitanism'.[2] Some blame for the anti-Semitism of the interwar years must, however, attach to Nicolae Iorga, a historian and politician whose reputation in western academic circles remains extraordinarily high even today.[2] It is seldom appreciated that Iorga was the founder in 1910 of the National Democratic Party, the central platform of which was 'the solution of the Jewish question through the elimination of the Jews'. Even after he had forsworn racial extremism, Iorga's intellectual influence on the younger generation of anti-Semites remained formidable.

The Jews had always been scapegoats and their victimization in the interwar years formed part of a trend in public behaviour stretching back several centuries. By contrast, the Hungarians were the erstwhile masters of Transylvania, who had only recently been displaced from power by their former Romanian underlings. Originally in December 1918, representatives of the Romanian community in Transylvania had met in Alba Iulia and had promised 'complete national liberty for all the peoples which inhabit Transylvania', including the Hungarians. The collective rights of the non-Romanian peoples who dwelled in the region were additionally guaranteed in respect to education, cultural provision and linguistic usage.

The promises made at Alba Iulia were rapidly forgotten and no collective rights were extended to the minority population in Transylvania. Instead, Hungarians living in Transylvania were dismissed en masse from the local bureaucracy and from employment on the railways and in the postal service. Their jobs were given over to Romanians in such numbers that persons had to be specially brought in from Moldavia and Wallachia to fill the vacancies. The lands and endowments belonging to Hungarian churches and institutions were seized, while Hungarian-owned estates and businesses were either nationalized or confiscated outright. A combination of emergency regulations and of administrative gerrymandering prevented Hungarians from ever achieving a majority on local councils for most of the interwar years.

The Germans in Transylvania suffered similar penalties and were gradually frozen out of business and state employment. A particular source of German grievance was that their municipal administration was taken over entirely by Romanians. By 1934 there was not a single burgomaster left in any of the historic German cities of Transylvania. This affected the Germans greatly since they had always taken a keen interest in their local self-government. In the Saxon churches of Transylvania, the stone effigies of patricians and town councillors bore silent testimony to a deep tradition of civic responsibility nurtured over 800 years of German settlement.

The doctrine of the Romanian unitary state failed to take into account not only the minority populations but the strength and persistence of regional sentiment as well. The new territories added to the Romanian kingdom in 1918 were never entirely reconciled to the government in Bucharest. The population of the Dobrudja remained sufficiently unruly for the region to be placed under the direct rule of the Ministry of the Interior in the 1920s. Bessarabia, likewise, retained its own separate political parties and its own vicious brand of anti-Semitism. In Transylvania, the local Romanian politicians were particularly distrustful of the leaders in Bucharest, whom they regarded as self-seeking and 'Levantine'. The Transylvanian Romanians had been schooled in politics under the legalist rule of the Hungarians and they retained a respect for constitutional procedures and for individual rights. The notorious corruption of the ruling National Liberal Party and its practice of giving public offices in Transylvania to political supporters from outside the region, pushed the Transylvanian Romanians into opposition to the government. It was largely from this group that the leadership of the rival National Peasants Party was drawn.

Except for two brief periods, Romanian politics in the 1920s was dominated by the National Liberals. The Liberals were responsible for framing the 1923 Constitution, for introducing full manhood suffrage, and for implementing a new round of agrarian reform which stripped the old landowners of their remaining large estates. But, having passed these measures, the National Liberals drifted sharply to the right and took over the role of the now defunct Conservative Party. Instead of embarking upon additional measures of social and political reform, the Liberals clung to power for its own sake, using methods inherited from the prewar period. They hugely expanded the bureaucracy to include the new class of dispossessed landowners, and used the centralized system of local administration to develop a patronage network in the regions. Political rivals were dismissed from positions of influence both at a national and at a local level and replaced with clients of the ruling party. Popular discontent was contained by the ruthlessness of the security police (*siguranta*) belonging to the Ministry of the Interior, and by an almost continuous state of martial law.

In order to rally opinion, the National Liberals pursued a nationalist economic policy, inveighing against 'international capital' and passing legislation aimed against foreign-owned companies. Although this policy coincided with the National Liberal slogan of 'By ourselves, alone', it inflicted widespread damage on the country's fledgling industry. The obsession of the National Liberals with 'Romanian' control of the 'Romanian' economy prefigured Ceausescu's own special brand of autarchy.

Despite the introduction of universal suffrage, elections continued to be manipulated and 'made' by the government in power. Opposition candidates were frequently disqualified from standing for election or were subjected to physical intimidation to prevent them campaigning. On the eve of the ballot, the Ministry of the Interior would customarily order the arrest of thousands of known opponents, and communities unsympathetic to the government were frequently quarantined on 'medical' grounds. Typically also, the polling clerks and commissioners would be government nominees and the electoral register would be falsified. In rural areas, however, the electorate customarily deferred to the advice proferred them by the local priest and policeman, and little overt coercion was necessary.

The overall consequence of these irregularities was to give the government party a landslide in every election. Thus, in 1920 the ruling People's Party obtained 224 seats as against the National Liberals' 9. Following the appointment of a National Liberal ministry, the former opposition won 227 seats, and the previous government-party took only 12. The Liberals repeated their success in 1927. Just to make sure that they retained the edge over their rivals, once they were in power the National Liberals passed the 'premium law', according to which the party taking 40 per cent of the vote automatically obtained a majority of seats in the parliament.

The principal rival to the National Liberals was the National Peasants Party. The National Peasant opposition was dominated by a Transylvanian-Romanian leadership and was committed to freeing the country from the slough of corruption into which the Liberals had led it. The programme of the Peasants Party included investment in agriculture to help small farmers, the opening up of the country to foreign capital, and the decentralization of government. Despite its name, the party largely eschewed the peasant populism of the nineteenth century. During the 1920s it adopted a broadly pragmatic approach, refreshingly free from emotive allusions to the soil and to native genius. Nevertheless, National Liberal control of the apparatus of government meant that the Peasants Party was deprived of influence at the polls.

The National Liberals owed their success to the support of King Ferdinand (1914–27), who broadly shared their philosophy. Ferdinand consistently promoted Liberal politicians to office from which vantage point they could rig elections. Whenever dissatisfied with their performance, the king wheeled out the People's Party to teach the Liberals a lesson and allow them time to gather their wits. The People's Party had neither an ideology nor an organization and its leadership consisted solely of the confused General Averescu. Although Averescu perceived himself as the saviour of Romanian politics, his party operated almost entirely as a stalking-horse for the crown.

Ferdinand died in 1927 and was replaced by a regency council ruling in the name of his grandson, King Michael (born 1921). Along with Ferdinand went both the People's Party, which perished leaving no trace, and the confidence of the Liberal politicians. The National Peasants thereupon proceeded to discomfort the government by arranging massive demonstrations and by embarking upon a Mussolini-style 'March on Bucharest'. The rally turned out a fiasco since the Peasants Party leadership had made no provisions for the homeward travel of its supporters; it was left to the government to arrange the necessary rail transport. Nevertheless, the show of support helped to topple the National Liberals from power. In November 1928, a Peasant Party government led by Iuliu Maniu was appointed by the regency council. The next month, it held an election and won 316 seats as against the Liberals' 13. Although the scale of the vote (78 per cent of the poll) for the Peasants Party suggests that some chicanery may have taken place behind the scenes, the 1928 election is generally considered to have been the fairest and freest election in Romania during the interwar period.[3]

Once in power, the National Peasant government rapidly engaged upon the wholesale dismantling of the Liberals' patronage network.

The civil service was halved and the top layer of bureaucrats dismissed. The centralized structure of government was abolished and the country divided up into five semi-autonomous regions. The tariff wall protecting the national economy from imports was lowered and capital was admitted from abroad. Massive foreign loans were contracted to assist industrial development, and the few remaining legal obstacles on peasant agriculture were lifted. At the same time, the party leadership committed itself to the rule of law. As Prime Minister Maniu declared at his first cabinet meeting, 'Our first aim will be to give the principles of the Constitution their real meaning and to impart a character of strict legality to the working of the administration'. His ministry proved to be the least corrupt in all Romanian history. Although the government continued to use violent methods against political opponents and retained the *siguranta*, Maniu abolished censorship of the press and ended the state of martial law.

It was Maniu and the National Peasants' singular misfortune to be in power at a time of economic and constitutional crisis. The depression which overtook Europe after the Crash of 1929, brought about a collapse in agricultural prices and closed the door to foreign loans. The industries which had been gradually developing during the 1920s, most notably oil-extraction and metallurgy, were forced to cut back production as world demand dropped. Between 1930 and 1933 Romanian manufacturing output fell by over a third and mining production by a half. Reductions in wages led to strikes, which were often put down brutally; and factory closures prompted a return to the countryside, where the unemployed found neither work nor land.

The Peasants Party fell, however, on a moral and constitutional issue rather than an economic one. According to the terms of the 1923 constitution, the late King Ferdinand should have been succeeded by his son, Carol. Even as a young soldier, however, Carol had demonstrated his unsuitability for the crown by deserting his post at the front to wed a commoner, Zsi-Zsi Lambrino. The marriage was promptly annulled by the government, and Zsi-Zsi along with the young son sired by Carol was despatched to Paris. In 1921, Carol entered into a more fitting marriage with Princess Helen of Greece and fathered, in the same year, Prince (later King) Michael. Shortly afterwards, Carol deserted Helen of Greece and took up instead with a divorcée, who variously went under the names of Magda Wolf and Helen Lupescu. Lupescu's presumed Jewish-Hungarian origin, previous marriage to a cavalry officer, and rumoured promiscuity were sufficient to ensure her lover's exclusion from the throne by parliamentary act.[4]

In 1930, however, Carol returned from abroad and had himself proclaimed King of Romania. The nine-year-old Michael was thereupon deposed to make way for his father and given in compensation the meaningless title of Grand Voevode. Carol's restoration was connived at by the Peasants Party leadership, which gave the king the legal sanction he needed by revoking the parliamentary act of exclusion. Doubtless, Maniu and his colleagues hoped thereby to win the king's permanent friendship and the sort of support which Ferdinand had previously given his National Liberal allies. At the request of the ascetic Maniu, however, Carol's return was made conditional upon him giving up Lupescu and reconciling himself with Queen Helen.

True to form, Carol reneged on his part of the bargain. Lupescu was reintroduced to the palace, although for a time her presence was concealed behind curtained carriages and broad-brimmed hats. Upon discovery of the king's continued infidelity, Maniu resigned. The Peasants Party government collapsed shortly after in a welter of recrimination and disillusion, from which it never recovered. The fall of Maniu and of the Peasants Party government put effective end to even the semblance of responsible and democratic rule. To paraphrase a later historian, the conflict between democracy and dictatorship was ultimately resolved in Romania on the improbable issue of sexual morality.[5]

Having gained the throne, Carol undermined the structure of parliamentary government entirely. Resuming the methods of his predecessor and namesake, Carol I, he alternated governments at dizzying speed. Between 1930 and 1940 Romania had altogether 25 separate cabinets and 18 different prime ministers. The resumption of the 'merry-go-round' meant that the only focus of political stability in Romania was the crown, and Carol II exploited this situation for all it was worth. His appointees took over as prefects and civil servants, and a royalist 'youth movement' began the intimidation of political rivals with the help of the police. In 1930, martial law was resumed; and in 1932 the universities were temporarily closed owing to student protests. A few years later the routine telephone tapping of local calls was begun and the activities of the *siguranta*, aided now by Carol's own private police force, became increasingly intrusive. Eventually, the political parties disintegrated altogether in the centrifuge of royal policy. At the beginning of 1938, Carol felt sufficiently confident to inaugurate his own dictatorship as head of the 'National Renaissance Front'. A new constitution, which drew heavily on the governmental organization of Fascist Italy, sanctioned Romania's descent into royal absolutism. Characteristically, the constitution received massive popular endorsement in a plebiscite at which voting was both compulsory and open.

The 1930s did, however, witness a measure of industrial recovery. Oil and armaments provided the principal engines for economic growth, and the state acted as the main banker (using foreign funds which had been declared state property in 1931). The grant of monopoly rights, special tax concessions and protectionist tariffs led to a resumed growth in heavy industry. It also helped that Carol II was a principal shareholder in the two largest cartels. Between 1933 and 1938 steel production doubled and the factory workforce expanded by 50 per cent. The index of Romanian industrial production rose altogether during the 1930s by a half, which was no small achievement given the parlous condition of the international economy.

These impressive gains affected only a small part of the population, over 70 per cent of which still worked on the land. Indeed, the success of industry during the 1930s was largely achieved at the expense of the rural proletariat who lost out in government grants while contributing nevertheless to taxation. Although the peasantry had received additional pieces of land following the new wave of agrarian reform in the 1920s, the properties released for their use were insufficient to remedy the persistent landhunger. Three-quarters of peasant plots were under five hectares (12.5 acres), which was the contemporary benchmark for subsistence. Additionally, the apportionment of new land had been undertaken inequitably, with preference given to government supporters. As in the nineteenth and early twentieth centuries, therefore, agrarian discontent remained the nub of domestic politics.

During the 1920s a fascist movement emerged in Romania and gained considerable ground in the 1930s. Romanian fascism divided into two wings. The lesser evil was the National League of Christian Defence, which rested its programme on a crude anti-Semitism. Its popular power base was the Bukovina and Bessarabia, where there were strong traditions of Jew-baiting. In 1937, the National League briefly assumed political leadership in a coalition government installed by the king. The prime minister was the Transylvanian poet, Octavian

Goga, whose collections of romantic verse – full of soil and peasant values – are still lauded in Romania today. Goga devoted his time in office to organizing pogroms with the help of the police and to insulting the king's mistress on account of her supposedly Jewish origin. Carol dismissed him after six weeks in office, thus putting an end to the League's political ambitions.

The National League was rapidly overtaken as the principal fascist organization by the Legion of the Archangel Michael. The founder of the legionaries was Corneliu Codreanu, a disillusioned follower of Octavian Goga. Codreanu had been gaoled in 1923 for compiling a list of Jews to be murdered and it was during his confinement that he had his 'conversion' to the legionary doctrine. While at prayer in the prison chapel he was moved by a statue of the Archangel Michael to found a new paramilitary fascist organization, which forswore the parliamentary road to power and which was committed to ridding the fatherland of Jews and communists alike. Shortly after his release, Codreanu murdered the police chief of Iasi on the grounds that he had recently shielded several local Jews from assault. Codreanu used his subsequent trial as a platform for his anti-Semitism and was rewarded by the sympathetic magistrate with a sentence of several months' imprisonment. In 1930 Codreanu set up a military wing to the Legion, known as the Iron Guard or 'greenshirts'.

Although the National Peasants Party employed legionary units to intimidate working-class agitators, Codreanu's fascists were of only minimal political significance in the 1920s. However, the failure of the Peasants Party, in which the rural population had vested their hopes, resulted in a groundswell of support for the Legion of the Archangel. Attempts to ban the Legion once its mass following became apparent, resulted only in it reappearing under a different name and did nothing to diminish its appeal. In 1937 the Legion polled together with the National League a quarter of the votes cast, even though the election had been rigged against it. There can be little doubt that fascism exercised a powerful fascination for a substantial section of the Romanian population. In its anti-Semitic, anti-democratic and anti-communist ideology, the legionary movement shared common characteristics with European fascism as a whole. According to Codreanu, democracy was a Jewish device designed to 'break the spirit of the Romanian people' and hand the country over to the instruments of 'high finance'. In Codreanu's scheme, the individual had to take second place to the nation, which he defined as a 'historical entity whose life extends over centuries, its roots embedded deep in the mists of time and with an infinite future'.[6] Nevertheless, despite the obvious similarities between legionary and Nazi beliefs, the Iron Guard possessed a sufficient number of unique features to distinguish it from other contemporary right-wing movements.

The Iron Guard ideology owed much to the peasant populist movement of the nineteenth century, but with the rational element burnt out leaving behind only a malignant emotionalism. Although the legionary movement offered no solution to the landhunger, its thinking was firmly rooted in the rural masses. The legionaries extolled the earth from which Romanians derived their legendary strength. In their initiation to the legion, recruits were offered a handful of 'blood-drenched ancestral soil', by the acceptance of which they became 'new men' imbued with a higher level of Romanian consciousness. The legionaries delivered their appeal to 'the peasant and his plot' and 'the man with his hectare' and singled out primitive folk virtues, including illiteracy, for special praise.

The orthodox religion, which touched so deeply the Romanian peasantry, was firmly embraced by the movement, and the support of the priesthood, one of whose members even became a legionary prefect in 1940, contributed in turn to the popular appeal of the Iron Guard. Legionary ideologists boasted that theirs was 'the only political movement with a religious structure'. Meetings of the Iron Guard were usually opened by a prayer and were accompanied with fiery crosses and other religious symbols. Legionary emphasis on the ritual of Christ's Passion and on the drama of the Resurrection led in turn to a perverted ideology revolving around the notion of 'political crucifixion' and the cult of death. Each cell of the Iron Guard was organized as a 'nest' (*cuib*), in which was believed to reside not only the present members but the spirits of those yet to come and of those who had already departed this life. Rallies of the Iron Guard were thus frequently accompanied by the exhumation of dead comrades, whose corpses were given seats at banquets and other celebrations. Legionary hymns gave similar prominence to death and to the prospect of 'resurrection' within the nest:

> Legionary! Do not fear
> That you will die too young.
> For you die to be reborn
> And are born to die ...

With a smile on our lips
We look death in the eye.
For we are the death team
That must win or die.[7]

Or, as the legionary newspaper *Dacia* explained in 1940, 'The finest aspect of legionary life is death.'

The Iron Guard drew its main support from the peasantry, the members of which were impressed by its mystic ideology as well as by the labours of rural reconstruction undertaken by legionary volunteers. However, the Legion also had a substantial following among the professional classes, who were resentful of Jewish business, and among university students. The Iron Guard was emphatically not a movement of déclassé and socially marginalized elements. Like the *Vatra*, its successor movement in contemporary Romania, it carried an appeal among the educated classes quite out of proportion to the limited intellectual content of its ideology. In this respect, it is not inappropriate that one of the principal theoretical works of the Legion was entitled *Wooden Skulls*.

The Iron Guard was the most dynamic element in Romanian politics during the 1930s. A large part of King Carol's time was spent, therefore, in devising ways to outmanoeuvre the legionaries, either by instituting bans on their activities or by stealing their clothes. In imitation of the Legion, Carol instituted a 'strength through joy' movement and put his own supporters into paramilitary uniform. Meanwhile, legionary death squads variously assassinated leading politicians (including no less than four former or incumbent prime ministers) and prominent Jews, and the rank and file disrupted everyday life with mass rallies and pogroms. In order to defend themselves against the Iron Guard, the other political parties formed their own private armies and fought it out on the streets with suicidally-inclined legionaries. The result was a culture and cycle of violence which paralysed Romanian politics. Eventually, the king took the only way out available to him: in 1938 Codreanu and the top legionaries were arrested and 'shot while trying to escape'.[8]

Carol's triumph was short-lived. The German conquest of Eastern Europe obliged the king to come to terms with the legionaries, who had the ostensible support of the Nazis. Carol admitted Codreanu's successor, Horia Sima, to the government and committed Romania to the side of the axis powers. But the accommodation with fascism came too late. In 1940, Hitler commenced the dismemberment of Romania; part of the Dobrudja was given to Bulgaria; northern Transylvania was returned to Hungary; and, by terms previously agreed between Hitler and Stalin, the Soviet Union received Bessarabia and northern Bukovina. Carol's reputation could not survive these territorial losses. On 6 September 1940, he fled the country taking with him Lupescu and a priceless collection of old masters. He left behind his teenage son, Michael, who thereupon resumed the crown for a second time.

In the wake of Carol's departure, a pro-Nazi government was formed consisting primarily of Iron Guardists and legionary sympathisers. Its leadership consisted of Horia Sima and Marshal Antonescu, a former Army Minister who enjoyed Hitler's confidence. The 'National Legionary State' promptly commenced its rule by slaughtering Jews, political opponents and civil servants. In an ironic gesture, one of the Iron Guard's first victims was Professor Nicolae Iorga, whose anti-Semitic and nationalist philosophy had contributed to the intellectual underpinning of legionary ideology.

The legionary state introduced a condition of virtual anarchy to Romania. In theory, Marshal Antonescu was the supreme political leader of Romania. He was known as the *Conducator* or 'leader' (the Romanian equivalent of *Duce* or *Fuehrer*) and was treated to the same popular adulation as his Italian and German counterparts. Antonescu was, thus, (in a striking anticipation of Nicolae Ceausescu), 'the leader, visionary, philosopher, apostle, father-saviour, synthesis of Latin genius, personification of the Daco-Roman tradition, and superman of dizzying simplicity'.[9] Despite the pageantry and vocabulary attending the *Conducator*'s appearances, Antonescu exercised no control over the national and local legionary commanders. These continued a reign of terror and of indiscriminate murder.

In anticipation of his invasion of the Soviet Union, Hitler needed a stable Romania. The hectic atmosphere brought about by the legionary death squads undermined Romania's contribution to the war and exposed a part of the axis flank to easy Soviet attack. Accordingly, Antonescu was prevailed upon by Hitler to bring the Iron Guard to heel. In December 1940 the *Conducator* began to disarm legionary formations, merging them into the armed forces. The Iron Guard, which still believed it enjoyed German support, responded by launching a rebellion. After three days of bloody fighting, the Iron Guard was finally suppressed by the army and in January 1941 the 'Legionary State' was abolished. A military dictatorship under

Conducator Antonescu remained in power on the side of the axis powers until 1944.

The Iron Guard has been variously explained as the instrument of international capitalism, of the Germans, and of scheming politicians. The lure of the legionaries and the curious philosophy they expounded suggests, however, that the Iron Guard was not a superficial phenomenon but that it had its roots in a frustrated peasantry, in popular mysticism, and in the abject failure of all other forms of contemporary political life. As the leading historian of this period concluded, the Legion 'was the nemesis of all the false constitutionalism and pseudo-democracy which have been observed in the course of recent Romanian history'.[10]

NOTES

1. Iuliu Maniu, cited by C.A. Macartney, *Hungary and Her Successors. The Treaty of Trianon and Its Consequences 1919–1937* (Oxford: Oxford University Press, 1937), p. 285.
2. On Iorga's anti-Semitism, see W.O. Oldson, *The Historical and Nationalistic Thought of Nicolae Iorga*, (Boulder, and New York: Columbia University Press, 1973) pp. 84–8.
3. Klaus P. Beer, *Zur Entwicklung des Parteien- und Parlamentssystems in Rumanien 1928–1933*, vol. 1 (Frankfurt-Bern: Peter Lang 1983), pp. 261–4.
4. The couple eventually married in Brazil in 1947.
5. Hugh Seton-Watson, *Eastern Europe Between the Wars 1918–41*, 2nd edn (Cambridge: Cambridge University Press, 1946), p. 204.
6. C.Z. Codreanu, *For My Legionaries, the Iron Guard* (Madrid: Editura Libertatea 1976), pp. 304–12.
7. Barbara Jelavich, *History of the Balkans. The Twentieth Century* (Cambridge: Cambridge University Press, 1983), pp. 205–6.
8. Codreanu was in fact garrotted.
9. Eugen Weber and H. Rogger, *The European Right*, (Berkeley and Los Angeles: University of California Press, 1966), p. 567.
10. Henry L. Roberts, *Rumania. Political Problems of an Agrarian State*, (New Haven, Conn: Yale University Press, 1951), p. 232.

3

THE COMMUNIST TAKEOVER

In August 1944 the Romanian Communist Party had no more than a thousand members, making it one of the smallest in Europe. Four years later, its membership exceeded a million and the party was firmly in control of every aspect of public and private life. The rise to power of the Communist Party was due almost entirely to a single factor: the intervention of the Soviet Union in Romanian domestic politics. The communist and Soviet takeover was facilitated by the 'percentage agreement' concluded between Stalin and Churchill in October 1944, which permitted the USSR '90 per cent predominance' in Romania in return for Britain receiving a free hand in Greece.

The performance of the Romanian Communist Party during the interwar years was inauspicious. In 1921 the party had been founded at a socialist congress in Bucharest. The decision to set up a communist group was largely the work of police *agents provocateurs*, who had infiltrated the congress with the aim of identifying extremists. Once the vote to set up the party had been taken, the genuine enthusiasts were arrested.[1] Although the party recovered from this clumsy start, it never attracted more than a few thousand members in the interwar years. As is typical of most organizations where ambition outruns resources, the leadership spent most of its time engaged in bitter internal disputes. The factional rivalry within the party was frequently so intense that Moscow had to intervene, appointing its own creatures to the position of General Secretary.

The lack of appeal of the Communist Party in Romania may be variously explained. Firstly, the country did not have the large industrial workforce in which socialist ideas most commonly spread. Secondly, the party consisted disproportionately of 'non-Romanians'. Hungarians and Jews made up almost half of party membership in the 1930s; ethnic Romanians comprised less than a quarter. The internationalism of communist ideology and its promise of a just society may account for the support which the party claimed among members of persecuted minority groups. As a consequence, however, most Romanians perceived communism to be an alien creed, of interest only to 'foreigners'.

During the Second World War, the Communist Party was split by circumstances into separate groups, from which there emerged rival factions. Some communists, like Ana Pauker and Vasile Luca, had found refuge in the Soviet Union, where they constituted what would later be known as the 'Muscovite' wing of the party. The 'home communists', those who had stayed in Romania, were divided between the faction led by Gheorghe Gheorghiu-Dej, which was confined in the Romanian prison camp at Tirgu Jiu, and the group in hiding which formed the party secretariat. Even before the war was over, rivalry within the ranks of the 'home communists' had resulted in the elimination of the leader of the 'secretariat' by Gheorghiu-Dej's 'prison-communists'. The contest between the 'prison' and 'Muscovite' wings took, however, longer to resolve and was only finally settled in Gheorghiu-Dej's favour in 1952.

The events of 1944 contributed significantly to Gheorghiu-Dej's eventual triumph. After three years of fighting on the axis side, and the loss of a substantial number of troops at Stalingrad, the Romanian army was in retreat. In April 1944, Soviet forces crossed the frontier. In anticipation of defeat, King Michael organized a coup d'etat with the help of the palace guard and a coalition of opposition political leaders brought together to form a 'Patriotic Front'. On 23 August, the *Conducator*, Marshal Antonescu, was arrested and the king announced an armistice. Three days later, Michael declared war on Germany. As in 1989, the organizers of the 1944 'revolution' are believed to have had the support of the chiefs of the secret police.[2]

Among the politicians who comprised the Patriotic Front was Gheorghiu-Dej, who had escaped from prison a fortnight before the coup, and the new leader of the 'secretariat-communists', Lucretiu Patrascanu. Compared to the role undertaken by the king, Maniu and other democratic politicians, the communists played only an insignificant part in the coup. Nevertheless, by the time the exiles had returned to Romania in the baggage train of the Soviet army, the 'home communists' had already established themselves in positions of influence both within the government and in the new party organization.

Despite the Romanian change of sides, the Soviet army entered the country more in the form of an invader than an ally. The Russian troops behaved with brutality, marking their passage with an epidemic of syphilis. Once they had occupied Romania, the Soviets confiscated a large volume of industrial machinery which they shipped homewards under the guise of reparations payments. Later on some of this equipment was returned as the principal Soviet contribution to joint industrial ventures (or *Sovroms*) from which Moscow reaped 50 per cent of the profits.

To begin with, the communists took only a small number of places in the new government. King Michael aimed at building a broad coalition, consisting of the parties which had previously joined together in the Patriotic Front: the National Liberals, National Peasants, Social Democrats and Communists. The communists were, however, not content with a junior place in the new government. In February 1945, they accordingly engineered a political crisis. A rally in the capital was fired upon by 'unidentified gunmen' (they used, however, Soviet ammunition) and the prime minister was falsely accused by the communist leaders of having instigated the violence. In an intemperate broadcast, the premier replied to these charges and referred to his critics as 'foreigners without God or country'. His words were understood as insulting the predominantly Jewish and Hungarian origin of the leading communists. In response to this slur, their supporters organized a wave of violence and protest.

At this critical moment, Andreia Vishinsky, the Soviet Deputy Foreign Minister, visited Bucharest and demanded that the king replace the present ministry with a new communist-led coalition government. When Michael temporized, Vishinsky told him that the Soviet Union could not otherwise guarantee the sovereignty of Romania. Vishinsky meant by this that the USSR might annex the country in the same way as it had already incorporated the Baltic states. Michael reluctantly gave way to Vishinsky's demand. In order to demonstrate the advantages of cooperation, the Soviet Union announced the return of northern Transylvania to Romanian rule only days after the king's capitulation.[3]

The new coalition, installed in March 1945, consisted almost exclusively of communists and fellow-travellers. Most of the latter were organized in phantom parties, like the Ploughmens Front and the Union of Patriots, which were simply communist organizations under another name. Only a few genuinely democratic politicians were members of the new government and these were rapidly sidelined. Communists were appointed to the key ministries of defence, justice, the interior and the economy. The political parties not included within the coalition were subjected to considerable obstruction; their members were routinely arrested and their papers were closed down.

The phase of 'bogus coalition' continued for two years and survived King Michael's attempts to have it replaced by a genuine coalition. Eventually, in 1947 the remaining democratic politicians were arrested and their parties were wound up. The Social Democrats were forcibly merged with the Communist Party to form the Romanian Workers Party, and the phantom parties were rearranged under communist leadership as the Popular Democratic Front. The curtain fell on 30 December 1947, when King Michael was visited by Gheorghiu-Dej and by the Prime Minister, Petru Groza. While Groza threatened the Queen Mother with a pistol, Michael was forced to sign an act of abdication. On the same day, Romania was proclaimed a People's Republic and Michael left the country.

The communist takeover was accompanied by considerable violence aimed against political rivals. The security service and the Ministry of Justice were controlled at an early stage by the communists who used the police and the courts to intimidate opponents. After a much publicized but highly irregular trial, Marshal Antonescu was shot. With even less justice, the leaders of the National Peasants Party were imprisoned and Maniu received a life sentence. During 1946 and 1947 'state terror' reached its climax resulting in the execution of 60,000 persons. (The Association of Former Political Prisoners of Romania has estimated than an additional 300,000 persons perished in Gheorghiu-Dej's labour camps.)

Beside their use of the courts, the communists did not baulk at 'extra-legal' methods. They regularly employed thugs to disrupt opposition meetings or, as occurred at a royalist rally celebrating the king's birthday, to shoot indiscriminately into a crowd. On one occasion, Gheorghiu-Dej himself broke up a factory demonstration, machine gun in hand. During the early stages of the take over, the Romanian army was deployed abroad in the task of 'liberating' Eastern Europe. Once the war was ended, most of its units were disbanded. In the absence of the regular army, effective control of the country was vested in the Soviet armed forces and in the communist 'Tudor Vladimirescu' regiment, both of which maintained law and order in a highly partial manner.[4] For many Romanians the casual brutality of the

communists set the seal on a long process of degradation and violence
going back to the days of the Iron Guard dictatorship.

The Communist Party grew rapidly in number after 1944 as
opportunists climbed aboard the ideological bandwagon. Its ranks
were swollen by former legionaries and *siguranta* officers, the
recruitment of which was specifically encouraged by Ana Pauker.
Repeating the methods of patronage used by the National Liberals in
the 1920s, the communists cleared the bureaucracy of all potential
opponents and appointed only party members to posts. The thousands
dismissed in the civil service purge of August 1947 were generously
paid off with back wages and compensation; within days a currency
reform had robbed them of their money.

Party membership was a necessary qualification both for rations and
for employment. For those who had held positions of responsibility
during the 1930s and under Antonescu, it was vital for just staying
alive. Thus the rapid numerical growth of the party – 700,000 in
January 1947; a million by the beginning of 1948 – cannot be taken to
illustrate popular support. Nor, any more than the elections of the
1920s, does the share of the vote obtained in the communist-run
ballots have any genuine significance. In describing the election of
1946, the last in which the democratic parties participated, one
historian has written:

> ·The electoral law gave every advantage to the communists. Polls
> were set up in factories and barracks where [their] agents could
> bring direct pressure on workers and soldiers. Electoral lists
> were hastily compiled so that no real check could be made on
> inaccuracies. Women were enfranchised for the first time, and
> fascists, Iron Guardists, and those who of their own free will had
> fought against the allies, were disenfranchised ... On November
> 19, 1946, the Romanian people went to the polls in an election in
> which every fraudulent, violent and unscrupulous device ever
> used in the Balkans was brought into full play.[5]

Even so, the communist-led coalition performed so badly that the
public announcement of the returns coming in from the constituencies
had to be suspended on the day of the count. After an inexplicable
delay of half a week, the government published that the communists
and their allies had received an 80 per cent share of the poll.[6]

Thereafter, all elections were open and featured only communist-approved candidates.

The communist seizure of power was accompanied by factional in-fighting among the communists. Essentially, the rivalry was between the old 'prison-communists', the former 'secretariat communists', and the 'Muscovites'. However, since the struggle was fought around personalities rather than policy, individuals were frequently able to cross from one faction to the other while some successfully managed to straddle several groups at the same time. The victory of the 'prison-communists' was ultimately achieved because they enjoyed Stalin's confidence. The 'secretariat communists', led by Patrascanu, were too ideologically flexible for Stalin, who was fearful of a 'Romanian Tito' taking power, while Ana Pauker and her Muscovite wing was considered too Jewish. Gheorghiu-Dej, by contrast, was of Romanian stock and sufficiently unimaginative to be doctrinaire.

The contest between these groups, nevertheless, was not settled until 1952, when Pauker and Luca were dismissed from the party leadership. Gheorghiu-Dej outfought his rivals by denunciation, by physical intimidation, and by using the party rank and file to vote his rivals out of power. His triumph was marked by the arrest of Patrascanu in 1948; the publication in the same year of a photograph of party leaders showing Ana Pauker and Luca in the second row; and the subsequent purging with the approval of the party hierarchy of Pauker's numerous appointees in the bureaucracy. It is quite possible that the years of bitter rivalry produced a 'faction fatigue' in the party and contributed to the leadership's subsequent willingness to rally round the person of Gheorghiu-Dej's unlikely successor, Nicolae Ceausescu.

Despite their differences, Muscovites and home-communists alike slavishly followed the Stalinist model. Once in power, they proceeded to convert Romania into a miniature version of the Soviet Union. Political influence was thus centralized upon the party and its organs: the Central Committee, Secretariat and the ruling Politburo. The Romanian parliament, the Grand National Assembly, was simply a rubber-stamp to decisions made by the communist leadership. A constitution, modelled on the Soviet one, gave this arrangement the force of law. All other institutions, from children's clubs to drama groups, were absorbed within the party apparatus. Imitating the religious policies pursued in the Soviet Union, the Greek Catholic Church, established in 1699, was abolished.[7] In further deference to

Russian leadership, the way in which the name of the state was spelled was even changed from 'Romania' to the more Slavic 'Rominia'.

In economic policy also, Romania followed a prearranged course. During the late 1940s and 1950s the Romanian economy was transformed by the nationalization of all businesses and by a massive reinvestment of state income into industry. A succession of plans were put in place with the aim of modernizing Romania and creating the factory proletariat in whose name the communists had come to power. During the 1950s, the Romanian growth rate averaged over 13 per cent every year and the workforce became increasingly urbanized.[8] By 1960 more than a third of the population consisted of town dwellers. These superficially impressive figures were won, however, at tremendous human cost: the virtual absence of consumer goods; barrack accommodation for workers; the forcible direction of manpower; and the use of slave labour. For all this, though, the results obtained were little different to the growth figures achieved in contemporary southern Europe where the process of rapid modernization took place more humanely and with much less official self-congratulation.

Agriculture similarly underwent rapid reform. Shortly after the war, the communists began a new round of property distribution. Estates over 50 hectares in size and plots relying on hired labour were confiscated, broken up, and given to the landless. The result of these expropriations was to remove from the rural economy the larger and more economically viable units, and to add to the number of households living on or below the margin of subsistence. The intention behind this latest agrarian remedy was to make a sufficient gesture to the peasantry to lend the communists some measure of support in the countryside.

In 1949, communist policy went into reverse. Evidently by this stage the leadership was confident enough to take on a more dogmatic stance with regard to the rural economy. In accordance with Stalinist practice, peasant plots were now joined together to create collective farms on which labourers worked in exchange for a share of the profits. In theory, the free consent of peasant proprietors was required before their land could be incorporated within the collective. 80,000 were prosecuted for failing to do so. Although the pace was slowed in the 1950s on account of popular resistance to change, the process of collectivization was completed in 1962. Only about 6 per cent of agricultural land remained privately owned, and most of this was organized as allotments and as small market gardens.

Stalin's death in 1953 and the subsequent programme of 'de-Stalinization' in the USSR was not welcomed in the upper reaches of the Romanian Communist Party. Khrushchev's calls for 'a return to Leninist norms', by which he meant political reform, and for the establishment of more broadly based party leaderships, threatened both Gheorghiu-Dej's policies and his position. Accordingly, he became all the more determined to resist the reforms pressed upon him by the Kremlin. Gorbachev would have a similar effect on Ceausescu 30 years later.[9]

During the late 1950s and 1960s, Gheorghiu-Dej adopted the position of an 'independent Stalinist' in an Eastern Europe which was steadily repudiating Stalinist techniques and ideology. Although he joined in the general denunciation of previous 'excesses', Gheorghiu-Dej blamed these on Pauker and claimed that her dismissal had been sufficient to put the Romanian house in order. To make sure that it stayed so, Gheorghiu-Dej eliminated from the ruling politburo those communists whom he suspected of reformist tendencies. Likewise, he refused Soviet attempts to bring the Romanian economy into line with Comecon policies and in 1958 he succeeded in having all Soviet forces withdrawn from Romanian territory.

As Romania began to distance itself from the Soviet Union, the propaganda of the Communist Party adopted a more national character. The title of the country was changed back to 'Romania' and streets called after Soviet heroes were renamed. As an insult and warning to the Soviet Union, the government published in 1964 Karl Marx's *Notes about the Romanians*, in which he criticized Russian imperialism and the annexation of Bessarabia. These measures, although largely symbolic, were enthusiastically welcomed by the population. Popular nationalism would be increasingly exploited as a way of mustering support by Gheorghiu-Dej's successor, Nicolae Ceausescu.

NOTES

1. C.T. Petrescu, *Socialnul in Romania 1835–6, Septembrie 1940* (Bucharest: undated), p. 359.
2. Walter Bacon, 'The Romanian Secret Police', in Jonathan R. Adelman (ed), *Terror and Communist Politics. The Role of the Secret Police in Communist States* (Boulder, Col. & London: Westview Press, 1984), p. 140.
3. Transylvania had been returned briefly to direct Romanian rule in autumn

1944; however, the extent of internecine fighting between Hungarians and Romanians forced the Soviet Union to place the region under its own supervision.

4. The Tudor Vladimirescu regiment comprised Romanian POWs who had embraced communism while in Russian captivity. The regiment was led almost entirely by Soviet officers.

5. Robert L. Wolff, *The Balkans in Our Time* (Cambridge, Mass: Harvard University Press, 1956), pp. 287–8. The election took place at the insistence of the western allies.

6. The communist coalition's real share of the vote is thought to have been about 20 per cent.

7. The Greek Catholic Church retains an orthodox liturgy while acknowledging the supremacy of the Pope in Rome. Between the wars the Greek Catholic Church had one and a half million adherents. The Church was reestablished in Romania in 1990.

8. The figure of 13 per cent is taken from Romanian sources and is probably inflated.

9. The analogy is noted by Mary Ellen Fischer, *Nicolae Ceausescu. A Study in Political Leadership* (Boulder, Col. & London: Lynne Rienner Publishers, 1989), p. 54.

4

THE RISE OF
NICOLAE CEAUSESCU

On 19 March 1965, Gheorghe Gheorghiu-Dej, the communist leader
who had affectively run Romania for over two decades, died of cancer.
His successor as party leader was Nicolae Ceausescu. Ceausescu was
at this time a shadowy figure, about whom little was known except that
he was Gheorghiu-Dej's protégé. Ceausescu's poor performance in
public speaking, apparent inability to mouth anything more convincing
than slogans, and reputed lack of intelligence, seemed at the time to
suggest that he had been selected as an interim measure. His task, so it
was thought, was merely to hold the government together while others
jostled for power behind the scenes. As it turned out, Ceausescu
would remain leader of communist Romania for almost a quarter of a
century.

Nicolae Ceausescu was born on 26 January 1918 to poor peasants in
the village of Scornicesti in Olt county. Photographs of Ceausescu's
parents, Andruta and Alexandra, published in the 1970s, show
crooked bodies and weatherbeaten faces: the inevitable consequence
of years of toil in the fields. Nevertheless Ceausescu was proud of his
background and not just for reasons of sentiment. In the top ranks of
the Communist Party, a working class upbringing and a Romanian
parentage were both rare commodities. Most of the leading
communists were the children of professional couples; and many were
also of Jewish or of Hungarian origin. Ceausescu's rural proletarian
and solidly Romanian origin made him popular among ordinary party
members, who largely retained the nationalist and anti-Semitic
prejudices of the pre-communist era.

The young Nicolae left his home village and full-time education at
the age of 11 to take up an apprenticeship with a cobbler in Bucharest.
According to the party histories, Nicolae was a precocious youngster
who took up left-wing politics at an early age. At 14, he was supposedly

arrested for distributing leaflets calling for a strike, and he is said to
have joined the Communist Party shortly afterwards. It seems likely,
however, that Nicolae Ceausescu's police and party records were
deliberately falsified in the 1960s. Most probably this was achieved by
doctoring papers which in fact referred to his elder brother, Marin. All
we know for sure is that Nicolae was imprisoned in the late 1930s and
that he spent part of his confinement in the company of
Gheorghiu-Dej.

On the eve of the Second World War, Ceausescu was elected
General Secretary of the Union of Communist Youth and he met for
the first time his future wife, Elena Petrescu. At that time Elena was a
communist and trade-union agitator at the Jacquard footwear factory
in Bucharest. Official histories record that the two met at a socialist
May Ball during the course of which Elena was elected 'queen'.
Photographs surviving from this period suggest that the two may
indeed have made a not unhandsome couple; his saturnine features
and her fixed frown were evidently acquired rather later. Both,
however, were rapidly separated once war was declared. Elena's
precise whereabouts during the next few years remain uncertain,
although Ceausescu's brother was later to gossip that she had been on
sexually intimate terms with several German officers. Ceausescu
himself was arrested in 1940 and later transferred to the prison at
Tirgu Jiu.

Tirgu Jiu was a light regime camp, and much of Ceausescu's time
was spent on work detachment outside the compound. He specialized
in fitting electrical cables and, in the 1970s, several buildings in the
Tirgu Jiu region still allegedly boasted his efforts at wiring. Shortly
after his release in the autumn of 1944, Ceausescu rejoined Elena
Petrescu, 'the young militant who had', according to one semi-official
biography, 'waited for him since those far-away days long ago ... The
prisons had separated them but not divided them. They were married
as soon as he was free'.[1] Thus was inaugurated a close partnership
which was to last right up until both were executed, side by side, on
Christmas Day 1989.

During the late 1940s and 1950s, Ceausescu remained close by the
Gheorghiu-Dej faction of the party. He faithfully towed the official
line and was seconded for a short time to the Frunze Military Academy
in Moscow.[2] Throughout his career, Ceausescu displayed an excellent
memory for detail and he prided himself on the preparation he put in
before every important meeting. Gradually, therefore, he acquired the

reputation of being an able administrator and his career progressed rapidly in the 1950s. As head of the Party Organization Bureau and subsequently a member of the party secretariat, Ceausescu was able to promote his own supporters to key positions within the hierarchy and to build up a formidable network of allies in the lower and middle ranks of the party apparatus.

Rather like Joseph Stalin, Ceausescu was a 'grey blur', whose accumulation of power and influence went largely unnoticed. Like Stalin also, Ceausescu was continually underrated by his rivals, who regarded him as slow-witted, unimaginative and good mainly for pushing paper. Nevertheless, Ceausescu enjoyed the favour of Gheorghiu-Dej who appreciated his unstinting loyalty. Ceausescu's readiness to fall rapidly in line with Gheorghiu-Dej's change of policy towards the Soviet Union in the late 1950s convinced the communist leader that Ceausescu was the best fitted to be his successor.

The process of changing from one leader to another was one of the weakest links in the structure of communist power in Europe. No clear order of succession was worked out in any of the Eastern bloc states. Usually therefore, the death or resignation of a leader was followed by fierce internal battles within the upper reaches of the party. During this period of uncertainty, an outward show of unity was preserved through the establishment of a collective leadership. Only gradually did a new leader emerge enjoying uncontested power within the party and government.

Following Ghorghiu-Dej's death in 1965, political power in Romania was formally shared between Ceausescu as party leader, Prime Minister Ion Maurer, and the new Head of State, Chivu Stoica. The ruling *troika* had necessarily also to heed the advice of Alexandru Draghici, the head of the security service, and of Gheorghe Apostol, who as boss of the communist trade union organization had quite considerable influence among working class members of the party. Although Ceausescu held the leading position in the communist hierarchy, he was at first no more than a *primus inter pares*.

Ceausescu was able to outmanoeuvre his rivals by relying for support on the party rank and file. Already by the time of Gheorghiu-Dej's death, he enjoyed substantial support among this group, largely because he had taken care to promote many of its members to positions of minor influence. Thus, the Party Congress, which met every four years, and the Central Committee, which operated very much as the party's parliament, acted as pliant instruments on Ceausescu's behalf. As a consequence, he was able to engineer the demotion of Stoica and Draghici in 1967–8, undermine Apostol's influence among trade unionists, and oblige Maurer to give up any personal ambitions of his own. By 1969, the collective leadership had been effectively superseded by the rule of one man. An accompanying reorganization of the Politburo, which was later renamed the Political Executive Committee (Polexco), and administrative changes in the localities ensured that Ceausescu's supporters also received their due prominence and reward.

It is always hard to estimate the extent of a leader's popularity in communist states. Where voting is conducted openly under the watch of party officials, election results cannot be taken as at all indicative of the national mood. Likewise, rallies and demonstrations of support may be attended by workers given the day off on the understanding that they clap and cheer on cue. Nevertheless, it does seem that in his first few years as party leader Ceausescu enjoyed quite considerable popular acclaim, although many Romanians nowadays deny this.

During his early years in office, Ceausescu 'liberalized' Romania and, even more importantly, put food on the shelves. Firstly, he directed investment and production away from heavy industry and towards consumer goods. Wages were increased, the number of private cars rose, and the price of household and of electrical goods actually fell. A new programme of construction was undertaken to relieve the housing shortage in the cities. Dull, grey blocks of worker accommodation thus sprang up to ring each of the major cities. Nevertheless, for families used to living in a single room and to sharing kitchen and bathroom facilities, the new apartments were a considerable improvement on what had gone before.

During the late 1960s, conditions in the workplace were similarly enhanced and poor managers were sacked so as to put an end to 'unrhythmical plan fulfilment and abusive supplementary hours'.[3] Ceausescu associated himself in dramatic style with all of these improvements. Anticipating Boris Yeltsin in the Soviet Union, the party leader descended unannounced on building sites and production lines, handing out advice and listening to complaints. He toured towns in the provinces, inspecting the provision of foodstuffs and stopping to receive petitions. Ceausescu's activities were duly recorded in the party newspaper thus contributing to his reputation as an energetic reformer. At the same time, Ceausescu laid special stress on 'socialist legality'. He criticized the way the security police had often in the past exceeded their brief and had detained persons on flimsy pretexts. By ameliorating the penal code and making the political police accountable to the party, he promised to prevent future abuses. In April 1968, Ceausescu took the momentous step of posthumously rehabilitating the party members who had been executed in the 1940s and 1950s. Additionally, he identified the late Gheorghiu-Dej as the main force behind 'the criminal frame-ups' of these years and began to distance himself from the policies of his former mentor.

In contrast to the numbing excesses of Gheorghiu-Dej's Stalinist regime, Ceausescu at first allowed a new freedom with regard to Romania's intellectual and cultural life. Poetry and the arts were to be released, he promised, from the constraints of party dogma and to be judged henceforward by aesthetic criteria. Although Ceausescu qualified his commitment to reform by declaring that artistic and literary expression should serve in the building of socialism, he did permit playwrights and poets to make guarded criticisms of life in contemporary Romania. Accordingly, Romania experienced in the late 1960s a literary renaissance, centred largely upon the 'Amphitheatre' group of young surrealist writers and poets.

Despite the ostensible break with the excesses of the Dej regime, Ceausescu retained his predecessor's independent policy towards the Soviet Union. He established diplomatic relations with the Bonn government and responded favourably towards the new West German *Ostpolitik*. Likewise, in 1967 Ceausescu refused to toe the Soviet line with regard to the Middle East and continued to retain friendly contacts with Israel. A telling and early illustration of Ceausescu's wish to distance himself from Moscow came in the spring of 1966 when Tito, Chou En-lai and Brezhnev consecutively visited Bucharest. The Yugoslav and Chinese leaders were feted with galas, trips to the seaside, and full-page spreads in the party newspaper, *Scinteia*. Their respective visits took place, so *Scinteia* declared, in a 'cordial, comradely atmosphere of warm friendship'. In complete contrast, the visit of the Soviet leader was kept a low-key affair which merited only a short announcement, and then only after Brezhnev had returned to Moscow. According to the Romanian communiqué, Ceausescu and Brezhnev had merely 'exchanged opinions on problems of continued development of cooperation'. Only their farewell dinner had taken place in a 'warm, friendly atmosphere'.[4]

The decisive breach with the Soviet Union came in 1968 with the invasion of Czechoslovakia. Ceausescu not only refused to participate in the Warsaw Pact occupation but vehemently criticized the intervention. In August 1968, Ceausescu declared before the Grand National Assembly:

> Our whole party, the whole Romanian people, looks upon the military intervention in socialist Czechoslovakia with profound anxiety. We consider this a flagrant transgression of the national independence and sovereignty of the Czechoslovak Socialist Republic, as an interference by force in the affairs of the brother Czechoslovak people, as an action in full contradiction with the fundamental norms of the relations that must reign among the socialist countries and among the communist parties, with the generally recognised principles of international law.[5]

At the same meeting of the Grand National Assembly, Ceausescu gave out that the Soviet intervention was a dangerous precedent and he warned that Romania might be the next target for invasion. Whether he actually believed this is uncertain. Nevertheless, the suggested threat of Soviet occupation provided a powerful stimulus to Romanian nationalism which Ceausescu proceeded to exploit for all it was worth. In speeches and rallies he posed as the defender of Romanian nationhood and independence, and conjured up the prospect of a new period of foreign servitude. Striking allusions to the Dacian Burebista who had resisted the Romans, and to the wars fought between Romanian princes and the Turks, established the close historical connection between the popular heroes of old and their modern-day counterpart, Nicolae Ceausescu. In order to maintain the nationalist tempo, squads of factory workers were drilled in the tactics of guerrilla warfare and a mass organization of 'Patriotic Guards' was urgently created. Within a few weeks, almost half a million volunteers had joined these new paramilitary units.

1968 was the high point of Ceausescu's career. Already popular by reason of the reforms he had introduced, Ceausescu's defiance of Moscow made him a national hero. He and the survival of the Romanian nation became for a time inextricably bound together in the public imagination and opposition to him because temporarily confused with betrayal of the country. Over the next 20 years, even as his popularity ebbed, Ceausescu would constantly recall the spirit and mood of this period in the hope of reawakening some enthusiasm for his government. 'Independence', 'sovereignty', 'fighting to the last man', and 'the lesson of 1968' were themes to which Ceausescu returned even in the last days of his career.

After 1968, it soon became apparent that much of what Ceausescu had promised in the first years of his rule was only empty posturing designed to broaden his political appeal. Once Ceausescu had consolidated his power and established his unique influence over policy, he felt free to go back on his earlier commitments and to revert to more traditional methods of rule. Consumer goods were thus withdrawn from the shops as the country buckled down once again to fulfilling impossibly high production targets. Political offenders were once again hunted down and detained, regardless of 'socialist legality'.

Finally in the notorious 'July theses' of 1971, Ceausescu denounced 'liberal' and 'intellectual' trends in the party and called for the re-establishment of a culture based firmly on the rock of 'socialist realism'. The return to traditional communist values is illustrated by the career of Adrian Paunescu, who had previously been one of Romania's most original young poets. In slavish conformity to the new line, Paunescu wrote in 1973, 'To commit a political act by means of your poetry is to be free to love in a collective way.' Thereafter, he became the leading 'court poet' and was responsible for some of the grossest literary examples of the Ceausescu personality cult.[6]

NOTES

1. Michel P. Hamelet, *Nicolae Ceausescu* (Paris: Edition Seghers, 1971), p. 49. The precise date of the Ceausescu's marriage has never, to this author's knowledge, been given. The suspicion thus lingers that no formal ceremony took place.
2. This aspect of Ceausescu's career was subsequently concealed.
3. Mary Ellen Fischer, *Nicolae Ceausescu: A Study in Political Leadership*, (Boulder and London: Lynne Rienner Publishers, 1989), p. 89.
4. Ibid, pp. 97–8.
5. Nicolae Ceausescu, *Romania, Achievements and Prospects Reports, Speeches, Articles. July 1965–February 1969* (Bucharest: Meridiane, 1969), p. 663.
6. Paunescu was appointed in 1990 editor of the popular weekly *Zig Zag*.

5
CEAUSESCU'S ROMANIA

Ceausescu's failure to carry through his previous undertakings was primarily due to his own intellectual shortcomings. He had been brought up in the political and moral climate of the Stalinist years and he lacked the imagination to break with the old style of thinking. He remained utterly convinced, therefore, of the party's right to rule and of its exclusive mission to lead Romania towards communism. Nor did he ever deviate from the principle of democratic centralism, according to which dialogue and discussion could only take place within the tight limits imposed by party discipline. Accordingly, his regime proved incapable both of adaptation and of accommodation. The only way it could be changed was by its violent overthrow.

In strictly Stalinist fashion, Ceausescu believed that the only true form of economic progress was rapid industrial modernization. Although he gave his political and economic programme the grandiose title of 'Towards a Multi-Laterally Developed Socialist Society', in every other respect it was predicated on a heavy industrial base and on an expanding factory workforce. Ceausescu's economic policy was rooted in prescriptions and plans taken from the Soviet Union of the 1930s, which even by the late 1960s were widely recognized as flawed. The reckless application of these outmoded formulas to the Romania of the 1970s and 1980s saddled the country with unprofitable industries and an increasingly dissatisfied population.

Perhaps the most inhuman aspect of the industrialization programme was the accompanying drive to increase the birth rate. A growing workforce was believed by Ceausescu to be a necessary precondition for economic 'take-off'. In 1966, therefore, abortions were declared illegal and contraceptives were made unavailable. There was, however, no corresponding improvement in maternity provision or in nursery care. The widespread resort to illegal remedies against

44

pregnancy resulted in the introduction during the 1980s of routine gynaecological examinations for women. Medical resources were, however, sufficiently overstretched to allow most women to avoid the required tests in exchange for a deduction from their monthly wage packets.

As the example of the population drive suggests, Ceausescu's rule preserved a sufficient number of unusual characteristics to make it unique among contemporary communist regimes. Although Ceausescu mouthed all the vulgar platitudes of Marxist theory and spoke in the language of class-struggle, his rule was suffused with idiosyncratic practices which combined to make it a caricature of a socialist government. Nevertheless, even the most extraordinary and perverse features of 'Ceausescu-ism' were directed towards a single, rational end: the legitimization of Ceausescu's rule. By appealing to nationalism and to history, by demonstrating on the streets the support he ostensibly enjoyed, and by developing a personality cult of his own, Ceausescu tried to justify his tyranny before the people and to lend a new aura of credibility to his government. In this respect, the very absurdity of Ceausescuism was an illustration of the leader's sense of personal weakness and of political vulnerability.

Ceausescu emphasised from the very first that he was a national and not just a communist leader and that the socialist future was rooted in Romanian traditions. Textbooks and newspapers loudly stressed, therefore, the continuities in Romanian history and explained how the advent of communism and of Ceausescu had fulfilled the national destiny. Gradually, the Communist Party was made responsible for the decisive developments in recent Romanian history: for encompassing the collapse of bourgeois government in the 1930s; for arranging the coup against Antonescu in 1944; and for driving the Germans out of Romania the next year.

As Romanian socialism became increasingly identified with patriotism, so the great events in Romanian history were shown to have foreshadowed the party's own access to power. In a series of extraordinary exhibitions held in 1980 to commemorate the '2050th anniversary' of the Romanian state, communism was presented as the goal to which the nation had striven for two millenia, and the party was portrayed as the guarantor of Romania's continued independence and statehood. In the same spirit, the 'prominent historian', General Ilie Ceausescu (brother of Nicolae) laboriously explained that the direct successor of the ancient Dacian state of antiquity was none other than the Romanian Communist Party: 'A brilliant standard-bearer of the Romanians' struggle for independence, perfectly identified with their historical ideas, the Romanian Communist Party has naturally set itself, since its very foundation in May 1921, as the fundamental target of its entire policy, to defend and strengthen national independence'.

By associating the party with the national destiny, and by constantly referring to the popular virtues which it embodied, Ceausescu's ideologists hoped to exploit the potent myth of Romanian 'exceptionalism' as a way of rallying support for the regime. They thus loudly extolled the achievements of the Romanian nation and emphasized the purity of its racial pedigree. Ceausescu himself even went so far as to praise the 'new man', distinguished by his athleticism, industry and revolutionary spirit, which socialism was forging in Romania. He promised his compatriots that genetic engineering would yield in time a more perfect strain.[1] Celebrations of national independence and of racial uniqueness were a persistent feature of the interminable *Song of Romania*, established in 1975 'for the assertion of the talent, sensitivity and creative genius of our people'.[2]

Ceausescu himself was the principal beneficiary of the rewriting of Romanian history. Not only did he become one of the main plotters of Antonescu's downfall but he was also portrayed as the last of the long line of national champions. He was likened to the warrior-princes of Moldavia and Wallachia and was frequently photographed posing beside the statues of previous Romanian heroes. A whole floor of the National Museum in Bucharest was given over to extolling Ceausescu's historic achievement. As Ceausescu's government became increasingly repressive during the 1980s, an attempt was even made to restore the reputation of the medieval Wallachian ruler, Vlad the Impaler. The rehabilitation of 'Dracula' and his conversion into a precursor of Ceausescu, provided a historical precedent for political ruthlessness.

The use of national symbolism was combined with a xenophobic foreign and domestic policy. Internally, Ceausescu adopted an antagonistic line towards the non-Romanian minorities. From the late 1960s, discriminatory measures began to be employed against ethnic Hungarians and Germans with regard to educational, linguistic and cultural provision. A decade later, anti-Semitism was revived and a series of scurrilous publications even went so far as to accuse the Jews of drinking the blood of gentile children. The slogan 'Romanians must be masters in their own home' was frequently employed to justify policies aimed against 'the cohabiting nationalities'.

In foreign policy, Ceausescu's exploitation of xenophobic sentiments was directed in the main against the Soviet Union. The Russians had historically always constituted one of Romania's main enemies and Ceausescu continued the policy, first espoused in the late 1950s and 1960s, of distancing Romania from the Soviet Union. He thus consistently rebuffed Moscow's attempts to draw Romania into its anti-Chinese and anti-Yugoslav campaigns, and he defended the Spanish and Italian Euro-communists against criticism. Likewise, he provided sanctuary in Romania for the anti-Soviet wing of the Greek Communist Party even going so far as to expel members of the pro-Moscow faction from the country.[3] Ceausescu also condemned the Soviet occupation of Afghanistan and, alone in the Eastern bloc, defied Moscow by sending athletes to the 1984 Olympic Games in Los Angeles. On occasions also, broad hints were dropped concerning the status of Bessarabia, although it was not until 1989 that Ceausescu mentioned the possibility of revising Romania's frontier with the Soviet Union. Even then, Ceausescu's references were oblique.

Ceausescu's anti-Soviet stance brought Romania immediate dividends in the form of western financial assistance: membership of the General Agreement on Tariffs and Trade, and the IMF and World Bank, and preferential trading terms with the EEC. In 1975 Romania was granted the status of 'Most Favoured Nation' by the United States government. Over the next decade, the country received one billion dollars of US-backed credits as well as access to advanced computer technology, light machine guns and military helicopters. Ceausescu also received a sympathetic welcome in Western Europe and America, and his visits there were accompanied by lavish receptions and the award of various titles and medals. Of these, the most notorious was the knighthood given to Ceausescu on the occasion of his state visit to London in 1978, and the most ridiculous his honorary citizenship of Disneyland. At the time, however, it was felt that Ceausescu's anti-Soviet stance was well worth rewarding by harmless appeals to his vanity.

During the 1970s, Romanians became increasingly cynical about Ceausescu's posturing as a national hero and defender of Romanian independence. Western displays of friendship to Ceausescu only seemed to confirm the suspicion of Romanians that America and its allies had decided to overlook their suffering in the interests of international power politics. Popular cynicism towards Ceausescu thus gradually broadened into a more general indifference towards the western democracies. In this way, Ceausescu's rhetoric and diplomacy led to a growing sense of isolation among Romanians and contributed to the belief that resistance was futile.

Ceausescu's exploitation of nationalist sentiments was frequently accompanied by mass demonstrations of support in his favour. From the very first months of his rule, he emphasized the importance of mobilizing the people into active participation in the party's collective rituals. For this reason, he had the party's official name changed from the Romanian Workers Party to the Romanian Communist Party, since he believed the latter to be more revolutionary and inspiring in tone. In accordance with the principle of popular participation, Ceausescu's trips around the country were invariably attended by rallies in which the entire local workforce was assembled. On the occasion of important events – meetings of the Central Committee, of the National Assembly, or of the Congress – several tens of thousands would customarily parade through the centre of Bucharest calling Ceausescu's name and chanting messages of support for the party. On the occasion of the last Party Congress in November 1989, 120,000 people demonstrated in the capital and expressed their 'ardent, vibrant homage to Nicolae Ceausescu'.

At gatherings of trade unionists or of political activists, similar manifestations of popular support and rejoicing were commonplace. During the course of such celebrations, the representatives of various groups would gather on a stage to heap praises on party and ruler. Girls with flowers (the symbols of Romanian youth) would sing; men in blue overalls holding spanners (the workers) would recite a few lines; people wearing glasses and white coats (representatives of the intelligentsia) would stutter out well chosen words of adulation. In a final display of unanimity and of Stalinist kitsch, the assembled audience would chant out on cue the initials 'P.C.R.', standing both for 'Communist Party of Romania' and 'The People, Ceausescu, Romania'. Nationalist and communist motifs thus coincided in a paean of praise for the leader.

In token of the support ostensibly enjoyed by the regime, Ceausescu threw the Communist Party open to three million citizens and about a third of the active population. Likewise, he introduced experiments in worker democracy and in multi-candidate elections so as to make his style of government more 'participatory'. None of these initiatives resulted, however, in any appreciable loss of power by either the party apparatus or the ruler.

During the 1970s, expressions of support for Ceausescu became ever more lavish and ever more artificial. Historical allusions to Ceausescu's greatness and to his place in the pantheon of Romanian national heroes became combined with even more incredible claims and adjectives. On the occasion of Ceausescu's appointment as President in 1974 (a new post created for him), *Scinteia* reported the following:

> March 28, 1974, will remain engraved in the history of the homeland and in the minds of our people. On this memorable day, the Grand National Assembly fulfilled the wish of the entire Romanian people and proclaimed Comrade Nicolae Ceausescu President. This most brilliant son of the Romanian nation, the leader who is the latest in a line of great Romanian statesmen is our first president.

The party newspaper went on to report how the 'symbols of worth and prestige and of state power' were given to Ceausescu: a sash in the national colours and the mace of office. His inauguration as Romania's new monarch in all but name was attended by the singing of the National Anthem. The 'discovery' two years later near Scornicesti, Ceausescu's home village, of remnants of the first *homo sapiens* in Europe is not only evidence of the incredible depths of the Ceausescu cult but also a metaphor of the new president's role as communism's 'missing link' between egalitarianism and royalty.

During the late 1970s and 1980s, scarcely a single achievement, from the building of a new school to a bumper harvest, did not owe something to the contribution of the party leader. Likewise, no book could be published during this period without a statutory reference to the intellectual guidance of Ceausescu. His portrait, airbrushed to conceal the lines of human frailty, hung in every public building and posters proclaimed his heroism from grass verges along every main road. Increasingly implausible descriptions attached to every mention of Ceausescu's name. He was, thus, in alphabetical order: the Architect; the Builder; the Creed-shaper; a Danube of Thought; an Epoch; Father; Genius of the Carpathians; our secular God; wise Helmsman; sweet Kissing of the earth; Lawgiver; tallest Mast; Nimbus of victory; Oak tree; Prince Charming; the embodiment of Romania (hence, 'When we say Ceausescu, we say Romania'); Son of the sun; Titan; and Visionary. Even his sign of the Zodiac was deemed worthy of special attention.[4]

The Ceausescu cult logically developed out of the events of the late 1960s when the new ruler had basked in popular acclaim as a consequence of his defiance of the Soviet Union. However, it also recalls the period of the early 1940s, when Marshal Antonescu had similarly bathed in the contrived adulation of the masses. Several of the terms previously employed to exalt Antonescu were adopted by his communist successor, including 'statesman of dizzying simplicity' and the title of *Conducator*.

The cult spilled over from the person of the president to his immediate family circle. According thus to a volume of homage published to commemorate Ceausescu's 55th birthday in 1973:

> We gaze with reverence and with respect at the harmony of his family life. We attach special moral significance to the fact that his life, together with that of his comrade for life, the former textile worker and young communist militant, member of the party since the days when it was banned, today Hero of Socialist Labour, scientist, member of the Central Committee of the Romanian Communist Party, Madame Comrade Elena Ceausescu, offer exemplary illustrations of the lives of two communists. And we should know that the three children of the President work, like all of us, to follow the example of their parents, to bring socialism to Romania ...[5]

The rise of Elena Ceausescu to prominence in the party began in the early 1970s when she became a member of the Polexco. She was given the reputation of a great research scientist and various works were attributed to her, starting with *Research Work on the Synthesis and Characterization of Macromolecular Compounds*, published in 1974. Although the accusation that she was barely educated and could hardly have composed the work herself was frequently levelled even in the 1970s, it does seem that Elena had previously spent some time as a student at the Polytechnical University in Bucharest.[6] It was additionally commonplace in Romanian academic circles for political appointees to appropriate the findings of junior researchers and to publish them under their own name.

Elena received praise and adulation quite out of keeping with her supposed intellectual achievements. According to party protocol, her correct form of address was 'Comrade Academician Doctor Engineer Elena Ceausescu, outstanding activist of Party and State, eminent personage of Romanian and international science'. Special subsidies allowed Elena's works to be published in the West, on the occasion of which the official Romanian media made great play of her scholarly reputation and credentials:

> The volume "Elena Ceausescu – Progress in Chemistry and Polymers Technology" appeared in Austria ... in the prestigious Bohmann publishing house ... The work was presented to the Austrian public at a homage-rendering event which took place at the Austrian Cultural Centre in the Palffy Palace ... [Among those present were] representatives from certain firms and institutes involved in research and production in chemistry, representatives of the Technical University of Vienna, businessmen and journalists ...[7]

According, however, to independent western observers:

> The Bohmann scientific publishing house in Vienna has just published Elena's latest, turgid set of papers. The original Romanian translation into German was so bad it had to be done again. The Romanian exchequer naturally had to pay a large share of the publishing costs. Accompanied by much fanfare in the Romanian press, she was due to appear in person on the evening of 5 January to launch the publication. She never showed up ... Practically the entire Romanian embassy staff in Vienna packed into the Palais to pay verbal homage to the leaderine. According to Romanian press accounts, the reception was attended by foreign press and scientists. In fact there were none at all. There was just one wretched official from the Austrian Ministry of Science and Culture who had to turn up because of Austria's cultural agreement with Romania ...[8]

In recognition of her contribution to Romania's development, Elena received a succession of medals and awards. The praise accorded to her reached in the 1980s a level almost equal to that given to her husband:

THE CEAUSESCU DYNASTY

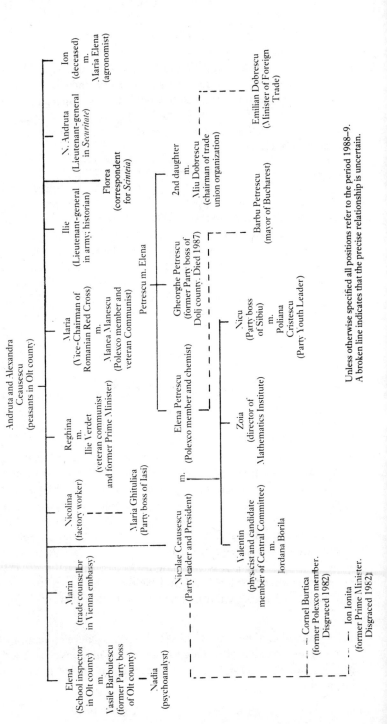

Unless otherwise specified all positions refer to the period 1988–9.
A broken line indicates that the precise relationship is uncertain.

Comrade Elena Ceausescu!
You, the stateswoman
And scientist of great renown,
Who brought
New prestige to Romanian science in the world.
To you we express our gratitude
From the bottom of our hearts.

In 1987 archaeologists also 'discovered' evidence in Elena's home village of human remains from the paleolithic period.

The Ceausescu's children were largely exempt from the personality cult, although their natural son, Nicu, received the Order of Labour (First Class) in 1983 and swiftly progressed to prominence as a candidate member of the Polexco. Nicu's reputation as a womanizer and drunkard, and notoriously bad relations with his father, seem to have ruled out any consistent eulogizing of his career. Despite Nicu's faults, however, it was anticipated that he would eventually succeed his father as ruler: 'like the saviour of a world which has been devastated by war'.[9] Zoia Ceausescu and Valentin, an adopted son, both played a fairly low-key role in Romanian politics.[10] Zoia was, nevertheless, awarded the Order of Labour (Second Class) in 1983, and Valentin was appointed a candidate member of the Central Committee in November 1989.

The family of the ruler not only served as a focus of adulation but provided also an important instrument of political control. Relatives of Nicolae and Elena were consistently advanced to key positions within both party and government. The army and the apparatus of state security were infiltrated at a high level by Ceausescu's brothers. The local party organizations in Olt county, Sibiu, Iasi and Bucharest were similarly put in the hands of close relatives (see diagram of the Ceausescu Dynasty on p.52. At the same time, the Ceausescu and Petrescu families forged links by marriage to other leading members of the communist hierarchy, most notably Manea Manescu and Ilie Verdet. 'Dynastic socialism' served to maintain stability by constructing a tight web of personal loyalties at the top of the political hierarchy. Nevertheless, the very use of these methods suggests the extent to which the ruling family perceived Romania to be their own personal property and the equivalent of a private landed estate. Ceausescu's casual seizure for his own use of national art treasures, seaside palaces and rural retreats, further indicates the same patrimonial aspect of his government.

Ceausescu did not, however, allow persons from outside the family circle to construct private fiefdoms of their own. He stated thus in 1971, 'No field of activity is anyone's personal property. Anyone who works in a ministry or trade union is placed there by the party, by the working class, and if he does not fulfil the mission entrusted to him he must be removed and replaced by someone who is capable of carrying out party policy'. He resolutely stood against those managers whose outlook was, 'This is my territory and none can interfere'.[11]

In accordance with this principle, ministers and party activists were constantly 'rotated' and moved from one job to another after only a couple of years. Officials would commonly move from party to state appointments and back again, and from the capital to the provinces. Virgil Trofin a Central Committee secretary between 1965 and 1971, therefore became head of the trade unions in 1971. After only a year he was moved on to Minister of Internal Trade and in 1974 sent to the countryside as First Secretary of Brasov County. The career path of Ion Iliescu, who succeeded Ceausescu as president of Romania in 1990, shows similar characteristics. In 1971 Iliescu held the rank of Central Committee secretary with special responsibility for propaganda. The next year he was moved into the provinces where he became party boss of Timis county and, a few years later, of Iasi. In 1979 Iliescu returned to Bucharest as a member of the largely honorific State Council.

Rotation not only prevented a rival for power accumulating a strong base of support but also contributed to Ceausescu's growing isolation. Around the stable core of family members who effectively ran Romania swirled a stream of rotating officials and managers. Because their careers were so uncertain and might be interrupted at the whim of the ruler, ministers and party functionaries concealed all evidence of failure from the ruler and told him only what they believed he wanted to hear. Ceausescu thus became increasingly remote from the realities of life in contemporary Romania. Between 1982 and 1989 he did not visit a single market in the country; when he eventually saw the state of food provision he was apparently appalled. There is also some evidence to suggest that Ceausescu was unaware of the reintroduction of rationing to basic foodstuffs.[12]

'Dynasticism' ensured loyalty in the highest echelons of government; and rotation prevented the emergence of rivals lower down the political hierarchy. As for ordinary Romanians, they were kept in check by a ruthless security apparatus and by frequent resort to physical and psychological coercion.

Responsibility for ensuring the population's quiescence lay with the Ministry of the Interior. Ordinary criminal investigation was conducted by the militia (police), although in the event of unrest special militia riot squads helped to put down disturbances.[13] However, the main instrument of political control comprised the security troops of the Ministry of the Interior who were more generally known as the *securitate*. The *securitate* was organized in directorates and undertook a wide variety of tasks. The most conspicuous branch of the *securitate* was the First Directorate which was empowered with internal newsgathering and with taking active operations against dissenters. Offices of the First Directorate were established in each county, town and village, and acted as centres of local surveillance. Operatives in the First Directorate tapped telephones, intercepted mail, and liaised extensively with a network of paid informers. As required, *securitate* officers also engaged in work of intimidation and of harassment. The ubiquitous security men, who hung around hotels and popular tourist locations belonged largely to the territorial branches of the First Directorate. Other directorates of the *securitate* were involved in routine counter-intelligence, diplomatic espionage, and the investigation of serious crime. Their work was supported by the General Directorate of Technical Operations which provided the expertise for electronic eavesdropping, and by the Seventh Directorate which was responsible for running the networks of informers.

The *securitate* functioned very much as the private army of the president. Members of the Second Directorate of the *securitate*, dealing with economic intelligence, were posted to key ministries where they compiled their own private statistics on industrial and agricultural performance. The reason for this was the widespread practice of exaggerating output which affected every enterprise and branch of the national economy. The information gathered by the Second Directorate may not in some cases have been given to ministers, who had to put up instead with false data provided by their subordinates. Only the inner circle of the government seems to have been fully aware of the extent to which the country was failing to meet the targets laid down in the national plan.

The Fifth Directorate of 'Guarding and Order' assisted in the harassment of dissidents, although its principal function was to protect personnel and installations. An elite formation within this directorate was the UMO666 presidential protection squad, the members of which guarded the Ceausescu family. The precise command structure of the *securitate* remains still uncertain. It is, therefore, unclear whether the so-called USLA anti-terrorist group, which seems to have numbered several thousand personnel, was a part of the Fifth Directorate or whether it reported directly to the overall head of the State Security Department. The USLA is, however, widely believed to have been informally located under the overall supervision of Elena Ceausescu.

The precise numerical size of the *securitate* remains similarly open to question. Throughout the 1980s, western intelligence sources estimated the *securitate* to include 20,000 full-time personnel.[14] This figure coincides closely with the figure of 25,000 subsequently published by Ion Pacepa, an intelligence chief who defected in the late 1970s, and with material subsequently released in Bucharest.[15] At the time of the revolution, however, a variety of figures were given in Romania ranging from 70,000 to 150,000 operatives with up to a million paid informers. The fact that a number of military units, including perhaps as many as 15,000 persons, were seconded to the *securitate* makes it even harder to establish the strength of the secret police apparatus.

The *securitate* were certainly well trained and proved reasonably efficient in the discharge of their duties. They had their own colleges, most notably at Bran and Baneasa. It was a constant (and accurate) complaint in military circles that the *securitate* received all the best equipment and salaries.[16] Rumour added to their reputation. Romanians thus widely believed that their telephones all contained microphones linked to *securitate* headquarters and that the ceramic ashtrays on hotel tables concealed sophisticated listening devices. Nevertheless, the overall performance of the *securitate* was hampered by the constant interference of local party officers. Furthermore, by the late 1980s senior offices within the *securitate* were showing signs of dissatisfaction. The demotion of the several *securitate* veterans and the spectacular rise of both Tudor Postelnicu as Minister of the Interior, and of his *securitate* henchman, Iulian Vlad, is thought to have introduced a new element of friction between professional officers and party-political appointees.[17]

Territorial units of the *securitate* were responsible for some of the worst infringements of human rights in Romania. Their interrogation methods characteristically involved beatings and imprisonment in leg-irons. On occasions, the intimidation of political opponents extended to murder. The thrall in which the *securitate* held the population was equalled only by the savagery of the courts in meting out vengeance for political crimes. An electrician who drove through the centre of Bucharest in a car to which he had fastened a portrait of Ceausescu and the notice 'We don't want you, hangman', received a sentence of ten years imprisonment. A catch-all law forbidding 'propaganda which advocates a change in the socialist order' was frequently used against dissident writers and carried a gaol sentence of five to fifteen years.[18] Characteristically such trials were charades of justice with a hired audience baying for the court to impose the maximum penalty.

Nevertheless, these methods of coercion were probably less important than the needling psychological pressure which the security apparatus was able to exert on ordinary Romanians. Arbitrary harassment by bureaucratic means and the invention of petty infringements of the law usually provided a sufficient incentive to conformity for the mass of the population. By preying on anxieties, the regime fostered a corrosive atmosphere of deceit and distrust which made personal acts of resistance seem both futile and self-defeating.

The absence of an opposition movement in Ceausescu's Romania may be partly explained by the rotation in office of rivals for power and by the pervasive influence of the security apparatus. Other factors contributed, however, to the profound sense of resignation and of powerlessness which everyday Romanians experienced. Of these perhaps the most important was the constant dissipation of intellectual and physical energy in the mundane task of obtaining sufficient food, warmth and medicines to go on living. Equally dulling was the impression of timelessness and of personal superfluity experienced by Romanians in their daily lives. This feature of Ceausescu's Romania is captured by Ana Blandiana in her poem, *All*:

> ... leaves, words, tears,
> canned goods, cats,
> occasionally trams, lines for flour,
> weevils, empty bottles, speeches,
> prolonged fantasies on television,
> red beetles, gas,
> pennants, the European Championship Cup,
> buses with gas cylinders, portraits of famous people,
> apples refused for export,
> newspapers, sentences,

mixed oil, carnations, welcomes at the airport,
cico-cola, breadsticks, Bucharest salami, dietetic yoghourt,
gypsies with Kents, eggs from Crevedia,
rumours,
Saturday serials, coffee substitutes,
the fight of the people for peace, choruses,
production by the hectare,
Gerovital, the boys on Victory Street,
The Song of Romania, tennis shoes,
Bulgarian compote, jokes, ocean fish,
All.

In a verse published in the same collection in 1984, Ana Blandiana went further, however, and implied that it was the disposition of the Romanian people which rendered them in some way uniquely incapable of resisting tyranny:

I think we are a vegetable people,
Whoever saw
A tree in revolt?[19]

Although it is difficult (and unwise) to measure innate national characteristics, Ana Blandiana's suggestion draws useful attention to how the survival of the regime owed much to popular psychology and attitudes.

Rural societies tend to be more deferential than urban ones, and it was only after the Second World War that Romania ceased to comprise an overwhelming peasant population. In addition, there was no tradition in Romania of civil disobedience or of resistance to tyrannical rule. In the face of adversity, the Romanian peasantry had historically adopted a fatalistic response, and had seldom openly questioned the authority of the local prince and landowner. Expressions of discontent had been usually confined to the casual theft or sabotage of the oppressor's property. Only very rarely, as in 1907, did they flare up into actual rebellion. In much the same way, Romanian workers in the 1970s and 1980s consistently plundered their cooperatives and deliberately wrecked industrial machinery. Like their peasant forbears, they were reluctant to engage in open, collective acts of opposition.

One may speculate about the way in which the Ottoman and

Phanariot inheritance encouraged docility and an undue respect for authority among the population at large. Such determinist explanations have their appeal, but are not altogether fruitful lines of enquiry. Nevertheless, it has to be admitted that the attitude of rural and urban workers in the Romanian heartlands of Moldavia and Wallachia differed from that of their counterparts in Transylvania. The tradition and practice of political autonomy fostered in western Romania by centuries of Hungarian and Habsburg rule had led to a greater sense there of individual responsibility and of personal rights. Notions of a contractual bond linking ruler and subject, and of inalienable personal freedoms, were and remain more deeply engrained in Transylvania. In retrospect, therefore, it is not surprising that the most open displays of resistance to Ceausescu's government should come in the 1980s, not from the 'old kingdom' but instead from the western part of the country, and that the revolution of 1989 should have had its origins in a Transylvanian city.

Amongst the middle class, traditions of conformity were similarly ingrained although out of different experiences. Members of the Romanian bourgeoisie have customarily found employment in the service of the state and have regarded government patronage as the key to material prosperity. Intellectuals have also sought out political preferment. As one leading socialist thinker put it in the early years of the century, 'The poet's odyssey will be a sad one', unless he is ready 'to sing the politician's glory'. Although 'a beaten path', sycophancy led straight to 'triumphal arches'. The readiness of so many Romanian writers and poets to bow at Ceausescu's knee in return for preferment indicates the persistence of older responses towards authority. As a leading Romanian novelist once confessed, nothing appeared to him more natural than he should publish a piece extolling Ceausescu in return for having one of his books republished.[20]

At the same time, Romanian intellectuals never perceived themselves as custodians of the nation's soul not as the potential leaders of society. Instead, they retained a distance between themselves and the working population, thus preserving the old distrust between the educated and the peasant classes inherited from the nineteenth century. Ceausescu's wedge-driving between the proletariat and the intelligentsia by his frequent criticism of 'intellectualism', widened the gulf between the two groups. Romania remained, therefore, largely without the intellectual dissident leadership which distinguished the movements of popular protest in Czechoslovakia and Poland.

The survival of the Ceausescu regime was its most remarkable feature. Despite the deprivations experienced by the majority of the population and the continuation of the worst Stalinist excesses, Ceausescu survived even to the extent of becoming a caricature communist. He surrounded his government with the aura of popular legitimacy by emphasising his strongly nationalist credentials and boasting the enormous support he enjoyed both at home and abroad. When this failed to convince, the *securitate* were ready to apply both physical and psychological pressure on the exhausted population. Resistance to the regime was, therefore, always muted and it never even remotely approached the scale found in neighbouring socialist countries. Thus, it was only at the very end of the 1980s that Ceausescu was brought down, and then only after the complete collapse both of the economy and of all remaining confidence in his government.

NOTES

1. RFE/SR (4 August 1989).
2. The role of history in buttressing the Ceausescu regime is brilliantly analysed by Dennis Deletant in *Slovo*, vol. 1, no. 2 (November 1988).
3. Vladimir Tismaneanu, 'Ceausescu's Socialism', *Problems of Communism* (Jan–Feb 1985), p. 61.
4. RFE/SR (Romania, 4 February 1989).
5. *Omagiu Presidentelui Nicolae Ceausescu*, (Bucharest: Editura Politica, 1978).
6. Probably as a political organizer; her course attendance was apparently perfunctory.
7. *Scinteia* (7 January 1988).
8. *Eastern Europe Newsletter* (27 January 1988), noted by Jonathan Eyal in *RUSI Soviet Warsaw Pact Yearbook* (London: RUSI – Jane's Defence Data, 1989), p. 267.
9. *Informatia Bucurestiului* (24 January 1988), noted by Julien Weverbergh.
10. Valentin was adopted by the Ceausescus in 1946 consequent upon a Communist Party appeal to adopt orphans from drought-stricken Moldavia.
11. *Scinteia* (10 July 1971), cited in Robert R. King, *History of the Romanian Communist Party* (Stanford: Hoover Institution Press, 1980), p. 96.
12. Report of Ceausescu's conversation with his guards at Tirgoviste, *Stern Magazin* (12 July 1990).
13. Riot squads were apparently first deployed in November 1987.
14. International Institute for Strategic Studies, *The Military Balance 1986–87*, (London: IISS, 1986), p. 54.
15. *The Free Romanian*, (July–August 1990); SWB/EE (27 August 1990).
16. In 1980, therefore, an army major received a monthly wage of 2500 lei; his *securitate* counterpart earned 5800 lei: Ivan Volgyes, *The Political Reliability of the Warsaw Pact Armies* (Colorado: Duke Press, 1982), p. 53.

17. *Eastern Europe Newsletter* (14 June 1989).
18. Amnesty International, *Romania. Human Rights Violations in the Eighties* (London: Amnesty International July 1987).
19. Both poems were published originally in *Amfiteatru* in 1984; the translation here is based on David B. Funderburk, *Pinstripes and Reds*, (Washington DC: Selous Foundation Press, 1987), pp. 68–70.
20. Quoted by Michael Shafir, *Romania. Politics, Economics and Society* (London: Frances Pinter, 1985), p. 148.

6

AUSTERITY, SYSTEMATIZATION AND RESISTANCE

Because of its natural oil resources, Romania had for long specialized in the production of petroleum-related products and had accordingly acquired a substantial refining capacity. During the 1970s, domestic demand for oil-based products grew significantly in Romania, even while the yield of the Ploesti oilfields started to fall off due to natural exhaustion. Romania thus became a net importer of petroleum at the very time of the oil price rise.[1] The fall of the Shah of Iran, with whom Ceausescu had worked out a profitable barter agreement, pushed up the cost of Romania's petroleum imports and obliged the country to purchase its oil on the international market in return for hard currency. The prohibitive cost of oil imports meant that Romania's petroleum industry continued to operate well below capacity.

By the early 1980s, Romania was seriously in debt to western bankers. After the default of Poland in 1981, Romania found it increasingly difficult to obtain extensions on its loans. The next year, Ceausescu had to go cap in hand to the IMF to get help for debt-servicing. In return for IMF assistance, Ceausescu promised to restructure Romanian industry and to release accurate statistics on the country's economic performance. In both cases, he failed to fulfil his part of the bargain.

Throughout the Ceausescu years, Romanian agriculture continued to be underfunded, despite its huge export potential. Following the dictates of 'socialist accumulation', profits from the land were put into industry and the provision of even the most basic machinery was neglected. In much of the countryside, the scythe and the horse-drawn plough remained the principal instrument of husbandry. In summer, the army and schoolchildren were regularly deployed to gather in the harvest. Conditions on the land were so bad that rural workers refused to let their cattle breed knowing that there was inadequate fodder available for larger flocks. As a consequence of this 'peasant intransigence', routine gynaecological examinations were extended to cows in the mid-1980s.

During the 1950s and 1960s, Romania had had one of the highest growth rates in the world and its industrial output had, according to official statistics, increased annually by over 10 per cent. Beginning in the 1970s, Romanian GNP began to slow down and recorded in 1981 a negative growth for the first time in the country's communist history. Thereafter, even the modest goals set out in Ceausescu's five-year plans could not be met. Despite its huge agricultural potential, Romania thus became a net importer of foodstuffs. In order to disguise this persistent and profound economic failure, Ceausescu continuously resorted to publishing false figures, which grossly overestimated Romania's economic performance. When these were challenged, he resorted to further deception. To the question why shops had no meat in them despite a 'record agricultural surplus', he replied at a news conference that it had all been bought by Romanians and was even now stuffed in their freezers.

Ceausescu's economic thinking was rooted in Stalinist beliefs about the primacy of industry and the benefits of centralized planning. Despite promises to the contrary, he never undertook any reform of the infrastructure nor allowed the devolution of decision-making to factory managers. Thus at a time when the rest of Eastern Europe was trying to overcome the rigidity of a command economy, Romania continued to be strangled by overplanning and overdirection. The text of Ceausescu's last plan was thus over 40 metres long. It laid down quotas for 1800 separate products and established for each 400 'target indicators'. When the economy failed to respond to direction, Ceausescu's solution was simply to speed up the pace of industrialization and to squeeze the workforce still further. When this did not yield any improvement, he blamed others for failure and cast around for new enemies. During the 1980s, therefore, the normal 'rotation' of officials was accompanied by a train of dismissals and demotions.

A particular target of Ceausescu's criticism were the foreign bankers, who by their high interest rates 'plundered' the Romanian economy. In 1981, he denounced western interest rates as a 'new form of exploitation', and called for an end to 'financial imperialism'. The next year, he announced that Romania would repay its entire ten billion dollar foreign debt by 1990. As it turned out, he managed to achieve this aim a year early.[2] The entire campaign of debt repayment was accompanied by an increasingly strident campaign directed against the 'financial and banking oligarchy' which 'purloined ... the people's income and, what is truly tragic, that of entire nations'.[3]

Ceausescu's selection of western financiers as the scapegoats for economic failure and the stress he placed upon self-sufficiency, typified the xenophobic nationalism he relied upon in order to mobilize the population to further effort. It does, however, recall the 'By ourselves, alone' economic policies of the former National Liberal Party and its equally vehement denunciation of foreign profiteering in the national economy. Whereas, however, the philosophy of the National Liberals was by no means unique in interwar Europe, Ceausescu's stress on autarchy was entirely unsuited to the global market and conditions of the 1980s. The repayment of the national debt was not accomplished by any dramatic upswing in Romania's economic performance. Instead, a trade surplus was achieved simply by restricting imports and exporting most of the country's industrial and agricultural produce. The 1980s, therefore, were a period of unrelieved austerity and deprivation for the majority of Romanians.

In 1981, after a gap of almost 30 years, bread rationing was reintroduced and foodstuffs such as sugar, coffee and rice became virtually unobtainable.[4] The next year, prices for other household commodities tripled and petrol was rationed. In 1988, the use of private cars was prohibited in the winter months (to prevent accidents on icy roads, so it was explained). To conserve power supplies, the use of vacuums and refrigerators was also banned and street lighting was forbidden in rural areas. Even in Bucharest, the main roads were only dimly illuminated and restaurants closed shortly after nightfall. Pharmaceuticals and antibiotics became quite unobtainable. Medicines listed on prescriptions could only be obtained by Romanians for hard currency or through the services of relatives living abroad. Needless to say, Ceausescu's own diabetes was treated with the latest medicaments and his private parties continued to be well-lit affairs.

While motorists queued for petrol or waited at tram stops, Ceausescu sped past in his Mercedes 600 along traffic lanes reserved for his exclusive use.

As the drive to repay the national debt became even more frantic, so the hardships imposed upon the population became unendurable. The rationing of power reduced the daily supply in winter to one hour's worth of a single bar on an electric fire, and the gas pressure in Bucharest was often too low in winter to permit cooking. The maximum temperature allowed for factories and offices in December was 44°F. Official prices and individual monthly rations (shown in the Table below) convey some impression of the scale of hardship experienced during the late 1980s.

Commodity	Amount per head per month	Price (in lei)
sugar	1 kilo	14
margarine	50 grams	7
rice	250	15
cooking oil	1 litre	20
pork	1 kilo	38
chicken giblets	1 kilo	30

At this time, the monthly wage averaged less than 2000 lei and the income of a rural worker might be as low as 600.[5] It should additionally be borne in mind that the official price was often very substantially less than the real price asked of customers and that even rationed goods were usually unobtainable for long periods. Meat, in particular, was largely unavailable for domestic consumption and what little reached the population consisted mainly of trotters and offal. A visit by Mikhail Gorbachev to Bucharest in 1987 was thus embarrassingly interrupted by Romanians stampeding a 'food and meat complex' newly erected in the capital to impress the Soviet visitor.

Since the leu was virtually worthless as an instrument of exchange, Romanians increasingly resorted to foreign currency transactions or, more usually, to barter. The usual barter commodity was a packet of Kent cigarettes, which was equivalent to a dollar or 15 litres of petrol. Transactions in lei on the black market usually involved spectacular prices, with a kilo of coffee reaching 1000 lei and a video recorder costing four years' salary or 70,000 lei.[6]

Wages not only failed entirely to keep pace with the inflation of black market prices but fell in real terms as well. During the 1980s, industrial workers only received a full pay packet if their plant had fulfilled production at the level laid down in its plan. Since a lack of spare parts and of raw materials meant that many industries were working at 50 per cent capacity, most workers suffered wage cuts. In the countryside, the owners of small plots were only allowed to sell home-grown food at fixed prices and even then they had to make available a fixed quantity of their produce to state procurement offices. By the late 1980s, doctors in Budapest were reporting evidence of malnutrition and of severe vitamin deficiency in Romanian tourists visiting Hungary.

Extraordinarily, however, as the condition of the population became ever more wretched, Ceausescu set himself increasingly grandiose ambitions, and praise for him in the official media reached a new intensity. During the 1980s, therefore, television viewing was reduced to two hours a day, a half of which was devoted to presidential activities. The newspapers now reported Ceausescu's speeches verbatim, inserting into their text the evidence of his enormous popularity: 'Speech interrupted by sustained applause', 'Further applause', 'Applause combined with cheers: *Ceausescu and Romania! Ceausescu and the People!*'

Ceausescu's visits to foreign heads of state similarly increased in number as the president sought to demonstrate his importance as a world leader. Between January and October 1988, Ceausescu paid state visits to no less than thirteen countries: Ghana, Liberia, Guinea, Mauritania, Pakistan, Indonesia, Australia, Vietnam, Mongolia, Kenya, Egypt, China and North Korea. On the occasion of Ceausescu's seventieth birthday, Romanian newspapers reported messages of congratulation sent by Carl Gustav of Sweden, Elizabeth II and Juan Carlos, all of which were in fact fraudulent. Personal vanity encouraged Ceausescu to seek to impress his permanent mark on Romania and this desire grew in intensity as his years approached the Biblically allotted span. During the early 1980s, huge efforts were made to complete the Danube-Black Sea Canal. When the canal was finally opened in 1984, the volume of shipping traffic passing along it was only 10 per cent of that previously predicted. Domestic traffic even had to be re-routed to make the waterway appear busy. Nevertheless, the new canal was hailed as a national triumph and another achievement on the road to 'a multilaterally developed socialist society'. Similar prestige projects completed in the 1980s included the Bucharest metro and Otopeni international airport and a new Romanian navy.

Most notorious of all Ceausescu's building ventures was the massive redevelopment of central Bucharest, which was begun in the mid-1980s. In the process, 26 churches and two monasteries in the old Uranus-Antim quarter were razed and 40,000 residents were displaced. Through the heart of the most picturesque part of old Bucharest was driven a wide street, a straight two miles long which was named the Boulevard of the Victory of Socialism. Both sides of the boulevard were flanked with blocks of flats, cast in the form of huge American beaux-arts railway stations and faced with marble (the so-called 'Ceausescu-style'). Because the stonework was not treated properly, parts of it rapidly yellowed and dissolved. Running through the centre of the boulevard were lanterns and fountains, which owing to power shortages were neither lit nor played. The redeveloped portion of Bucharest rapidly earned the nickname among Romanians of 'Ceaushima'. Crowning the Boulevard of the Victory of Socialism was built a colossal square edifice, 300 feet high, and faced with Corinthian porticos. Although designated the House of the People,[7] the building was intended to accommodate the Polexco, the Central Committee, and office of the President as well as all the ministries of state. It represented therefore the visible symbol of the centralization of authority in communist Romania, and epitomized the blurring and overlap of responsibilities between government, party and president.

Ceausescu himself took a close personal interest in the building of the House of the People. It was largely due to his relentless interference in the work of the architect, Anca Petrescu, that the edifice was not finally complete by the time of his fall.[8] Construction of the 'pyramid' (as it is now commonly known) required tens of thousands of workers, up to 25,000 of whom were on site at any one time. The actual cost of the House of the People has been variously put at between 16 and 20 billion lei ($760–950 million), with one estimate even going so high as to suggest 70 billion lei ($3.3 billion).[9]

The destruction of the old quarter of Bucharest met with criticism from Mikhail Gorbachev on the occasion of his visit to the city in May 1987. Having publicly rebuked Ceausescu for his complacency with regard to living standards, Gorbachev commented on his plans for the redevelopment of Bucharest: 'I hope the historical architecture will be preserved. We failed to do that in some places in Moscow and now we are regretting it'. Gorbachev's warning, which was subsequently printed in *Pravda*, was interpreted at the time as a measure of the distance between the Soviet leader and his Romanian counterpart. Nevertheless, as a statement of international concern, Gorbachev's advice proved modest in comparison to the outcry which greeted the publication of Ceausescu's plans to 'systematize' the Romanian countryside.

In March 1988, Ceausescu announced details of a far-reaching plan for rural redevelopment, which foresaw the reduction of the number of villages in the countryside from 'around 13,000' to 'at the most 5000 to 6000'. Ceausescu explained that the surplus villages were to be razed and the land upon which they lay was to be given over to agricultural use. Following the loss of their homes, about eleven million villagers were to be moved to new 'agro-industrial complexes', which would act as points of concentration for the rural population. Ceausescu envisaged that the process of 'systematization' would be carried through at breakneck speed and would be complete by the year 2000.

Ever since coming to power, Ceausescu had spoken of the need to reform agriculture and to follow through the process of collectivization with measures aimed at 'obliterating the differences between town and countryside'. In the early 1970s, substance was given to these ideological generalities and the concept of transferring the rural population to new sites, which were half urban and half village, was first promoted. Nevertheless, the idea was no sooner raised than it was buried in committees. It was not until the mid-1980s that rural systematization found its way back on to the agenda in the context of the 1986–90 five-year plan. As a prelude to systematization, all land in the Romanian state was declared the national property of the state. The concept of private ownership thus ceased to retain any legal value.

Systematization caused rapid and widespread alarm throughout the Romanian countryside. Although government statements sought to portray life in the villages as primitive and lacking in essential comforts, the truth was that most rural communities consisted of well-appointed dwellings, often set around leafy courtyards and surrounded by spacious plots. In their gardens, countryfolk were able to cultivate fruit and vegetables and to rear livestock, thus supplementing their meagre wages and rations. Most of Romania's villages were centuries old and contained closely knit communities, conscious of their shared traditions and kinship.

By contrast, the new agro-industrial complexes promised a life in identical apartments set in rows of low-level accommodation blocks. From their new homes, the inhabitants would either be bussed out to the collectives or would work in nearby factories. Few of the housing units were, however, connected to the water supply. A well and lavatory block at ground-floor level was deemed sufficient for the inmates' needs. Apparently this decision was endorsed by Ceausescu on the grounds that 'not even in Paris are all the houses connected to the water and sewage system'.[10] Additionally, kitchens were communal, and despite promises to the contrary, there was little opportunity for private cultivation on the small stretches of compacted earth which surrounded the new accommodation blocks. Many of the new buildings were constructed of unsuitable materials which proved incapable of withstanding the Romanian winter.

The systematization of the countryside was justified both as a vital agricultural reform and as an ideologically necessary development. Firstly, by squeezing the rural population into a smaller geographical area, an additional 4.5 per cent of the total agricultural land surface of Romania would be handed over to collectivization. According to the economic thinking in the Communist Party, villages and private plots were far less efficient vehicles of agricultural production than state farms with their superior economies of scale. The fact that village smallholdings accounted for over a third of the national production of meat, for 40 per cent of Romania's milk and eggs, and for a quarter of its fruit, was conveniently overlooked. Secondly, the existence of a class of smallholders was resented on grounds of theory. The 'autarchic cultural existence' of villagers stood in the way, so it was explained, of the socialist homogenization of Romanian society.[11] As one party ideologist argued, moving the villagers into agro-industrial complexes would effect a transformation in their everyday thoughts, customs and attitudes:

> They will learn a new type of social relationship and of collective behaviour by living in common; they will help one another, communicate between themselves and evolve personally in an atmosphere where ideas are shared. All of this will specifically and realistically lead towards a new state of being and to a new type of man.[12]

The stress repeatedly laid in party propaganda on the forging of a new cultural and socialist identity in the countryside suggests that the main aim of the systematization programme was to break the spirit of peasant enterprise and individualism.

In order to win over the rural population, the success of two pilot projects in Ilfov district and at Scornicesti was widely trumpeted. At Scornicesti, Nicolae Ceausescu's home village was uprooted to make way for an agro-industrial complex holding a population of several tens of thousands, and for one of Romania's largest football stadiums. Only a single original dwelling was left standing: the home where Ceausescu had been born and which had subsequently been converted into a museum devoted to his personal history. In Ilfov, four villages (Buda, Demieni, Odoleanu and Vladiceasca) were bulldozed to make way for lines of identical buildings, 'designed according to an inspired architectural vision'.[13] Unsurprisingly, neither example succeeded in convincing villagers that the new agro-industrial complexes represented a superior style of accommodation.

Although the party press continually extolled the material benefits which systematization would bring to villagers, the programme met with resistance. In several places, in Petrova in Maramures county and at Parva and Monor in Bistrita-Nasaud, local rebellions were reported. Elsewhere, officials concealed villages by administratively merging them into larger units. Nevertheless, the programme went ahead, having its greatest effect on the Wallachian plain and in the western region of Transylvania near the Hungarian border. A particular cause of concern among the rural population was that no lists of the villages scheduled for removal was published, thus leaving the entire countryside in a state of anxiety. Villagers were normally only given notice of several weeks (in one case 48 hours) that their houses were to be destroyed and they were additionally required to undertake the work of demolition themselves.

The systematization policy was widely publicized in the United States and in Western Europe where it elicited very substantial criticism. The unique qualities of Romanian rural life were variously extolled and the Ceausescu government's disregard for humanitarian considerations was widely deplored. Concern over the villages additionally drew attention to Romania's appalling human rights record and forced a substantial shift in diplomatic policy towards the regime. Increasingly, western governments distanced themselves from the ruler they had been so keen to court in the 1970s. In July 1988, therefore, Romania was forced to relinquish its status as a Most Favoured Nation trading partner of the United States.[14] The British and West German governments expressed similar concern at Romania's continued violation of the basic norms of civilized behaviour. In September 1988, the British Foreign Secretary, Sir Geoffrey Howe, complained in a letter to his Romanian counterpart that the systematization programme would do 'irreparable damage to our common European cultural and architectural heritage'. Despite pressure in the House of Lords, however, Ceausescu was allowed to retain the honorary knighthood awarded him in 1978.[15] Pressure from the West did, however, oblige a slowing of the systematization programme in late 1988 and a promise that the destruction of villages had never really been intended.[16] In order to sow confusion, the rumour was deliberately put around that the ancient German settlement at Gottlob (Kisosz) had been demolished. Western visitors were then allowed to the site to report that the village was still intact.

It was, however, not so much Western Europe as the People's Republic of Hungary which acted as the most profound and persistent critic of Ceausescu's human rights violations and of the systematization programme. Hungarian concern was aroused for several reasons. Firstly, there was considerable evidence to suggest that the Hungarian minority communities in Transylvania would bear the brunt of systematization. In the 1960s and early 1970s, the forerunner of the state planning body presently in charge of the systematization programme had directed most of its destructive impulses on buildings and monuments belonging to Romania's national minorities. More recently, a number of Transylvanian villages in Satu Mare, Bihor, Arad and Timis counties had been demolished and more were expected to follow. As the Hungarian parliament pointed out in a resolution passed on 31 July 1988, 'For the national minorities in Romania the implementation of the plan [of systematization] would mean the destruction of their material and spiritual cradle, the dispersal of their communities, human tragedies, and in the last resort, forced and accelerated assimilation'. The parliament additionally stressed that, 'the villages of Romania contain inestimable historical and cultural treasures. They are part of the inalienable spiritual and material heritage of mankind'.[17] Secondly, there had been, during the 1980s, a considerable worsening of the plight of the Hungarian

minority in Romania. Hungarian educational facilities had been pared
back and minority-language publications reduced both in number and
in volume. A whole series of unpublished 'internal regulations'
discriminated against Hungarians, preventing them from putting up
notices in their own language and forcing them to take up jobs
elsewhere in the country. Traditional Hungarian centres were opened
up to large scale Romanian immigration and Romanian teachers and
recent graduates were seconded to minority areas. The largest
discrimination was practised, however, against the Hungarian *csango*
community in Moldavia. Following the 'discovery' that the *csangos* were
'magyarized Romanians', a campaign of forcible assimilation was
begun. The *csangos* were deprived of their schools and were even
forbidden to speak Hungarian in public.

Equally alarming was the government-inspired 'hate campaign'
which was inaugurated in the mid-1980s. A collection of novels
published at this time portrayed Hungarians as cruel and morally lax,
and blamed them for the Stalinist excesses of the post-war years.[18]
Pseudo-historical works dealing with Hungarian fascism in the 1940s
and the Austro-Hungarian 'rule of terror' in the nineteenth and early
twentieth centuries lent a specious air of retributive justice to the
persecution of Hungarians. During the late 1980s, a flood of ethnic
Hungarian refugees from Transylvania and bodies in the Mures River
floating past the border confirmed the steady worsening of conditions
and of morale in socialist Romania.[19]

Following the publication in Hungary in 1987 of a three-volume
history of Transylvania, which refuted some of the more exaggerated
claims of Romanian nationalist historiography, the violation of the
minority's rights was combined with accusations of 'territorial
revisionism'. The Hungarian state was accused of plotting to seize
Transylvania and of harbouring fascist ambitions. Although these
claims were steadfastly denied by the Hungarian government,
Ceausescu constantly reiterated his talk of a Magyar threat to
Romanian independence with the aim of whipping up popular
nationalist support for his ailing government. So alarmed was the
Hungarian government at the scale of Romanian propaganda that it
put its border troops on special alert.

Hungary was politically the most developed of the Warsaw Pact
countries with both a highly influential dissident movement and a
powerful reformist wing actually within the Communist Party. Under

pressure both from the streets and from the apparatus, the party boss Janos Kadar and his successor after May 1988, Karoly Grosz, were constantly forced to up the tempo of their criticism of the Ceausescu government. On 27 June 1988, 40,000 Hungarians demonstrated in Budapest against the systematization programme and against the abuse of human rights in Romania. This was the largest protest on the streets of Budapest since 1956 and it immediately established the good political credentials both of the main organizers, the Hungarian Democratic Forum, and of the Forum's close ally, the reforming Minister of State Imre Pozsgay. By the same token, the demonstration emphasised the impotence of Hungary's communist government in its dealings with a fellow socialist country. In the course of the next fifteen months, Pozsgay and the HDF used their accumulated political capital to break the enfeebled grip of the Communist Party and together they transformed Hungary into a modern democracy. In this way, the systematization programme had the indirect and unexpected consequence of speeding the process of democratic change in neighbouring Hungary.

During the 1980s, early signs of incipient opposition began to appear in Romania itself. These fell into two main categories: conspiratorial attempts at military coups and disorganized popular protests. Both were occasioned by the increasingly wretched conditions and by the policies of the Ceausescu government. It was in response to the latter, and more particularly to the lack of funding given to the armed services in contrast to the *securitate*, that an army coup may have been arranged in 1983.[20] The next year, a second plot to overthrow Ceausescu was allegedly hatched by some senior officers and party members. The putsch is said to have failed due to key military units being coincidentally sent out of the capital to help gather the harvest. The precise identity of the figures involved in this second plot (if indeed it existed at all) is still uncertain due to continued disinformation in the top ranks of the present government.[21]

The most serious popular demonstration of opposition to the government came on 15 November 1987. Angered by wage cuts and fearful at what new nightmare of deprivation the winter would bring, several tens of thousands of workers marched through the centre of the Transylvanian city of Brasov demanding meat, bread and milk. In the course of the protest, local party offices were ransacked. The rising, which lacked both organization and clear purpose, was swiftly put down by the army. In the attendant fighting, three persons were killed. The government's response was to arrest the ringleaders and to mollify the rest of the workforce by rushing food supplies to the town. During the next few weeks, further disturbances were reported in Iasi, Timisoara and Bucharest.

Anxiety over the systematization programme, combined with the new international attention focused on Romania, inspired and gave courage to a dissident movement.[22] One of the principal forces behind the intellectual opposition to the regime was Doina Cornea, a former lecturer in French at the University of Cluj and a member of the outlawed Greek Catholic Church. Despite having been placed under house arrest since 1982 for recommending religious and philosophical texts to her students, Cornea continued to publicize violations of human rights in Romania. In a series of letters smuggled out to the West, she criticized Ceausescu's plans for rural development and the damage done to Romanian cultural traditions. Strong expressions of diplomatic support for Doina Cornea, including a foiled attempt to visit her in Cluj by the British ambassador, prevented Ceausescu from arranging her imprisonment.

Over the course of 1989, Cornea was joined in her protest by a number of leading Romanian intellectuals, led by the writer Mircea Dinescu. Dinescu appealed to his fellow Romanians to make a stand 'against the dinosaurian Stalinism in whose belly we will find one day the corpses of those who had the courage to express their despair'.[23] Dinescu and other writers who joined his protest were summarily placed under house arrest. Although Ceausescu's firm response to dissent resulted in a further wave of international protests, his ruthlessness at least ensured that the intellectual opposition in Romania remained fragmented. Thus, unlike Czechoslovakia, where semi-clandestine clubs and a burgeoning underground literature united dissidents and intellectual groups in a common programme of opposition, Romania almost entirely lacked the foundation of a civil society equipped and able to threaten communist hegemony.

Under these circumstances, it is not surprising that the principal challenge to Ceausescu should have come from the ranks of the Communist Party itself. Unlike Hungary, however, where the communist reform movement was led by a younger generation of activists, the lead was taken in Romania by the party veterans. During the second half of the 1980s, a succession of 'old communists' came into open conflict with Ceausescu. In 1985, Janos Fazekas, who had joined the party in 1944 and subsequently been a deputy prime minister, attacked Ceausescu's policies with regard to the Hungarian minority. He was accordingly relieved of all his posts and sent into internal exile. Several years later, Silviu Brucan, another party veteran, and Dumitru Mazilu, who had first come to prominence in the early 1960s, publicly criticized the Ceausescu government's human rights record.

The most significant challenge from within the party came, however, in March 1989. In that month, six distinguished members of the 'old guard' who had led the party in the 1940s, wrote an open letter to Ceausescu. They complained firstly of the systematization policy, appealing for its prompt suspension on humanitarian, cultural and economic grounds. Thereafter, they requested the president to restore Romania to the rule of law and to cease his violation of human and of constitutional rights.[24] The six signators – Gheorghe Apostol, Alexandru Birladeanu, Silviu Brucan, Corneliu Manescu, Constantin Pirvulescu and Grigore Raceanu – were all promptly placed under house arrest.

The disassociation of the party veterans from Ceausescu provides in retrospect strong evidence that the regime was beginning to unravel. Economic hardship, combined with the systematization programme and mounting international pressure imposed tremendous strains on political loyalties. Yet, even as the regime began to crack, no alternative government was ready and waiting in the wings to take over power. Unlike Poland, Romania lacked an independent trade union apparatus and, unlike Czechoslovakia, no *samizdat* society had yet emerged. When a massive popular uprising spontaneously erupted on the streets of Timisoara and Bucharest in December 1989, the only group sufficiently well organized to assume power were the disaffected elements within the party. Pre-eminent within this group were the communist 'old guard', and it was they who were to be among the main beneficiaries of the Christmas Revolution.

NOTES

1. Romania largely avoided the economic dislocation caused by the 1973 rise in oil prices since the export price of Romanian refined petroleum products rose in accompaniment. This happy coincidence was not repeated in 1978.
2. *Financial Times* (14 April 1989).
3. Michael Shafir, 1985, op. cit. p. 119
4. Rationing was initially introduced region by region. By 1986–7 it was nationwide.
5. According to government figures the average monthly wage in January 1989 was 3018 lei; this figure is exaggerated.
6. *Eastern Europe Newsletter* (9 November 1988).
7. Its original name was the House of the Republic.
8. Ceausescu had apparently still not settled on the design of the roof by the time of his death. Quite why an inexperienced architect in her mid-20s should have been chosen as the architect of the House of the People must remain uncertain. Although Anca Petrescu has always denied this, she may just conceivably have been a relative of Elena Ceausescu.
9. *Romania Libera* (8 February 1990); the House of the People is presently used to accommodate the sessions and staff of parliamentary committees.
10. *Lumea* (19 January 1990).
11. *Scinteia* (17 July 1988).
12. *Flacara* (8 July 1988), cited in Stephane Rosiere, 'Le programme du Systematisation du territoire Roumain', *Les Temps Modernes* (Paris, January 1990), pp. 54–5.
13. *Actualites Roumaines* (8 July 1988).
14. Ceausescu repudiated MFN status when it became clear that the US Senate would not agree to its renewal.
15. *The Independent* (21 September 1988; 11 April 1989).
16. The Romanian ambassador to Bonn, Marcel Dinu, as reported in the *Stuttgarter Zeitung* (3 December 1988), cited by Anneli Ute Gabanyi, 'Ceausescu's "Systematisierung". Territorialplanung in Rumanien', *Sudosteuropa*, vol. 38 (1989), p. 241.
17. *New Hungarian Quarterly* (Autumn 1988), p. 56.
18. Ion Lancranjan, *Cuvint despre Transilvania* (Bucharest, 1982), *Toamna fierbinte* (Bucharest, 1986); Doru Munteanu, *Vinerea neagra* (Bucharest, 1986).
19. RFE/BR (20 July 1989).
20. The details of this event still remain patchy.
21. In interviews on Romanian television and the weekly *Cuvintul* (28 February 1990), General Kostyal asserted the involvement of Ion Iliescu. This claim was later dropped and the names of Silviu Brucan, Nicolae Militaru and Ion Ionita were emphasized instead (*Adevarul* 23 August 1990); SWB/EE 28 July 1990). At the time of writing, the coups of the 1980s are being employed as ways of buttressing up the authority and legitimacy of rival factions in the government.

22. On intellectual dissidents in Romania more generally: H. Gordon Skilling, *Samizdat and an Independent Society in Central and Eastern Europe* (Basingstoke: Macmillan, 1989), pp. 191–5.
23. Cited by Dennis Deletant, *Sunday Correspondent* (17 December 1989).
24. The text is reproduced in *Les Temps Modernes* (Paris, January 1990), pp. 25–41.

7

ENVIRONMENT AND AIDS

The emphasis placed by the Ceausescu government on breakneck modernization had catastrophic consequences for the Romanian environment. In order to fulfil the national plan at a minimal cost, factory complexes were hastily thrown up with neither the proper filtration equipment nor basic provision for health and safety. Industrial sites spewing out chemical pollutants were placed close beside population centres. So as to ensure the 'harmonious distribution of industry', other plants were located in the heart of previously unspoiled countryside. By the time of the revolution, 40 per cent of the Romanian population was suffering from chronic bronchial and chest disorders, and large areas had been converted into industrial wastelands. According to incomplete material released at the beginning of 1990 by the newly-formed Ecological Movement, there were in Romania at least 625 centres of serious pollution.[1]

By the time of Ceausescu's downfall, there was scarcely a single town in Romania not threatened by environmental disaster. On the edge of Baia Mare, an ore-processing plant churned out annually 50,000 tons of sulphur dioxide and 3000 tons of metal powder. The whole town was frequently enveloped in a smog, comprising poisons up to a hundred times higher than the legal limit.[2] The Pulp and Paper Works at Suceava similarly discharged every day 20 tons of cellulose and fibre waste, and was responsible for a unique respiratory and nervous disorder known as 'Suceava syndrome'. Outside Tirgu Mures, the *Azomures* fertilizer plant released a plume of toxic gas across a wide area of countryside.

Almost certainly the worst example of industrial pollution was the 'carbon black' processing plant at Copsa Mica, which was greatly expanded in the 1970s with British assistance.[3] The *Carbosin* factory at Copsa Mica pumped thousands of tons of soot annually into the atmosphere and every fissure in its brickwork seemed to exude fumes. The detritus of Copsa Mica blackened the surrounding countryside, staining the trunks of trees at 20 kilometres and killing the vegetation at six. No animal life could survive in the immediate area except for wildfowl, the flesh of which was sufficiently noxious to be inedible. The town resting on the edge of the Copsa Mica plant was permanently shrouded in a sticky dust and the skin of the inhabitants was impregnated with soot. In a sad attempt to brighten their lives, the residents of nearby cottages painted the walls of their homes a dazzling blue and pink. The colours were soon swallowed up by the pervading filth and gloom.

Within individual factories, machinery was frequently left unguarded, the equipment was notoriously unsafe, and the workforce was insufficiently trained. Employees at the EPN factory in Timisoara, which provides furniture for the British market, are thus said to be easily recognized by their lack of a full set of fingers.[4] During the 1980s, explosions at the weapons factories at Mirsa and Zarnest were not uncommon and are thought to have claimed several hundred lives. For its part, the Cernavoda nuclear power station, a prestige project begun in 1978, was so shoddily built that its concrete foundations cracked and a third of the welding joints came apart under stress. Rather than admit these errors, the local managers falsified test records. Only the intervention of Cernavoda's Canadian partners prevented the station going into operation prematurely with potentially appalling consequences.

Within urban centres the collapse of the basic municipal infrastructure resulted in the contamination of water supplies by effluent and human waste. Throughout the 1980s there was a succession of outbreaks of cholera in cities along the Black Sea coast. The sewage system in Bucharest frequently failed to cope and discharged instead into the streets. In order to prevent an epidemic, the supply of mains water was so heavily chlorinated as to be virtually undrinkable. Roads both in the capital and in provincial cities were pitted with potholes and new housing complexes were frequently completed with only rutted mud tracks for streets.

The economic thrust of the last decade of the Ceausescu regime was attended by a widespread scarring of the rural landscape. The building materials needed for systematization were obtained by quarrying on such a scale that a range of hills near Huedin was largely obliterated. On the Danube delta, an ambitious and unsuccessful attempt to recover the region for agriculture resulted in the destruction of a fifth of this unique forest and marsh environment. The indiscriminate use of pesticides additionally resulted in dairy products containing such a dangerous quantity of carcinogens that they were ineligible for export. Nor was the seascape spared. In order to obtain hard currency, a European dumping ground for chemical and nuclear waste was opened near the port of Sulina.[5] The materials were stored in steel barrels which were either left exposed to the elements or buried close to the surface. Escaping dioxins rapidly killed off fish shoals and polluted part of the Bulgarian coast. In 1988, the Soviet Mir spacecraft identified radiation leakage at Sulina and international pressure was applied to clear up the site. The task of recleansing the dump is thought to have cost rather more than the paltry $2 million which it had previously earned.

The scale of the environmental pollution in Romania was widely appreciated before the revolution through private reports and through clandestine groups working within the country.[6] However, it was not until 1990 that the extent of the contemporary AIDS epidemic affecting Romania came to light. Even then, precise figures proved hard to obtain and the information provided by the authorities was frequently contradictory.

The first Romanian AIDS victim was identified in 1984 by Dr Ludovic Paun, director of the Clinic for Infectious and Tropical Diseases at the Victor Babes Hospital in Bucharest. However, it was not until 1987 that the Romanian government formally admitted the presence of the infection. The next year, Dr Paun published a text on the disease, which was confidentially circulated among members of the medical profession. He established 38 cases of patients suffering from AIDS, of which five were reported as having died. Almost certainly the figures provided by Paun were far too low. It seems that he had confined his investigations to the adult population and had not taken into account the spread of the disease among children. Attempts to rectify Paun's findings by including the alarming evidence of sample tests taken in orphanages were blocked in 1989 by the Ministry of Health. Government officials concealed all evidence of infection among children for fear of the adverse publicity and attention it would cast on the parlous state of Romanian medical provision. Figures provided in June 1990 put the number of AIDS infected children at 3000.[7] This was, however, a tentative estimate. Statistical analysis based on sample testing suggested that the total for the population as a whole might be nearer 130,000, with the overwhelming majority of victims thought to be children.[8] Government statistics released in September 1991, claiming 1557 cases of HIV infection and 552 AIDS deaths, are thought to be underestimates.

The spread of the AIDS virus among the youngest section of Romanian society was due to several related circumstances. Owing to the Ceausescu government's prohibition on contraception and abortion a large number of unwanted babies were born. These were taken into state care and put into orphanages. Hospitals and psychiatric institutions were similarly filled with children for whom their parents were unable to take proper care. The scale of health and medical provision in these institutions was minimal. Often the inmates shared beds and in psychiatric hospitals the children frequently huddled in rags and blankets. Since the supply of hypodermics was inadequate, needles were customarily reused. In the absence of specialist drugs, malnutrition and anaemia were treated by intravenous feeding and by blood transfusions. The equipment for these operations was often unsterilized. Once the AIDS virus had entered an institution, it was therefore rapidly passed on among the patients.

Even after the Revolution, the scale of the AIDS epidemic among the adult population could only be speculated upon. The high incidence of hepatitis B indicated that the virus might be still more widely distributed than had hitherto been thought. The continuing lack not only of condoms but also of treatment for genital lesions and of advice on personal hygiene, also suggested that a high rate of transmission could be expected. It is additionally believed that a large number of adults volunteered before the Revolution for 'mini-transfusions' of blood in the hope of obtaining intravenous nourishment, and that most of these operations were performed with unsterilized equipment. The most savage legacy of the Ceausescu era, with all its talk of increasing the population, may therefore prove to be not just the wasting of the environment but the decimation of a whole generation of Romanians.

NOTES

1. *Romania*, no. 2–3 (1990), p. 20; *Daily Telegraph* (19 January 1990).
2. RFE/REE (11 May 1990).
3. I owe this information to a former manager at Copsa Mica. He did not, however, recall the name of the British firm involved.
4. Romanian furniture is sold widely in the UK, although the place of origin is

concealed under a number of misleading brandnames. Whereas East German self-assembly items occupy the lower end of the UK furniture market, examples of 'quality workmanship' are frequently Romanian.

5. The transfer of waste to Sulina was undertaken by a company based in Lichtenstein using Turkish vessels.

6. Most notably Romanian Democratic Action, which published a 22-page report on the environment in 1988.

7. Given at the Sixth International AIDS Conference in San Francisco, June 1990; cited in RFE/REE (17 August 1990).

8. Ibid.

8

LASZLO TOEKES AND THE *SECURITATE*

It is not surprising that the revolution which overthrew the Ceausescu government should have begun in Transylvania. This was always the more developed part of Romania with traditions of civic responsibility and of popular opposition to oppressive rule. As recently as November 1987, riots in the Transylvanian city of Brasov had yielded the most serious challenge in 20 years to the Ceausescu government. Additionally, the Hungarians of Transylvania had been singled out by Ceausescu for especially harsh treatment and they anticipated that their communities would bear the brunt of the systematization programme. Already in the early months of 1989, there had been sporadic village uprisings in Transylvania against the plans for rural development. Hungarians were also prominent in the international campaign against the agro-industrial centres and sustained through the *Ellenpontok* (Counterpoints) newspaper and the *Transylvanian Information Service* the two leading Romanian *samizdat* sources of the 1980s.

Nevertheless, Ceausescu reckoned that the national animosities he had deliberately cultivated in Transylvania would be sufficient to prevent any common front being established there against his government. In the event of disorder breaking out in Transylvania, he hoped to appeal to traditional Romanian patriotism by suggesting that there was a plot afoot to have the region returned to Hungarian ownership. Even as the Christmas Revolution spread from Transylvania to the streets of the capital, the president continued to claim that the insurrection was the work of 'reactionary, imperialist, irredentist, chauvinist circles': the familiar codewords for Hungary and for Romania's Hungarian minority. It is certainly the case that there is a substantial gulf of distrust between the various ethnic communities in Transylvania. This ill-feeling has its roots in the history of the region,

83

but it was deliberately fostered by Ceausescu as part of a 'divide and rule' policy. What was remarkable about the events of December 1989 is that the Romanians of Transylvania should have joined together with the region's Hungarians to defend Laszlo Toekes, a Hungarian pastor who had been pilloried by the government as a 'chauvinist, anti-communist and anti-Romanian enemy of the state'.

For two centuries the family of Toekes has provided pastors for the Calvinist Reformed Church in Transylvania. Like the Gereb, Juhasz and Soos families, the 'Toekes dynasty' is one of the leading lines of Protestant churchmen in Romania. The Calvinist church claims some 700,000 adherents in Transylvania, almost all of whom belong to the

The *Securitate* Apparatus

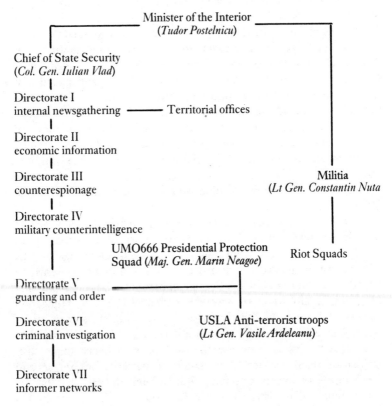

(names in italics refer to office-holders in December 1989)

Hungarian minority. Under Ceausescu, however, the Reformed Church was reduced to little more than an instrument of government. It was deprived of its rights of self-government and subjected to continued interference by the Department of Cults, the ministry responsible for religious affairs. The Reformed Church bishops of Cluj and Oradea were simply the placemen of the government appointed without reference to the established procedure of election. They were additionally susceptible to manipulation by the First Directorate of the *securitate*, which as part of its brief undertook the surveillance of the clergy. The contempt in which the Ceausescu government held the Calvinist community is amply demonstrated by the seizure of a shipment of 20,000 Hungarian language Bibles sent to Transylvania in 1972. A large part of this consignment is thought to have been subsequently recycled into lavatory tissue at the Braila paper mill.[1]

During the 1980s, the corrupt and supine character of the Reformed Church hierarchy was singled out for particular criticism by Istvan Toekes, deputy bishop of Cluj and a lecturer at the Reformed College in the same city. Istvan Toekes accused the church leadership of 'brutal arbitrary behaviour' and of behaving in the fashion of a 'marionette'. He drew attention there to the disregard shown by his superiors for the constitution of the church, sharply criticized the personality cult surrounding the bishops of Cluj and Oradea, and demanded the convocation of a General Synod. Toekes's opposition resulted in his dismissal in 1983 both as a deputy bishop and as a lecturer. In 1989 he was barred from preaching altogether.[2]

Whereas the elder Toekes had confined his criticism to the church hierarchy, using legal arguments to support his case, his son, Laszlo Toekes (born 1952) was ready to take on the entire apparatus of church and state. During the early 1980s, Laszlo Toekes contributed to the dissident publication, *Ellenpontok*, drawing attention to breaches of civil rights in Romania. Additionally, he sought to preserve Hungarian cultural traditions by holding special classes in literature and history for his parishioners in Dej, and by the establishment of amateur dramatic companies. When the state publishing house refused to print sufficient hymn books and wall calendars for his congregation, Laszlo Toekes organized a nationwide petition and eventually obtained both. It is, however, illustrative of the difficulties facing the church that the wall calendar had also to include the date of Ceausescu's birthday.

Toekes's activities rapidly brought him to the attention of the Department of Cults. Acting through the bishops of Cluj and Oradea, Gyula Nagy and Laszlo Papp respectively, the department sought to have Pastor Toekes despatched into ecclesiastical exile in the remote parish of Sinpetru de Cimpie. The bishops proved amenable to such persuasion on the part of the department not only because Toekes had singled them out for criticism but also because they resented the prestige attaching to the 'Toekes dynasty'. Both bishops Nagy and Papp were clergymen of humble origin who had been promoted precisely because of their obscure background. In Nagy's case, his low intellectual achievement was matched only by his distinction as a former Olympic athlete. Rather than accept exile, Laszlo Toekes chose unemployment. For two years he was jobless and living with his parents in Cluj. Nevertheless, the harassment of Toekes had been brought to the attention of the Foreign Relations Committee of the United States Senate and considerable diplomatic pressure was brought to bear on his behalf. Accordingly, in 1986 the ecclesiastical authorities relaxed their harsh treatment of Toekes and appointed him to the post of assistant pastor in the ethnically mixed city of Timisoara.[3]

During the late 1980s, Laszlo Toekes's criticism of his superiors and of the Romanian government became increasingly severe. He was a vocal opponent of the systematization programme which he denounced on Hungarian State Television as a measure aimed at eliminating the peasantry: 'the only section of society which disposes of the moral and material background that makes it possible to resist the regime'. He drew attention to the way villagers had been coerced into signing petitions in support of the agro-industrial centres and he rebuked his fellow clergy for their reluctance to criticize the government. In his sermons, which attracted many hundreds of worshippers, he made scarcely veiled attacks on Ceausescu and he urged prayer for the threatened villages. Nevertheless, he made it clear that his concern was for the spiritual welfare not just of his Hungarian congregation but of the Romanians of Transylvania as well. Both were equally the victims of a corrupt, brutal and degrading dictatorship and he called for solidarity between the nations of Transylvania as the preliminary to democratic transformation in Romania. He stressed that he acted as 'above all else the servant of Christ' rather than as the spokesman of any single section of society. In this way he sought to refute the accusation that he was a tool of the Hungarian minority and an agent working on behalf of neighbouring Hungary. It is likely that Toekes's statements were known not only to Romanians who understood some Hungarian but also to those who listened to the Romanian language services of Radio Free Europe and the BBC.[4]

Toekes's defiant stand against the church and state authorities resulted in an increasingly obtrusive campaign being waged against him. At the end of 1987, the dossier on Laszlo Toekes was taken out of the hands of the *securitate* Office for the Study of Nationalists, Fascists and Hungarian Irredentists (First Directorate) and given over to Colonel Traian Sima, head of the territorial *securitate* office in Timisoara. Previously, the First Directorate had largely confined its activities to disseminating false rumours about Toekes. Under the direction of Colonel Sima, who had gained experience in the intimidation of clergy while serving in Oradea, increasingly violent methods were deployed.[5]

During 1988 and 1989 the harassment of Laszlo Toekes took the form of threatening visitors to his church flat and members of his congregation. When these tactics failed to halt Toekes's criticism of the government, Colonel Sima embarked upon more ruthless methods. Accordingly, members of Toekes's congregation were arrested and beaten up. Others were intercepted at bus stops and railway stations and charged with foreign currency offences. Most gravely, on 14 September 1989, the church elder Erno Ujvarossy, who had previously organized a petition in Toekes's defence, was found murdered in the woods outside Timisoara. Toekes himself was charged with black marketeering and was briefly detained.[6]

At the instigation of the *securitate*, Bishop Laszlo Papp of Oradea launched a new campaign against Toekes from within the church hierarchy. On 31 March 1989, the pastor was ordered by Papp to cease preaching in Timisoara and to take up instead a new appointment in the distant parish of Mineu. When Toekes refused to leave his congregation, eviction proceedings were begun by the church authorities so as to force him out of his home. Since Toekes was deemed no longer to be an employee of the church in Timisoara, his ration book was confiscated and power supplies to his flat were interrupted. At great personal risk to themselves, Toekes's parishioners brought him food and fuel.

Although Toekes enjoyed considerable support from his congregation and elders, some of whom went into hiding rather than be forced to denounce him, his fellow clergy failed to rally to his defence. Thus, the authors of an open letter appealing to the bishop of Oradea to cease his harassment could not find one practising Reformed Church minister who was prepared to add his signature.[7] It is unlikely, however, that the reluctance of the Reformed Church clergy stemmed from a lack of courage on their part. The majority were convinced that Toekes was engaged in a pointless suicide mission and that his defiance would only result in further difficulties for their own congregations. A few churchmen also perceived the dispute between Toekes and his superiors to be primarily a private feud which stemmed from the rivalry between the old, established families of churchmen and the new generation of Ceausescu appointees.

Laszlo Toekes received, nevertheless, open support in Hungary. He continued to give interviews to Hungarian reporters and his sermons were tape recorded and broadcast on Hungarian radio. In November 1989, the Romanian ambassador was summoned to the Hungarian Foreign Ministry and informed of the Hungarian government's concern for Toekes's welfare. Hungarian protests at the behaviour of the Romanian authorities were similarly lodged with the United Nations. The Hungarian parliament additionally proposed Toekes for the Nobel prize. In order to avoid the accusation that they were supporting Toekes for 'nationalist and revisionist' motives, the parliament symbolically coupled Toekes's nomination with that of Doina Cornea.

The importance of this support was subsequently recognized by Toekes's wife. As she later explained, 'The international publicity held them off. If he had been an unknown and nameless figure, they would have killed him sooner or later'.[8] It was probably for this reason that the authorities sought to maintain an illusion of legality in their treatment of Toekes, proceeding as much by court orders as by physical intimidation.

During the autumn of 1989 the *securitate* operation against Toekes redoubled in intensity and the Minister of the Interior, Tudor Postelnicu, took effective charge of Toekes's case. He ordered material to be gathered establishing the pastor's complicity in treason with reference either to the Hungarian or Canadian intelligence services (Toekes had a brother living in Canada), and he instructed Sima to enforce the eviction order on Toekes. Groups of workers drawn from a local machine factory were mustered to demonstrate aggressively in front of his flat. On 2 November, an unidentified four-man team broke into Toekes's home, threw the furniture around

and wounded the pastor in the forehead. A week later, the windows of
his flat were smashed.

Shortly after these incidents, the *securitate* visited Toekes and
promised an end to the violence if he went off to the parish of Mineu
and stopped 'creating scandal for the Romanian authorities'. At about
the same time, Bishop Laszlo Papp obtained a court judgement
ordering Toekes to quit his church accommodation forthwith. On 15
December, the first attempts were made forcibly to evict Toekes from
his flat. However, a human chain formed by members of his
congregation around the block in which he lived, prevented the
enforcement operation. The pastor thanked the crowd but advised
them to leave before they incurred the wrath of the authorities. His
warning was met with chants of 'We won't leave'. The next day, the
few hundred Hungarian protesters were joined by several thousand
more, consisting mainly of young ethnic Romanians. In a historic
gesture, Romanians linked hands with Hungarians. They then went on
to hold a procession through the centre of Timisoara, where they
chanted Toekes's name and slogans against the government. In
conscious imitation of the events in Brasov in November 1987, the
demonstrators sang the song, 'Romanians Awake'. As Laszlo Toekes
was himself later to relate:

> The crowd was mostly Romanian and it was there again the next
> day. A demonstration of solidarity became a revolt in solidarity. I
> could not have imagined this. Hungarians and Romanians had
> always been opposed to each other. The regime had fostered real
> hatred between the two peoples. The support I received from the
> ethnic Romanians during these days was an overwhelming
> experience. How moving to see the Romanian crowd under my
> windows chanting their national hymn. Until that day, that hymn
> had separated us. From that day on, it united us ... [9]

Having received instructions from Bucharest to act toughly, an intense
securitate action was undertaken to evict Toekes. On the night of the
16–17 December, the pastor's house was forcibly entered. He and his
wife took refuge in the church, where they were seized and assaulted
standing beside the communion table. After Toekes had been bullied
into signing an acceptance of his eviction, he and his wife were driven
some 200 miles to the northeast to the village of Mineu. Over the next

five days Toekes was interrogated and put under pressure to confess to being a foreign agent.

A statement by Bishop Laszlo Papp, justifying the eviction of Toekes, was published on 21 December. Bishop Papp accused Toekes of 'indiscipline', of 'grossly violating the statute of organization and functioning of the Reformed Church in Romania and the laws of the Romanian state', and of 'denigrating and making a tendentious presentation of the realities in our country'.[10]

Laszlo Toekes was released from arrest on 22 December following the flight of his captors. Laszlo Papp fled Romania a week later.[11]

NOTES

1. Hungarian Democratic Forum, *Report on the Situation of the Hungarian Minority in Romania* (Budapest: H.D.F., 1988), pp. 109–10.
2. Keston News Service (25 August 1988; 6 June 1989).
3. The Calvinist pastor whom Toekes was deputed to assist was Leo Peuker. Following Peuker's death in December 1986, Toekes was appointed his successor.
4. RFE/REE (2 February 1990).
5. *Kapu* (April 1990), pp. 6–7.
6. Keston News Service (2 November 1989).
7. Ibid., (19 October 1989).
8. *Erdelyi Figyelo*, No. 9–10 (1990) p. 11.
9. RFE/REE (2 February 1990).
10. SWB/EE (23 December 1989).
11. Laszlo Papp escaped to Hungary and thence made his way to Metz, where his son lived.

9

TIMISOARA

During 1989 the communist system in Eastern Europe fell apart. In August of that year, a Solidarity Prime Minister was appointed in Poland. Throughout the summer, the democratic opposition in Hungary achieved a series of impressive victories, which culminated on 23 October in the proclamation of a new non-socialist Republic. At midnight on 8–9 November, following the collapse of the East German government, the Berlin Wall was breached. By the end of November, the old hard liners had been ousted in Czechslovakia and Bulgaria, and both countries stood on the brink of democratic transformation. Albania and Romania remained alone in Europe as islands of totalitarian communism.

Ceausescu was obstinately opposed to any measure of change in Romania. In an extraordinary interview which he gave on West German television in November 1989, Ceausescu condemned the betrayal of socialism in Eastern Europe and affirmed his own ideological intransigence. 'At the turn of the century,' he explained, 'Romania will have achieved communism. The Romanians know that they have to make sacrifices and they do so gladly.' At the 14th Party Congress which opened in Bucharest a few days later, the 3308 delegates unanimously re-elected Ceausescu as leader of the Romanian Communist Party. In a speech lasting six hours, Ceausescu reiterated the same uncompromising message he had given on television. 'The party cannot give up its revolutionary responsibility,' he declared, 'it cannot give up its historical mission to another political force.' Only when pears grew from poplar trees would the party relinquish its leading role in Romanian politics and society. The assembly gave Ceausescu's speech more than sixty standing ovations; outside the hall students hung fruit on bushes as a symbol of their defiance.

Ceausescu was firmly convinced that the collapse of communism in Eastern Europe had been masterminded by an international conspiracy with its headquarters in Moscow and Washington. As he explained at a meeting of the Polexco on 17 December 1989:

> Everything that happens and happened in Germany, in Czechoslovakia and Bulgaria now, and in Poland and Hungary in the past, are things organized by the Soviet Union with American and Western support ... What has happened in the last three countries, the German Democratic Republic, Czechoslovakia and Bulgaria were coups d'etat organized with the help of the scum of society with foreign support. This is the only way of understanding these things.

He advised the Polexco members that in view of his analysis, they should consider themselves 'in a state of war'.[1]

Ceausescu's concern with the danger spreading from a reformed Eastern Europe and his determination to resist all measure of change contributed to his eventual fall. His belief that domestic protest was entirely the work of foreign agitators stirring up class enemies and hooligans made it impossible for him to consider any form of political dialogue or compromise. To negotiate with such elements would, in his opinion, imperil not only the leading role of the party but also the integrity and independence of the Romanian state. Accordingly, he embarked upon a policy of the violent suppression of dissent which, both in Timisoara and later on in Bucharest, pushed the population into confrontation.

From the very first, Ceausescu believed that the demonstrations in support of Laszlo Toekes in Timisoara were the work of 'foreign espionage circles' but that they could be contained once sufficiently ruthless measures were put in train. By 16 December the scale of the unrest in Timisoara had grown substantially. Several thousand persons proceeded noisily through the central square of Timisoara, shouting Toekes's name, demanding an end to rationing and privation, and chanting slogans against the government. Bookshops were broken into and their contents, which chiefly consisted of books written by the president, were burnt. A number of his portraits were also torn down, defaced and thrown in the Bega River. Since the local militia proved incapable of containing the unrest, units of the *securitate* and army were hastily brought into Timisoara. These, however, responded to the disorder without recourse to shooting, using at this stage only clubs and truncheons to break up the crowds. That night a number of arrests were made and a large military convoy, supported by tanks, moved westwards across the city to a barracks in the suburbs.

All the next day protests continued, being swollen by students from the Polytechnical Institute and the University of Timisoara, and also by groups coming from the industrial suburbs of the city[2]. The demands expressed by the demonstrators became increasingly radical. Whereas on the previous day, the protesters had chanted mainly for Toekes's release and had shouted slogans against the government, they now expressed more ideologically coherent demands: 'Free elections', 'Democracy', 'Freedom for all'. Imitating the earlier actions of protesters in Czechoslovakia and East Germany, Romanian flags were held aloft with the communist symbol in the centre torn out. Still though, the armed forces in the city did not resort to firing, using baton charges instead to break up the crowd. Covert signs of support made by individual soldiers led to repeated and premature cries of 'The army is with us!'. Partly as a consequence of the forbearance of the military and security forces, a group of protesters were able to fight their way into and then ransack the local party headquarters.

In his original instructions to the army and *securitate* commanders, Ceausescu had ordered that every measure be taken to put down the demonstrations in Timisoara; as he later put it, they were 'to fight and not to make manoeuvres'. His command, however, had been ignored by the two members of the Polexco responsible for internal security: the Internal Affairs Minister, Tudor Postelnicu, and the Defence Minister, General Vasile Milea. Their decision not to issue live ammunition to their troops probably derived from a conviction that the shooting of civilians was unnecessary and would only inflame the protesters. As Milea was later to recall, 'It did not enter my mind that it would reach so serious a proportion.'

At a meeting of the Polexco held on the afternoon of Sunday 17 December, Ceausescu bitterly criticized the disregard shown for his instructions which he blamed for escalating the crisis. Additionally, he upbraided General Milea for failing to establish a convoy of armoured vehicles in the centre of the city and for moving his forces instead into barracks. In the course of a histrionic performance, Ceausescu recalled events in 1945, when he had organized the shooting of demonstrators himself, and he made his instructions unambiguously clear. The disorder in Timisoara must be brought to an end even at the cost of widespread slaughter. The alternative as Ceausescu saw it, was quite simply 'the liquidation of communism' in Romania.[3] The meeting concluded with various members of the Polexco abasing themselves before Ceausescu as a sign of their renewed allegiance. The only objection to Ceausescu's hard line policy was voiced by Milea, who reported that he had, 'rummaged last night through all the military regulations and found no paragraph stipulating that the people's army has to fire at the people'. He was told to shut up.[4]

The same afternoon Ceausescu repeated his talk of an international conspiracy in a closed-circuit 'teleconference' to county party secretaries. These were by now aware that something grave had occurred in Timisoara for their lines of communication to the party headquarters in the city had been cut earlier that day. In a broadcast lasting several hours, Ceausescu informed the secretaries that the disturbances in Timisoara 'had been arranged by foreign agencies and by anti-socialist and anti-Romanian circles in East and West alike'. He recalled the events of 1968 and implied that once again Romania's political independence was under threat.[5]

Early the next day, Ceausescu left Romania for Iran on a three-day visit, the purpose of which was to secure certain valuable defence and military contracts. Before his departure he received early reports of the crackdown he had ordered in Timisoara and, throughout his brief stay in Iran, he remained closely informed of developments at home. During his absence, leadership of the country was vested in the Permanent Bureau of the Polexco, headed by Elena Ceausescu and Manea Manescu. Ceausescu's decision to leave the country even before the suppression of the disorder is a measure both of his confidence and also of his desire to maintain the outward show of normality.

During the course of 17 December, Ion Coman, the secretary of the Central Committee with special responsibility for military and security affairs, was given full responsibility for operations in Timisoara.[6] He was joined shortly afterwards in the city by the chief of militia, Constantin Nuta, by the *securitate* head of directorate, Emil Macri, and by the Prime Minister and his deputy, Constantin Dascalescu and Cornel Pacoste respectively.

The appointment of Coman resulted in an immediate escalation of military and security activity. Under Coman's direction 'Operation Timis' was put into effect by combined units of the *securitate* and of the anti-terrorist USLA. These attacked the demonstrators during the afternoon of the 17 December, firing on the crowds from armoured vehicles. Groups of persons were bayonetted and others were deliberately run over. Evidently, the army was also involved in the crackdown, although later on it would be claimed that it was not soldiers but *securitate* men dressed in their uniform who had actually shot at civilians. The thanks which Nicolae Ceausescu later paid to the army for its help in suppressing the demonstration makes it seem likely, however, that soldiers were indeed involved in the shooting.

The crackdown in Timisoara appears to have been largely successful. The number of demonstrators was reduced to a few hundred people who defied the checkpoints and cordons by continuing to assemble in the centre. During 18 and 19 December, the various parts of the city were sealed off one from another by military checkpoints to prevent the coordination of resistance. Meanwhile, the *securitate* used its network of informers to identify and round up participants in the protest. The hospitals were also visited and wounded demonstrators arrested. Some of these were executed or tortured. Following Ceausescu's overthrow, the naked and mangled corpse of one such victim was found in the local mortuary and widely publicized.

The events in Timisoara were witnessed by a number of foreign observers who, once they had left the country, gave highly coloured accounts of what they had seen. Estimates published in the European press and broadcast to Romania by foreign stations put the number of fatalities in Timisoara at several thousand. In reality, the figure was about seventy. Accordingly, Elena Ceausescu felt confident that the recent events could be concealed and explained away later on as gross exaggerations. On 18 December, therefore, the country's borders were closed, and a determined attempt was made to hide what had passed in Timisoara. The bodies of those killed in the fighting were accordingly removed from the hospital mortuary in Timisoara and taken to Bucharest for incineration. Apparently, Elena Ceausescu planned later to give out that the victims of the fighting had in fact defected abroad. The smuggling of the corpses out of the mortuary was accomplished with the assistance of Professor Traian Crisan, a *securitate* agent employed at the local hospital.[7] With order apparently restored in Timisoara, a mass rally in support of the government was planned for the city in order to demonstrate to the outside world that normal conditions now prevailed in the city. A detachment of 20,000 workers was gathered and entrained in Oltenia ready to attend meetings scheduled for the end of the week.

With the opposition to the government driven off the streets and out

of the central portions of the city, the initiative passed to the factories
and to the suburbs. As work resumed on Monday 18 December, the first
strike committees were set up among the largely female workforce at the
ELBA electrical works and at the *Solvent* petrochemical plant.[8] By
Wednesday, a general strike prevailed throughout Timisoara: only
bread loaves continued in production. A 'Committee for Socialist
Democracy', together with an 'Action Committee of the Timisoara
Romanian Democratic Front', sought to coordinate the work of the local
strike committees and to negotiate on their behalf with representatives
of the local party. The establishment of these bodies represented a vital
stage in the escalation of the protest, for it introduced the first element of
organization in a popular movement which had hitherto been almost
entirely spontaneous.

On the afternoon of 20 December, protests began again in central
Timisoara in response to an appeal by relatives for the return of the
bodies of those who had been slain in the recent fighting, and for the
publication of lists of those who had been arrested. Once again, Coman
instructed the streets to be cleared by gunfire. Evidently, however, by
this time the morale both of the army and of the *securitate* had broken.
Individual soldiers refused to carry out orders to fire on protesters; some
joined in the demonstration and others abandoned their positions. By
the evening, several T55 tanks were in the possession of the protesters.
Units of the *securitate* also defected. *Securitate* officers intercepted at the
railway station three of the first trainloads of workers rallied previously
in Oltenia. Having been apprized of the true situation in the city, the
workers joined the side of the protesters.[9] By the evening of Wednesday
20 December, there was in the centre of Timisoara a crowd numbering
no less than 100,000 persons: about a third of the city's entire
population.

During that same evening, the army left the city and returned to
barracks, with some of its vehicles flying white flags. The decision to
retire the army was probably taken by the commanders on the spot who
realized that the only other option left to them was to engage in a
massacre, the order for which their troops would almost certainly
refuse. Surviving accounts, however, tell of the complete confusion
reigning among the government and party officials who were in the city
at this time. Most appear to have regarded the situation as already lost
and returned to Bucharest to await further developments there. The
threat by the strike committee in the *Solvent* petrochemical works to
blow up the plant if the army did not leave the city may also have

influenced the decision to withdraw.

Following the evacuation of the army, the Timisoara Action Committee of the Romanian Democratic Front established itself in the Opera Theatre in the centre of the city under the chairmanship of Lorin Fortuna. In its first manifesto, the committee made all negotiation with the government conditional upon the resignation of 'the tyrant Nicolae Ceausescu'. It demanded the organization of elections, a free press, respect for civil rights, and improvements in medical and social welfare. The committee also demanded a full inquiry into who precisely had instructed the army and *securitate* to fire on the demonstrators. In order to protect the city against renewed assault, the committee recruited a citizens' guard and installed a system of loud speakers in the city centre so that the population could be rallied in an emergency.[10]

On the afternoon of 20 December, Ceausescu returned to Bucharest from Teheran and took full charge of the government. He ordered his speech writers, Eugen Florescu and Gheorghe Sprinteroiu, to prepare the text of an address, which be delivered on Bucharest radio at 7.00p.m. local time. In this broadcast, Ceausescu informed the population that 'hooligan elements' had been responsible for demonstrations, violence and looting in Timisoara and that these 'terrorist actions' had been 'organized and unleashed in close connection with reactionary, imperialist, irredentist, chauvinist circles, and foreign espionage services in various foreign countries'. He congratulated the army and security service for 'the firm and patient way in which they had fulfilled their duty towards the homeland, the people and socialist achievements'. He repeatedly stressed the threat to Romania's territory and independence posed by the disorder in Timisoara in order to explain the tough line adopted over the past few days.

During the early hours of 21 December, Prime Minister Constantin Dascalescu began direct negotiations with the Action Committee in Timisoara and conceded their demands for an investigation into the recent violence. Clearly, however, Dascalescu was acting on the president's instructions and was only playing for time. He had done the same in November 1987 when he had led discussions with strikers at Brasov, only to have them arrested when the situation had cooled. The simultaneous order of a state of emergency in Timis county suggests that Ceausescu was planning a fresh assault on the city of Timisoara on the pretext of its illegal defiance of a constitutional regulation. In the meantime, however, he sought to make a symbolic display to the Romanian population of the support which his regime could still muster with the aim of overawing the opposition. As it turned out, this proved to be a fatal miscalculation.

NOTES

1. *Lumea* (19 January 1990).
2. The Polytechnical Institute had 12,000 students; the university 4000.
3. *Lumea* (19 January 1990).
4. *Romania* no. 2–3 (1990) p. 64.
5. *Romania Libera* (9 January 1990).
6. Coman had apparently arrived in Timisoara the preceding day.
7. *Nepszabadsag* (5 March 1990).
8. The strike in the ELBA factory may have been occasioned by the army's shooting of a woman worker.
9. Rompres, *Romania December 1989–December 1990*, p. 9; *Kapu* (April 1990).
10. *Curierul Romanesc* (30 December 1989).

10

THE REVOLUTION
IN BUCHAREST

'Television made the Revolution; television is the Revolution.' With these words, the first director of Free Romanian Television, Aurel Munteanu, identified the critical role played by the media in the making of the Christmas Revolution. Throughout the preceding autumn, Romanians had followed the fall of the communist dominos in Eastern Europe through the Romanian language services of foreign radio stations and, where possible, on Bulgarian, Hungarian and Yugoslav television. The symbol of the national flag with its communist emblem ripped out and the chant, first heard in Bucharest on 21 December, of 'We are the people', both derived from media accounts of recent events in Prague, Berlin and Leipzig. Importantly also, Romanians were able to draw the conclusion that the Soviet Union would not intervene to save Ceausescu should his regime run into difficulties.

In December 1989, Romanians followed the events happening in their own country through these same foreign channels and they learned the truth of what had passed in Timisoara. Both inspired and appalled by the news coming from the city, Romanians took to the streets in Tirgu Mures, Arad, Cluj and Constanta, taunting the government and demanding an end to bloodshed. Once reports of these secondary disturbances had reached the media stations abroad, they were promptly relayed back through the airwaves to Romania, thus setting in train further protests. On 21 December, the tide of protest spilled uncontrollably on to the streets of Bucharest and swiftly brought down the Ceausescu government.

Television and radio did not just maintain the impetus of the revolution but acted as the channel through which Ceausescu's vulnerability was first made plain. On the official service of Romanian television and radio, broadcasting before the revolution on 21

December, a breach in the facade of the Ceausescu regime was suddenly exposed at a decisive moment and projected around the country. Ceausescu's public humiliation on this occasion emboldened the opposition to his rule and speeded his own demise.

Ceausescu, of course, had not planned it thus. With typical bravado, he intended on the morning of 21 December to make a media display of the strength and resolve of his government in the face of the continuing disorder in Timisoara. In factories throughout the countryside, employees were summoned to attend meetings to deplore the demonstrations in Transylvania. For nine hours, workers were bussed continuously into the centre of the capital itself, ready for a rally which the president had scheduled for midday. Once they had disembarked, the crowd was handed out such typical posters as 'Long live the Party; Long live Ceausescu', as well as more pertinent placards condemning hooliganism and calling for discipline. By late morning approximately 100,000 persons were crammed into the Square of the Republic in front of the Central Committee Building ready to hear Ceausescu's address which was to be carried live on Bucharest radio and television.

A few minutes after midday, Ceausescu appeared on the first floor balcony of the Central Committee Building and began to speak. He never was an impressive orator nor a telegenic performer. His speeches comprised slogans strung together to make sentences and he made his points more by repeated assertion than by reasoned argument. To add cogency to his words, he customarily pounded his fist or gesticulated into the air. The fatuity of the cult of personality stood never more starkly revealed than in the actual presence of the object of worship.

Typically, Ceausescu began his speech by offering 'revolutionary greetings' to the crowd gathered before him; and the crowd equally typically responded with orchestrated chants of 'Ceausescu; Romania: Our Esteem and our Pride'. Suddenly however, the president was interrupted. Shouts of 'Murderer', 'Timisoara' and screams were heard.[1] The live television transmission was interrupted, but not before viewers had caught the blank look of confusion and disbelief on the president's face. Over the next few minutes, militia-men sought to restore order among the crowd, sections of which were already engaged in tearing up posters and in improvising new chants against the government. During the delay, listeners to the radio and television heard only the prerecorded songs of a patriotic choir.

With a semblance of order restored, Ceausescu reappeared on the balcony and transmission of his speech recommenced. After a few empty phrases about strength and unity, and the independence and integrity of Romania, the president adopted a more placatory tone. He announced a string of improvements in wages, pensions and allowances in the hope of mollifying the crowd. This only confirmed, however, the impression that the initiative lay no longer with the president and that popular discontent was forcing him to make concessions. Throughout the remainder of his speech, Ceausescu was continually interrupted by agitated shouting and he was able to watch the failure of the militia to restore order in the main body of the rally. Later that day, Ceausescu's speech was rebroadcast with loud chants of support dubbed over the original soundtrack. It is unlikely, however, that this remedy proved at all convincing to those who had previously witnessed Ceausescu's humiliation live on Romanian television and radio.

Once assembled, the crowd gathered in the Square of the Republic proved hard to dislodge. Armoured cars were brought into the city centre and water cannon and tear gas were used to disperse the protesters. When these failed to have effect, armed units opened fire on the crowd from street corners and from rooftops. The demonstrators, however, broke up into small, running groups of several hundred and evaded all attempts to bring them to order. When the police received reinforcements from units of the army and *securitate*, protesters built barricades across the streets. As in Timisoara a few days earlier, bookshops were broken into and armfuls of the president's collected works were consigned to flames. Ceausescu's posters were defaced and the walls of the capital were covered with slogans denouncing his rule. Of these, the most popular proved to be, 'Today Timisoara, tomorrow the whole country'. By that evening, Magheru Boulevard, the university quarter and the nearby Intercontinental Hotel had been taken over by the protesters. By all accounts, most of the demonstrators consisted of young people and students.

Following his humiliation before the crowd, Ceausescu ordered a meeting of the Permanent Bureau of the Polexco. At an extended session, its members sought out ways to contain the unrest. As a first step, the president confirmed the wage increases he had announced during his recent speech. Realizing the futility of this gesture, he instructed the patriotic guard units in factories to be put on full alert,

commanded the army to shoot on demonstrators as necessary, and
ordered the military reinforcement of the Central Committee building
and of the inner quarter of the capital. That evening he held a
teleconference with local party secretaries, advising them of the new
measures he was putting in train to counter the unrest. On this
occasion, Elena repeatedly intervened in the conference, imploring her
husband to be more decisive in his instructions.

Reports from eyewitnesses actually within the Central Committee
building at this time tell of the considerable confusion among officials
and party functionaries. The overwhelming consensus of opinion was
that the Ceausescu government was on the verge of collapse and was
sure to be replaced within the next 24 hours, if not sooner. This
conviction was supported by reports that individual units of the army
were failing to obey instructions to shoot and that some indeed had
already defected to the side of the demonstrators. The belief that the
collapse of the regime was imminent prompted a number of important
groups within the political and military elite to move towards forming a
successor government. The full details of these events have yet to be
revealed, while conjecture and deliberate disinformation on the part of
the main actors have served to confuse the historical record still
further. The rapidity with which the new government of the National
Salvation Front was formed, strongly suggests that close discussions
between members of the party 'old guard', the army and the *securitate*
may already have been underway by the time of Ceausescu's flight. It
has yet to be shown, however, that these groups had worked out in
advance 'a carefully prepared blueprint for taking power'.[2]

In the immediate wake of the revolution, members of the newly
constituted government took pains to establish that they had not
plotted the President's downfall. Indeed, at the time a certain amount
of regret was expressed that no such conspiracy had existed since this
would have added to the new government's legitimacy and
revolutionary credentials.[3] Over the course of 1990, however, it was
gradually divulged that a major 'breach' in the army and *securitate* had
been achieved, which involved some 20 generals gathered in a Military
Resistance Committee.[4] The membership and affiliation of this
committee continues to vary according both to the informant and to
the political score he is endeavouring to settle. Suffice it to say that had
the generals been as committed to despatching Ceausescu as is now
commonly maintained, they would surely have turned against him with
rather more alacrity and purpose than they in fact displayed. Still, on

21 December, the army was shooting civilians in Cluj, Sibiu, Brasov, Tirgu Mures and Arad as well as in the capital itself. In fact, responsibility for the army's eventual defection probably owed less to the alleged work of any Military Resistance Committee as to the endeavours of the Defence Minister Vasile Milea, the memory of whose deeds has been deliberately effaced by the apologists of the 'military conspiracy' school.[5]

Already on 17 December General Milea had experienced Ceausescu's wrath on account of his failure to issue live ammunition to his troops in Timisoara. On this occasion, he had only narrowly kept his job. Milea's continued reluctance to issue unequivocal instructions to the units of the Ministry of National Defence apparently resulted in a fresh outburst from the president on the evening of 21 December. Evidently by this time, Milea's exasperation with Ceausescu was complete. During that night, he issued instructions to various commanders both inside and outside the capital to hold their fire and not to shoot on demonstrators. A further uncorroborated report also tells that Milea deliberately failed to implement Ceausescu's instruction to reinforce the Central Committee Building. Instead, he simply ordered vehicles to parade through the centre of the city to give the impression that something really was being done. Later on, Ceausescu was apparently to complain that he had spent a sleepless night on account of the noise created by all these manoeuvres.[6]

When daybreak came, the extent of Milea's disobedience became clear. The Central Committee Building was only lightly guarded and the streets leading up to it were inadequately protected. At the same time, the earliest reports began to come in from local party secretaries and *securitate* offices that the army was no longer taking any action to put down demonstrations in the provinces. Thus whereas the previous day, the army had shot down six demonstrators in Tirgu Mures, it had now assumed a passive position, simply guarding the party headquarters and leaving the streets to the crowds.

In view of this worrying information, Ceausescu urgently summoned Milea to his conference rooms on the third floor of the Central Committee Building. He instructed Milea to order the army to recommence active operations immediately and to open fire on such units as proved recalcitrant. General Milea refused Ceausescu's order. Accordingly, at about 9.30a.m. he was taken out of the room and shot by members of the president's personal protection squad. (In some accounts, he was murdered by the president's brother, Ilie Ceausescu.)

In what would turn out to be its last lie for Ceausescu, Bucharest radio reported that Milea had committed suicide.[7]

Throughout the night, there had been running battles between demonstrators, the army and units of the *securitate*. The latter were able to make full use of their highly sophisticated radio communications and their network of command centres to surprise and harass the crowds.[8] In a few places they detonated bombs in the hope of spreading panic. The morale of the demonstrators remained, however, firm. They lit candles to the memory of those slain in the fighting and continued improvising songs against the government. Their spirits were kept up by news from the rest of the country telling of demonstrations and strikes for, remarkably, telephone contact between the capital and the provinces had not been lost. During the night of 21–22 December, several shops opened to allow the purchase of fresh supplies of bread. In university halls of residence and in a number of work places, committees were formed to coordinate the swelling movement of protest.

At daybreak, the confusion within the ranks of the army was plain. It seems that the last firm order which the commanders on the spot had been given was Milea's command not to fire. Already the earliest reports of the death of the Minister of Defence had been received, adding to rumour and sapping the army's resolve. One officer later reported, 'As soon as the news of Milea's death broke, the army was in rebellion. That was the turning point. Milea was a true army man and a good commander who had come up through the ranks.'[9] Other accounts tell of how exchanges of news between soldiers and demonstrators led to open fraternization and of how officers looked on uncomprehendingly as Christmas trees were planted on gun turrets.

The bewilderment in the army was matched by equivocation among the security forces. By the morning of 22 December, sections of the *securitate* had plainly defected to the side of the revolution. Whether these groups were acting on their own initiative or on the order of their superiors, who saw which way the tide was turning, is uncertain. It seems probable, however, that a part of the *securitate* USLA changed sides at a very early stage in the revolution and may even have been manipulating some of the crowd on the morning of 22 December.[10] It is certainly the case, as photographic evidence records, that unidentified persons in plain clothes were directing the demonstrators and exercising an unusual level of control in the events immediately preceding the storming of the Central Committee Building.

Conceivably, these were *securitate* men belonging to the USLA group deputed to guard the Building, for their commander, Vasile Ardeleanu, is known to have changed sides at an early stage in the revolution.

From about 9a.m. on Friday 22 December, the centre of the city began once more to fill up with demonstrators; on this occasion, however, the army took no ostensible measures to control the crowd. Gradually emboldened, and shouting cries of 'The army is with us', a vast throng pushed its way towards the Central Committee Building. Shortly before midday, groups eventually broke into the party offices, climbing through the ground floor windows. As they made their way up the staircases inside, Nicolae and Elena Ceausescu appeared briefly on a balcony. For a moment, it seemed as if the president might address the crowd laid out along the square before him. But he was pulled inside by his wife. A few minutes later, a helicopter landed on the roof of the building and the Ceausescus clambered inside, pulling in after them Manea Manescu and Emil Bobu, two of their closest collaborators. As it turned out, the inclusion of Manescu and Bobu overburdened the helicopter, forcing it shortly afterwards to descend. In the meantime, a second helicopter dropped leaflets, advising the citizens of Romania of the imminent threat to the independence and integrity of the country. Even as the Ceausescus made their undignified flight from the capital, the president hoped that he could rally support behind his regime by repeating the outworn appeal to national unity.

Within a few minutes of Ceausescu's departure, students appeared on the balcony of the Central Committee Building. They proclaimed the fall of the Ceausescu government, and shouted out the names of those they would like to see serving in its successor. Over the next few hours, a bewildering succession of speakers variously denounced Ceausescu, sang revolutionary songs, and announced the formation of new democratic governments.

Throughout those final 24 hours, Romanian television had devoted itself to playing martial music and to relaying the latest statistical information on the country's economic performance. Only in response to a state of martial law, proclaimed by Ceausescu an hour before his flight, did the official media suggest that anything unusual was happening in the country. Shortly afterwards, a group of young people broke into the television and radio studios. At just before one o'clock, television transmission was interrupted by a crowd headed by the dissident poet, Mircea Dinescu. With the words, 'Brothers, thanks to

God, we have won', Dinescu announced the fall of the Ceausescu government and that Romania was free. A few minutes later, Bucharest radio declared in a formal communique that after 23 years the door of the Romanian media had been opened to the people and proclaimed the triumph of the revolution in Bucharest. As news of the events in Bucharest flashed on television screens throughout Romania, crowds poured out into the streets of the country's villages and towns, ransacking party offices and holding huge celebratory processions.

The rejoicing was, as it turned out, premature. Not only would forces loyal to Ceausescu continue to fight on, but the allegiance of the army was still uncertain. The soldiers had stopped shooting, but they had not yet joined the side of the revolution in force. They awaited instead for instructions from their commanders, and these were still uncertain as to the course of action they should take. As Mircea Dinescu later recalled, the generals were on the whole in favour of the overthrow of the Ceausescus, but they were reluctant to commit themselves to a revolution headed by what they saw as 'a few crazy poets and intellectuals'.[11] In this period of indecision, one possible outcome was that either Ceausescu's brother-in-law, Ilie Verdet, or Prime Minister Constantin Dascalescu would assume power at the head of a government purged only of the Ceausescu name.[12]

During the early afternoon of 22 December, a determined attempt was made to convince the army commanders to commit themselves to a new government led by 'serious politicians'. The principal figures in this movement were Ion Iliescu and General Nicolae Militaru. Both were former high-ranking communists who had merited Ceausescu's displeasure. Militaru had been forced to leave the army in 1978 and a few years later had lost his seat on the Central Committee. For his part, Iliescu was former party chief in Iasi who had been dismissed from the Central Committee in 1984. The extent to which these two had previously refined their plans and won backing in advance from army and *securitate* commanders is a matter of considerable interest and speculation.

Immediately after Ceausescu's flight, Iliescu made contact through intermediaries with the Ministry of National Defence and obtained the agreement of the generals that they would actively support a government of experienced ex-communist politicians.[13] In the meantime, General Militaru drove to the radio station, arriving there only a hour after its capture.[14] He immediately went on the air, broadcasting an appeal directly to Chief of Staff, General Gusa, and to the other generals. Militaru asked his former colleagues to order the army back to barracks and he advised that they should commit themselves at once to the side of the revolution. As evidence that 'serious politicians' were now indeed about to take charge, Ion Iliescu was duly summoned to the radio station where 'as a good patriot' he lent his own support for the revolution which had taken place. Mircea Dinescu was later to comment that had Iliescu delayed his visit to the radio station by an hour, then 'the revolution would have failed'.[15]

The negotiations with the generals proved successful. Over the following hours, the military commanders together with General Gusa and the head of the militia, broadcast their support and called upon all units to cease firing. Early that evening, they instructed their subordinates to show full obedience to the newly constituted Front for National Salvation. This was the first indication given to the Romanian population that a new government had already been installed and that it enjoyed the support of the armed forces.

The National Salvation Front was set up in the Central Committee Building by Ion Iliescu at about four o'clock on the afternoon of 22 December. By this time, Iliescu knew that he could count on military support for any new government he planned and that he had the support of a part of the *securitate*. Additionally, he had been in contact with the Soviet Embassy in Bucharest to let them know in advance of his plans and he was subsequently able to claim that he enjoyed Soviet backing. Thus, even before the meeting which established the new government, Iliescu had built up a formidable position for himself.

In attendance at the inaugural session of the National Salvation Front were gathered the representatives of the most powerful organizations within the Romanian state. These were the men who would shortly take charge of the Romanian revolution. The core of old communists, who had fallen out with Ceausescu over the systematization programme, were represented by Alexandru Birladeanu and Silviu Brucan. Vasile Nicolcioiu, head of the party chancellery, was there on behalf of the functionaries of the communist *nomenklatura*. The armed forces were present in the form of Generals Militaru and Gusa, who were accompanied by a certain Captain Mihai Lupoi. In attendance also was Vasile Ardeleanu, head of the elite anti-terrorist branch of the *securitate*, Ion Pircalebescu, chief of the paramilitary Patriotic Guard, and Petre Roman, a member of the younger generation of communists.[16] Roman's subsequent claim that he had joined the meeting by accident, having previously been speech-making on a nearby balcony, is implausible. Roman was a close associate of Ion Iliescu, and his inclusion at the inaugural meeting of the Front suggests the degree of influence which Iliescu had already succeeded in accumulating.

A part of the discussions held that afternoon concerned the name of the new government. It was pointed out that an obscure organization calling itself a National Salvation Front had been established a few months before with the aim of preventing Ceausescu's re-election as party secretary at the 14th Congress. But since this organization was known to few and in any case seemed to lack all influence, it was felt nevertheless justifiable to take over its name. This conversation was subsequently misreported as implying that the National Salvation Front government had been planned well in advance.[17] During the course of the meeting, a basic political programme was sketched out, the details of which it was agreed would shortly be published. It was felt, however, that for the time being it would be best to confine all statements of intent to broad generalities. Militaru's suggestion that the new government define itself as an 'organ of the party' was unanimously rejected, and Iliescu was elevated to presidency of the new government.

Shortly before midnight, Ion Iliescu published the text of a communiqué from the National Salvation Front (NSF). The message announced that 'the entire state power' had been taken over by the ruling Council of the NSF and that the army and security forces were subordinate to its authority. The programme of the Front contained the establishment of multi-party democracy, the holding of free elections, the separation of the branches of government, a radical reform of industry, agriculture and education, full rights for national minorities and observance of human rights.

Membership of the Council of the NSF was similarly defined. Along with such distinguished old communists as Birladeanu, Mazilu, Brucan and Manescu were listed the generals who had played such a vital role in ensuring the triumph both of the revolution and of Ion Iliescu. However, their names came low down the list. First given were the dissidents, Doina Cornea, Ana Blandiana, Mircea Dinescu and Laszlo Toekes. The decision to include their names on the list of council members was taken without their approval and was intended to convey the impression that the NSF represented a 'broad front'. True to its origins, however, the Front would soon be exposed as the instrument of Ion Iliescu and of the forces he had gathered round him at the inaugural meeting in the Central Committee Building on the afternoon of 22 December.

The fighting which began on the night of 22 December is commonly presented as a contest between the *securitate* and the army, with the people supporting the latter. In fact, by this time, most units of the *securitate* were already supporting the army and the new government. As we have seen, Vasile Ardeleanu, head of the *securitate* USLA, was among the group that established the NSF. Likewise, Iliescu is known to have already established close links with a senior *securitate* officer, Professor Virgil Magureanu, whose support and influence are likely to have been decisive over the next few days.[18]

The supreme commander of the *securitate*, General Iulian Vlad, also defected to the side of the revolution no later than the night of 22 December. In the appeal which he delivered in the early hours of the next day, Vlad drew attention to the fact that the units of the Interior Ministry were already 'fighting shoulder-to-shoulder with the Romanian army for the survival of the national being of the Romanian people'.[19] It seems, however, that a number of *securitate* units gave up the fight gradually in return for guarantees and promises of amnesty; some officers may even have been released unconditionally after they had surrendered. The present Romanian government has, however, never given a full account of the activities of the *securitate* during the period of the revolution, thus giving good reason both for speculation and for the accusation of a cover-up.

Rather than being the work of the *securitate* as a whole, the fighting was undertaken by only a dwindling number of security units. In the main, these belonged to the Fifth Directorate of the *securitate* organization and, more particularly, to the UMO666 presidential protection unit led by General Marin Neagoe. The Fifth Directorate was supported by members of the Counter-Espionage Fourth Directorate, the command structure of which appears to have split down the middle. By reason of their superior training and equipment the groups of *securitate* remaining loyal to Ceausescu were able to inflict substantial physical and psychological damage. Nevertheless, the electronic command centres of the *securitate* in Bucharest were rapidly made inoperative by army units, thus preventing the proper coordination of resistance to the revolution.[20]

The renegade *securitate* units had the apparent aim of recapturing the administrative and communications centres of the new government. Thus, fighting took place in the centre of Bucharest, around the Central Committee Building and presidential palace, and beside the television station. At one point, a *securitate* unit even managed to disrupt power supplies to the television building. Shooting and artillery fire around the *securitate* headquarters in the centre of Bucharest resulted in the destruction of the Central University Library (which is next to the Central Committee Building) and damage to the National Museum. In Timisoara, Brasov and Arad, gun battles were similarly reported, while in Sibiu a machine gun on the roof of the Hotel Continental raked the surrounding streets. Individual snipers shot at random from buildings both in Bucharest and elsewhere, provoking widespread panic and the formation of citizens vigilante groups. In the capital, the 'terrorists', as they were now universally known, made use of a network of tunnels linking the main government offices in the centre. Their sniping forced members of the NSF government to travel around Bucharest in tanks. The chaos caused by the 'terrorists' was exaggerated by rumours of Palestinian assistance and by reports of mysterious foreign vessels approaching the coast.[21]

Both the new Romanian government and its supporters in the army gave out that the counter-offensive was part of a prearranged master plan, known variously as 'Plan M' or 'Operation Genocide'. According to a statement published on 29 December by Mihai Chitac, NSF Minister of the Interior, 'reconnaissance-diversion' teams had been previously equipped by Ceausescu with night sights, helicopters and armoured cars as part of a well-prepared counter-strike. As Chitac explained, 'The actions we all had to put up with went hand in hand with an intense psychological war. Rumours were spread to intimidate and many individuals were threatened on the phone. Which only leads to the conclusion that all actions had been prepared in advance, that they broke out on signal.'[22]

The fragmented organization of the *securitate* makes it seem unlikely that any such master plan had indeed been prepared. When, therefore, General Iulian Vlad was ordered to report on the contingency arrangements of the security forces, he reported that he could find no evidence of any emergency planning at all. At the time, his negative answer was taken for prevarication and he was promptly dismissed from his post. Nevertheless, it seems that while individual units of the Fourth and Fifth Directorate might have previously been allocated speciasl tasks to fulfil in the event of any attempted coup, no comprehensive plan had been worked out. Most probably, some units were simply following standing orders for action in the event of a

Soviet invasion, while others were just trying to fight their way out of Bucharest. Additionally, their level of equipment was certainly rather less lethal than commonly supposed, consisting only of hand-held firearms.[23]

In the week following 22 December, there were repeated incidents of gunfire on the streets of Bucharest. In order to encourage the remaining units to surrender, threats of execution and promises of amnesty were made and a succession of *securitate* officers delivered personal appeals over the radio. On 23 December, the former Minister of the Interior, Tudor Postelnicu, published a communiqué advising that 'all actions of a terrorist nature ... were useless and irresponsible'. On the same day, Lieutenant-General Stamatoiu, a directorate chief, delivered his own declaration of support to the new government. Nevertheless, the situation remained sufficiently tense and uncertain for members of the new government to suggest that assistance be asked from President Gorbachev and the forces of the Warsaw Pact. Gorbachev, however, rejected this request before it could even be delivered. Nevertheless, troops were placed on alert in Soviet Moldavia and a 1000-bed hospital was made available there for casualties from the fighting in Bucharest.

Throughout the period of confused fighting and gunfire, crowds remained on the streets, sheltering behind tanks and in doorways and bringing food to the soldiers. The vast majority of these consisted of young people, aged between 16 and 25. The extaordinary courage they displayed in this part of the conflict may be explained in terms of a genuine desire to help the army and in terms also of a natural wish to be present in the making of history. Surviving accounts suggest, however, that the willingness of young people to participate in this phase of the struggle assumed early on the dimension of a profoundly moral act. By showing support on the streets and by braving the random gunfire, a sense of personal purification and of redemption was achieved, which obliterated the sense of personal shame and of moral compromise instilled by the Ceausescu government. As Ana Blandiana was later to put it, 'the innocent and tempestuous blood' shed on the streets of Bucharest had in some mysterious way purified 'the stale and dirty waters' thrown up 'from the desperate bank' of Romania's recent history.[24]

NOTES

1. Conspiracy theorists have argued that the crowd was incited to abuse Ceausescu by *securitate* officers who were already planning Ceausescu's downfall. There seems little evidence for this claim.
2. Michael Shafir, in RFE/REE (13 July 1990).
3. See thus, the statement by Silviu Brucan, Reuters (4 January 1990), and reproduced in RFE/REE (19 January 1990); and the statement by the new chief of staff, Vasile Ionel, given in the *Daily Telegraph* (4 January 1990).
4. Details of the 'generals' plot' against Ceausescu were disclosed by Silviu Brucan and Nicolae Militaru in the *Baltimore Sun* (22 May 1990), *Adevarul* (17 July 1990; 24 July 1990; 23 August 1990). An English language translation of the last of these pieces is given together with a commentary by Mark Almond in the *East European Reporter* (Autumn/Winter 1990), pp. 74–7.
5. The reasons for the 'disclosure' of the Military Resistance Committee's existence and activity are suggested by Silviu Brucan's comments in *Adevarul* (24 July 1990): 'People who found they had courage after 22 December [1989] are now doing their best to diminish the merits of those individuals who worked against the Ceausescu dictatorship and to present the plan to topple it as a 'confiscation of the revolution' ... The generals' plot must be praised as the high point of Romanian dissidence'. On the 'myth-making' of the revolution, see also Michael Shafir in RFE/REE (12 October 1990).
6. RFE/REE (26 January 1990; 11 May 1990).
7. Photographs published after the revolution indicate that Milea was shot through the chest, which strongly suggests that he did not take his own life. The funeral oration for Milea given by General Hortopan on 29 December mentioned also that he had been 'killed by Ceausescu's dictatorial clique at the crucial moment'.
8. *Romania Libera* (23 January 1990; 26 January 1990; 27 January 1990).
9. *The Independent* (6 January 1990); the officer was, in fact, only partially correct. Although Milea had 'come up through the ranks' and been the commander of the Cluj garrison in the late 1960s, he had subsequently adopted an overtly political role as commander of the Patriotic Guards.
10. *Baricada* (7 October 1990).
11. RFE/REE (26 January 1990).
12. Another bid for power was separately pursued at this time by former foreign minister Corneliu Manescu.
13. The intermediaries usually named are Generals Kostyal and Stanculescu, but the precise activities and whereabouts of neither officer can be established with any certainty at this time.
14. RFE/REE (11 May 1990).
15. *Frankfurter Allgemeine Zeitung* (13 January 1990).
16. *Romania Libera* (12 May 1990).

17. According to Silviu Brucan, the first NSF was set up during the autumn of 1989 by a Professor Milian.
18. Magureanu emerged in public view as a spokesman for the NSF on 24 December. Interestingly, the communiqué he delivered over the radio on that occasion dealt largely with relations between the Ministries of National Defence and of the Interior, and with exonerating the *securitate*.
19. SWB/EE (28 October 1989).
20. Statement by General Stanculescu, given in SWB/EE (22 February 1990).
21. After the revolution, government spokesmen denied that any Palestinians had participated in the fighting. In August 1990, Militaru and Brucan claimed, however, that 30 foreigners from *securitate* training schools, mainly Palestinians, had assisted the terrorists: SWB/EE (28 August 1990).
22. SWB/EE (1 January 1990).
23. Statement by Ion Iliescu, (23 December 1989), given in SWB/EE (28 December 1989). Nor indeed is there any evidence for a Plan Z-Z, according to which five unspecified states agreed to despatch intervention forces to Romania to prop up Ceausescu at time of crisis. It has been suggested that the new government deliberately exaggerated the threat posed by the *securitate* as a way of consolidating its authority during the period of transition: Matei Calinescu and Vladimir Tismaneanu, 'The 1989 Revolution and Romania's Future', *Problems of Communism* (Jan–April 1991), p. 47.
24. *Romanian Review*, no. 1 (1990) p. 4.

11

TRIAL
AND EXECUTION

The helicopter which plucked the Ceausescus and their two closest collaborators from the roof of the Central Committee Building was overloaded. Accordingly, it had shortly to put down outside Bucharest to allow Manescu and Bobu to disembark. Both, as it turned out, were rapidly captured by members of the army. The helicopter took off again with instructions from Ceausescu to fly to Olt County. It is possible that Ceausescu intended even at this late stage to try and organize support for a counter-strike in his home region. The pilot, however, fearing that the helicopter might at any moment be fired upon by ground forces, convinced Ceausescu that it was dangerous to continue his flight by air. Accordingly, the helicopter put down at Titu, a small town near Boteni military airport. At this juncture, the Ceausescus were forced to hijack a car. They were, however, spotted by two militiamen who promptly gave chase. In the town of Tirgoviste, some 50 miles northwest of Bucharest, Nicolae and Elena Ceausescu were finally halted and arrested. Following their capture, the couple were transferred under guard to a nearby military garrison. After many contradictory reports, announcement of the Ceausescus' capture was broadcast on the evening of 23 December.[1]

Other members of the Ceausescu family were rounded up in the hours immediately following the flight of the president. During the afternoon of 22 December, Nicu Ceausescu was arrested in Sibiu and brought as a prize to the television station in Bucharest. Shortly after his appearance on Free Romanian Television he was stabbed and wounded in the stomach. Nicu's sister and stepbrother, Zoia and Valentin, were captured by the army shortly afterwards. According to Bucharest radio, a search of one of Zoia's apartments had revealed 'stolen' jewellery and other items, as well as $97,000 in cash. Various luxury items found in Zoia's kitchen would subsequently form part of the prosecution case against the Ceausescus. Leading members of the Polexco either gave themselves up or were captured. Tudor Postelnicu's arrest was announced in the early afternoon of 23 December, and that of Ilie Ceausescu, Dinca and Bobu a few hours later.

It seems that members of the new government originally intended to give Nicolae and Elena Ceausescu a public trial during the course of which the democratic and legal procedures of the new Romania would be displayed. In announcing the Ceausescus' arrest, Ion Iliescu had thus promised their 'just and harsh judgment by the people'. Radio Bucharest similarly declared that the former president and his wife would be referred to 'public justice'. When Nicu Ceausescu had been paraded before the television cameras on 22 December, repeated warnings had been given against passing a hasty judgement on him.

The decision to have the Ceausescus tried in secret and summarily executed was taken on the evening of 24 December by the small group of politicians and army commanders who constituted the inner circle of the National Salvation Front. It was ostensibly occasioned by fear that the Ceausescus might be released from captivity by loyal units of the *securitate*. On the day after the execution, Petre Roman reported that, 'we had information about a possible attack on the place where they were being held,' and that this news 'did not permit us to wait'. In later interviews he spoke of the threat posed by an airborne landing of *securitate* paratroops.[2] Silviu Brucan subsequently supported Roman's story. 'It was a political decision,' he said. 'The situation was too critical for us to afford the luxury of a civilian trial. It was a crucial moment, a momentous decision in the battle for the revolution.' Already on 24 December, so Brucan explained, renegade *securitate* units had learnt where the Ceausescus were being held and were even bombarding the garrison at Tirgoviste.[3]

The trial and execution of the Ceausescus would, so it was hoped, also discourage further resistance to the revolution. Throughout the days immediately following the overthrow of the Ceausescu government, there were repeated rumours of an impending invasion by foreign mercenaries. These were fuelled by 'authentic' reports that the Romanian navy was engaged in sea battles with unidentified warships.[4] Large contingents of *securitate* forces were said to be preparing a major counter-offensive in conjunction with terrorists brought back from Iran on the president's recent visit. In the prevailing mood of panic and uncertainty, the decision to kill the Ceausescus seemed eminently sensible. Moreover, their death was perceived not only in terms of expediency but as entirely justifiable. The death toll in the fighting of the last few days had been placed at 60,000 persons, a figure which indeed confirmed the belief that the Ceausescus had plotted a war of genocide on the people. The gruesome disclosure of a pit full of corpses on the outskirts of Timisoara similarly supported earlier reports of a massacre in the city involving several thousand victims. Only later was it discovered that these were the bodies of paupers and vagrants who had been interred at least several months before.[5] The impression of a monstrous tyranny which had sucked the lifeblood of the people was reinforced by revelations of the ostentatious lifestyle of the presidential family. Depictions of Ceausescu as a dehumanized ghoul or vampire were a common motif on the sides of tanks and on the walls of Bucharest in the early days of the revolution.

We may presume, furthermore, that a number of high-ranking army and *securitate* officers would have had a vested interest in the execution of the Ceausescus. Both the army and security services had played a leading part in suppressing popular disturbances before the decision to switch sides on 22 December. Commanders guilty of bloodshed must have been relieved to see the execution of the leading witnesses to their own misdeeds. Whether this played any part in the decision to hold a summary trial can only be a matter of speculation. According, nevertheless, to Silviu Brucan, the final decision to execute the Ceausescus was preceded by a close argument within the ruling council of the National Salvation Front.

The trial of the Ceausescus took place at Tirgoviste military garrison on the afternoon of Christmas Day. The charges laid against Nicolae and Elena consisted of genocide and of encompassing the death of 60,000 persons, organizing armed action against the people and the state, causing explosions and damaging property, and seeking to flee the country 'with funds in excess of one billion dollars deposited in foreign banks'. None of these offences were proved in the trial which followed. Indeed, in the weeks that followed, the figure of 60,000 would be reduced to a thousand, and the extent of the Ceausescus' foreign deposits revised to less than a million dollars.[6] Owing to the severity of the charges, the trial had necessarily to be presented in a military tribunal so as to accord with a presidential decree of 1968 which placed all serious offences within the jurisdiction of courts martial and denied also the right of appeal. In the case of the Ceausescus, the relevant indictment was laid by the Directorate of the

Military Prosecutor's Office and the requisite court was the Bucharest Area Military Tribunal under the presidency of Colonel Gica Popa. Altogether, about a dozen persons were present at the Ceausescus' trial, including Gelu Voican Voiculescu, General Stanculescu and Captain Mihai Lupoi, who were there on behalf of the new government, and the *securitate* Colonel, Professor Virgil Magureanu.[7]

The trial itself took place in makeshift surroundings with the dock comprising two formica tables laid together in the shape of a V. In most other respects, the courtroom drama coincided closely with the norms of judicial conduct characteristic of the Ceausescu regime. There was an ostentatious and scrupulous regard for proper procedures; Nicolae Ceausescu's blood pressure was therefore taken to ensure that he was sufficiently fit to stand trial and both defendants were offered the services of a defence lawyer. At one point in the proceedings, the Ceausescus were even asked if they wished to plead not guilty on grounds of insanity. Instead of seizing this opportunity, which would have made their execution almost impossible to justify, Elena swiftly answered the court, 'You are the rhinoceroses who are suffering from psychological problems.'[8]

On the other hand, however, the charges laid before the Ceausescus were never proven, rumour was treated as certain fact, and the examination frequently broke down into insults and abuse. The veneer of legality thus scarcely concealed the substance of gross judicial irregularity. Most strikingly, the court was uncertain as to whether it constituted a conventional military tribunal or whether it was a 'people's court' operating with powers delegated to it by the new government. The decision was only made later that the tribunal constituted a court martial and the record of its verdict was published thus.[9]

Throughout the trial, which lasted altogether about three hours, Nicolae Ceausescu refused to recognize the competence of the court. He demanded that in accordance with the constitution he be tried by the Grand National Assembly and 'the representatives of the working class'. Repeatedly, he pounded the table with his fist as he made the point that the court was only the instrument of those who had staged a coup d'etat. As Ceausescu made clear, 'I am President of the country and Supreme Commander of the Army. I do not recognize you. You are ordinary citizens and I answer only to the Grand National Assembly. I do not answer those who, with the assistance of foreign organizations, carried out this coup.' On other occasions, Ceausescu feigned boredom and stared pointedly at his watch.

The prosecution case rested largely on putting together current rumours along with generalized accounts of Ceausescu's misrule. The former president was criticized for the lack of medicine and heating in the country, for reducing the people to poverty, for destroying villages, and for driving the 'cream of society' into exile. He was asked to explain why he had sought, 'to bring the Romanian people to this state of humiliation today? To export everything they have produced?' Why had he starved the nation that he represented? At the same time, Ceausescu was upbraided by the military prosecutor for the opulent lifestyle enjoyed by his family. 'I have seen the villa of your daughter,' he said. 'She had golden scales for weighing meat brought from abroad.' This interrogation was interspersed with questions about the recent events in Timisoara and in Bucharest. Ceausescu was asked who had given the order for a bloodbath in Timisoara and Bucharest and where the 'foreign mercenaries' had come from. As the military prosecutor went on, 'Innocent children have been crushed by tanks. You have dressed *securitate* officers in army uniforms to raise the people against the army … You have ripped out oxygen pipes in hospitals, you have blown up the blood plasma depot … ' Did the former president really know nothing about what the *securitate* units were up to?

No separate charges were laid against Elena Ceausescu, but throughout the trial it was presumed that she had acted as the willing accomplice of her husband. Elena was nevertheless accused of having paid to have her books published abroad, and in any case of not having written these herself. Additionally, she was chastised for allowing herself to be dressed 'in the most luxurious clothes, receiving more fuss than a queen – all of this done by robbing the people'.

Yet if the case against the Ceausescus was laid without strict regard for judicial process, the responses of the Ceausescus showed their striking failure to comprehend the events of the last few days. As one commentator has pointed out, 'His [Ceausescu's] actions were those of a man kidnapped in the middle of the night, severed from all external information, and squarely faced with the most – for him – fantastic charges, uttered by persons who had long been his trusted accomplices.'[10] Both Nicolae and Elena therefore asserted that they had been overthrown by a military coup organized by a 'gang of traitors with foreign help'. They denied that there had been any shooting in Bucharest, and claimed that the people would soon rise up against the new government. As for the *securitate*, Elena claimed, in what may have been a reference to Colonel Magureanu, 'they are sitting across from us here'.

Ceausescu additionally rebutted all criticism of his rule and of the hardships inflicted by his government. In an extraordinary outburst, he declared, 'I will tell you that for the first time a cooperative worker received 200kg of wheat per person, not per family, but per person ... There has never been such a level of development in the villages as there is today. We have built schools, ensured that there are doctors, ensured that there is everything for a dignified life.' As for the industrial workers, Ceausescu asked the members of the court whether they had not witnessed 'how the people cheered when I went to the factories?' As the military prosecutor commented, a rational dialogue with the Ceausescus was impossible. Indeed, he went on to say, it was hard to sentence people who failed so signally to appreciate that they had committed any crimes at all. Nevertheless, the prearranged verdict was given: confiscation of all the defendants' property and capital punishment. There then followed an unseemly scuffle as the hands of Nicolae and Elena Ceausescu were bound and they were led out to a courtyard. When Elena saw the firing squad drawn up in readiness for the execution, she is alleged to have cried out in disbelief, 'And I was like a mother to you!' This last fond delusion failed to sway the firing squad. Indeed, even before the Ceausescus and a cameraman recording the event could assume position, the members of the execution squad together with other soldiers present in the courtyard had opened fire.

The bodies of both Ceausescus were kept at Tirgoviste for several more days before being transferred to the capital. On 30 December, the Ceausescus were interred without ceremony beneath wooden crosses in Bucharest's Ghencea cemetery. Nicolae Ceausescu's grave was marked 'Col. Popa Dan 1920–1989' and Elena's with the equally commonplace 'Col. Enescu Vasile 1921–89'. The secrecy with which the Ceausescus were buried derived from a concern in the government that their final resting-place should not become a shrine or place of pilgrimage.

A heavily edited video of the trial of the Ceausescus was broadcast continuously on Romanian Television on 26 December. At first it was not intended to show any pictures of the execution itself. Nevertheless, it was felt by the new government that renegade *securitate* units would be more likely to surrender if presented with incontestible evidence that the Ceausescus were no longer alive. As Silviu Brucan later recalled:

Two [*securitate* men] who had been caught said they would not consider themselves free of their oath [of loyalty to Ceausescu] until they had seen the film or picture in which it is clear that they are dead. And since in the first film there was no such scene, we ordered that the final scenes be added to the old film, scenes in which one can see they are dead, plus two colour pictures taken after they died.'[11]

Brucan was later to gloat that the Ceausescus broke down shortly before their execution and that they showed evidence of terror at their impending fate. The video of their last minutes reveals little of this. Both seem instead to have accepted their fate defiantly, refusing pointedly to ask for mercy. Both, moreover, gave touching examples of their mutual affection.[12]

It is certainly the case that the execution of the Ceausescus made all further resistance to the new government hopeless. Furthermore, the use of capital punishment revealed the tough line which the government was prepared to take. Exploiting the execution of the Ceausescus, an NSF communiqué published on 27 December threatened that 'terrorists' who refused to surrender within the next 24 hours should expect to face the same punishment as the former president and his wife. By this time, however, it was admitted that only a few units of desperadoes were still at large.[13]

Although it proved expedient, the execution of the Ceausescus represented the first failure on the part of the new government. In its programme published on the 23 December, the NSF had promised to separate the executive and judicial powers of the state. The trial of the Ceausescus, rather than providing a lesson in democracy and justice, was a set-piece show trial. The verdict and sentence had been prearranged by the NSF and the prosecution proceeded in complete disregard of judicial norms. Accordingly, although there was substantial sympathy for the predicament of the new government, western governments felt obliged to advise the NSF that they would formally protest at any future use of drum-head court martials.

NOTES

1. First-hand accounts of the Ceausescu's flight tend to coincide; a detailed description obtained from the Ceausescu's helicopter pilot, Lt-Col Vasile Malutan, is given in Edward Behr, *'Kiss the Hand You Cannot Bite'. The*

Rise and Fall of the Ceausescus (London: Hamish Hamilton, 1991), pp. 4–11. It remains, however, possible that Malutan's account is deliberate disinformation. Malutan does not mention the role played by General Stanculescu in organizing the escape, and the Ceausescus certainly believed their flight to have been betrayed by Stanculescu (Behr, p. 21). Malutan was promoted to the rank of full colonel after the revolution.

2. RFE/REE (26 January 1990); SWB/EE (3 January 1990; 10 January 1990); the *securitate* were not in fact equipped with aircraft.
3. Other uncorroborated accounts speak of the garrison coming under helicopter attack.
4. This was subsequently denied by the Deputy Minister of National Defence, SWB/EE (5 January 1990).
5. Only in mid-January were the grave pits of those slain in the fighting discovered; they contained 60–70 bodies.
6. The official death toll for the period of the revolution, as given by Rompres in 1991, was 1033 persons with a further 2383 wounded. These figures are generally considered an overestimate. In January 1990, French officials gave a precise figure of 746 fatalities, while in the same month the judge presiding over the trial of Ceausescu's four leading officials cited a figure of 689 dead and 1200 wounded.
7. Others in attendance were Ioan Nistor, Corneliu Sorescu, Daniel Condrea, Ion Zamfir, Dan Voinea, Jan Tanasa, M. Florescu. Popa's suicide was reported on 2 March 1990.
8. According to later accounts the defendants were also offered the opportunity to appeal, a right to which in fact they were not strictly entitled.
9. Rompres. 'Romania – Documents, Events', no. 13.
10. Ken Jowitt, cited in Calinescu and Tismaneanu, 'The 1989 Revolution and Romania's Future', *Problems of Communism* (Jan–April 1991), p. 47.
11. SWB/EE (5 January 1990).
12. There is speculation that Nicolae Ceausescu died of a heart attack before he could be actually executed and that an elaborate mock-up was staged with a propped-up body. The evidence for this appears negligible.
13. Corneliu Bogdan, cited in *The Independent* (28 December 1990).

12

ION ILIESCU
AND HIS FRIENDS

In an article published on 20 February 1990 in the Bucharest daily, *Dreptatea*, Adrian Marino proposed the concept of a Romanian 'double revolution'. In the preceding December, so Marino argued, there had first of all been a spontaneous, popular and anti-communist uprising which brought about the fall of the Ceausescu government. Marino defined this movement as a 'bottom-to-top' revolution, led primarily by the country's young people. This first revolution was, however, swiftly taken over and redefined by a second movement, originating in the upper reaches of the communist hierarchy. This 'top-to-bottom' revolution had more limited aims than the first and was organized by a group of reform-minded communists who were anxious to preserve as much of the old power system as possible. In Marino's view, the two revolutions were incompatible: the 'bottom-to-top' revolution demanded a complete break with what had gone before; the 'top-to-bottom' revolution was aimed at preserving the old system with only a minimum of concessions. Until the contradictions between the two revolutionary movements could be resolved, Romanian politics was, according to Marino, likely to remain violent and volatile.

Marino's analysis of the December revolution is both shrewd and accurate. Incontestably, the demonstrations which led to the overthrow of the Ceausescu government were prompted by a tremendous explosion of popular wrath. The crowds which overthrew the regime in Timisoara and Bucharest lacked at first any organization and any clear ideological purpose. In the political vacuum which followed the flight of the Ceausescus, leadership of the revolution was taken by a small band of party officials, led by Ion Iliescu. It was this group of former communists who made up the core of the National Salvation Front and who directed the course of the revolution in the days which followed.

Once their leadership of the country was secure, the same band of politicians decided the organization and membership of the new Romanian government, thus sealing the fate of the 'bottom-to-top' revolution.

The NSF government is frequently criticized for having 'hijacked' the revolution and for having deliberately diverted Romania away from the path towards true parliamentary democracy. There is justice in these accusations. Nevertheless, it should be remembered that, had it not been for the speedy responses of Iliescu and Militaru on the afternoon of 22 December, the generals might have proved rather less ready to commit themselves to the side of the revolution. By the swift measures which they put in train on the day of Ceausescu's flight, Iliescu and his supporters did not so much hijack the revolution as ensure its ultimate triumph over the remnants of the Ceausescu government.

The governing body of the National Salvation Front consisted overwhelmingly of former communists. From the very start, the dominant personality within this group was Ion Iliescu. Iliescu (born 1930) had for most of his career served as a loyal supporter of the party and of Nicolae Ceausescu. His credentials as a revolutionary socialist were impeccable. The son of communist parents, he had joined the party when both he and it were still in their infancy. During the war, he was interned in the Tirgu Jiu prison camp along with Ceausescu and Gheorghiu-Dej. Subsequently, he had trained in Moscow as an engineering student during Stalin's last years and had worked his way up the Romanian party apparatus as a student organizer. As the chairman of the Romanian Union of Students Associations, he had led the reprisal actions against young people who had demonstrated in 1956 in support of the Hungarian Revolution. Subsequently, he became secretary of the party youth organization. In 1964 he was appointed to the Central Committee where he held special responsibility for ideology and propaganda. During the 1960s, Iliescu was one of the first party officials to promote the personality cult of the new party leader, Nicolae Ceausescu. It was he who organized some of the earliest adulatory receptions which were to become the hallmark of 'Ceausescuism'.[1]

The system of rotating party officials led to Iliescu being moved to the provinces during the 1970s. Nevertheless, he continued to rise. He was party boss of Iasi and served on the fringes of the Polexco. He was on close personal terms with the president and photographs released after the revolution show him playing chess and badminton with Nicolae and Elena. As State Secretary of the National Water Council Iliescu had a significant role in the construction of the Danube-Black Sea canal, which together with Bucharest's House of the People, must stand as the most expensive and stupendous folly of the Ceausescu period.

In 1984, however, Iliescu lost the president's favour. He was dismissed from the Central Committee and appointed director, instead, of the *Technica* publishing house. During the late 1980s, Iliescu cultivated close links of his own with members of the party bureaucracy and of the technical intelligentsia, among whom he had the reputation of being a 'charming and kind man'. During this period, Iliescu is also thought to have cultivated close links with the senior *securitate* officer, Professor Virgil Magureanu. Magureanu subsequently attended the Ceausescu's trial and was appointed in 1990 head of the new *securitate* apparatus, the Romanian Intelligence Service. Since Magureanu's role in present-day Romania is a highly controversial one, it is perhaps unsurprising that details of his previous career and contacts with Iliescu have not been made public.

Iliescu was later to claim that he had opposed Ceausescu from the very first and that he had moved into opposition to the regime as early as 1971. This is not true. Only in September 1987 did he make a veiled attack on Ceausescu in the journal *Romania Literara*, where he advocated a transition towards Soviet-style *perestroika* and criticized 'voluntarist arbitrariness' in government. The fact that Iliescu could get away with this suggested at the time that he enjoyed protection in very high places and that he was probably Gorbachev's preferred choice for succeeding Ceausescu.[2] Since Iliescu studied in Moscow at roughly the same time as Mikhail Gorbachev, there is considerable speculation that the two men got to know each other personally at this time and maintained contact subsequently. Certainly, to begin with, Iliescu used his rumoured connection with Gorbachev as a way of ensuring his own primacy in the National Salvation Front. He was able to hint, therefore, on 22 December that should the revolution go awry, his personal links with Moscow would alone ensure speedy Soviet assistance. Later on, Iliescu would deny any personal acquaintance with Gorbachev, although well-placed Soviet sources suggest otherwise.

Iliescu's pedigree as an opponent of the Ceausescu regime was sufficiently ambivalent for the NSF to decide not to publish a full biography during the run-up to the elections in May 1990. No such impediment, however, affected Iliescu's closest companions within the NSF. Both Silviu Brucan and Dumitru Mazilu enjoyed considerable early influence and reputation within the National Salvation Front largely on account of their previous resistance to the Ceausescu government.

Silviu Brucan (born 1916) had like Iliescu joined the Communist Party in 1944. He was subsequently appointed deputy chief editor of the party newspaper, *Scinteia*, and played a key role in the propaganda activities which accompanied the show trials of the opposition party leaders in 1947. Between 1956 and 1962 he was Romanian ambassador to the United States and to the United Nations. Brucan's Jewish and intellectual background made him unpopular with Ceausescu. After a brief period in charge of Romanian television, Brucan took up the post of Professor of Marxism at the University of Bucharest in 1966. For a long period, he was used by the regime as a propaganda instrument in the West and was allowed to attend foreign conferences and to give lectures abroad. His mild criticism of the government on these occasions was used to demonstrate the tolerance of the Romanian authorities and their readiness to allow divergences of opinion. In 1987, however, Brucan boldly condemned the suppression of the riots in Brasov, predicting with great accuracy that, 'repression will generate a rupture between the party and the working class'. This proved too much for Ceausescu who had him placed under house arrest. Nevertheless, Brucan used contacts in the Soviet Union to ensure that his activities were not too greatly circumscribed. Indeed, in 1988 he was allowed to visit the United Kingdom at the invitation of the Foreign Office in London and of the Sandhurst Military Academy. Only in March 1989 was Brucan placed under stricter confinement, following his participation in the 'letter of the six'. Brucan was later to use his criticism of the regime between 1987 and 1989 as evidence of his qualifications as a dissident.

After Iliescu and Brucan, Dumitru Mazilu (born 1934) was the third most important member of the National Salvation Front. Mazilu was a former professor of law at the Ministry of the Interior training school in Baneasa and is widely reported to have held the rank of colonel in the *securitate*. He is thus believed to have been an important link between the new government and the older generation of senior *securitate* officers who had been eclipsed by the rise of Postelnicu and Vlad. Subsequently, Mazilu had worked in the foreign ministry and was Romanian representative on the Human Rights Commission of the United Nations. His threat to make public the abuses of the Ceausescu regime resulted in his recall from Geneva in 1987 and to his being placed under house arrest. Mazilu managed, nevertheless, to smuggle out to the West the text of his report listing Romanian violations of human rights. Thus, like Brucan, Mazilu was able to use his record of opposition as evidence of his qualifications for membership of the post-revolutionary government. Mazilu proved, however, to be one of the earliest victims of faction-fighting within the new government. His previous connections with the *securitate* were exploited by Iliescu in a successful bid to discredit him. Having resigned his membership of the Front on 25 January 1990, Mazilu returned greatly embittered to Geneva.[3]

In the first days of the revolution, effective leadership of the NSF was vested in Iliescu, Brucan and Mazilu. As a consequence of the negotiations he had played with the army during 22 December, Iliescu enjoyed the support of the generals. Iliescu was pre-eminently the 'serious politician' the military commanders wanted to see put in power, even though his own background appeared tainted by his association with the old regime. Iliescu additionally enjoyed support within the ranks of the party technocracy and *nomenklatura*. We may guess that through Magureanu, Iliescu also had connections of his own with the *securitate*. For their part, Brucan and Mazilu were both able to employ their previous quarrels with Ceausescu as evidence of their reformist inclinations. Additionally, Mazilu had close connections with the *securitate*, and Brucan provided a link to the old guard communists who had signed the 'letter of the six'. In this way, the leadership of the NSF reflected the interests of the group who on the afternoon of 22 December had first thrown their weight behind the establishment of the NSF: the dissident party veterans, the *nomenklatura*, the army and the *securitate*.

Until the beginning of January 1990, the composition of the NSF was deliberately concealed behind a flood of misinformation. Iliescu was named as its president on 22 December, and Mazilu as vice-president four days later. In the meantime, a host of well-known dissidents and intellectuals were listed as members of the 'ruling' Council of the National Salvation Front: Doina Cornea, Ana Blandiana, Laszlo Toekes, Geza Domokos and Mircea Dinescu. Officers and military commanders who had joined the side of the revolution on 22 December, were similarly named. Thus, the impression was conveyed that power rested jointly in the hands of the intellectual leaders of the revolution and of the representatives of the armed forces. Given the vital role both had recently played in the revolution, the union of these two groups within the framework of the NSF Council seemed at the time entirely appropriate.

Over the succeeding week, the membership of the NSF Council was expanded from some 39 persons to a total of 145. However, the full membership list of the Council was never disclosed and it soon became evident that the institution was powerless. Rather than residing with the Council, authority lay instead with a self-appointed Executive Office of 11 persons. Among this group, there was only one representative of 'intellectual' circles (Ion Caramitru), and no army officers. Instead veteran communists, such as Iliescu, Mazilu, Brucan, Karoly Kiraly and Dan Martian (Iliescu's successor as secretary of the Communist Youth Organization), were joined by obscure middle-ranking members of the old Communist Party hierarchy. Even within the Executive Office, so it was claimed, decisions were only taken by a small cabal headed by Iliescu and Brucan.[4]

The organization of the National Salvation Front bore a striking resemblance to the old structure of Communist Party government. Like the Central Committee of the Romanian Communist Party, the NSF Council was a facade institution, shouldering little responsibility and wielding even less power. It existed solely for the purpose of conveying the illusion of consensus and of a popular mandate. Real power was vested in the Executive Office, which functioned very much as the successor of the party Polexco, and in the narrow group of individuals clustered around the person of the president. In a fashion similar to the Polexco, the authority of the Executive Office remained ill-defined and, for that reason, diffuse. Each member of the Executive Office headed up a commission of the NSF with responsibility for a specific activity of government. Thus, they were able to intervene directly in affairs of the state administration.

Although the decree establishing the political organization of the NSF declared, 'all power structures of the former dictatorial regime' to be dissolved, the powers pertaining to the Executive Office derived from a constitutional sleight of hand typical of the communist government it claimed to have replaced. Theoretically, the 145 members of the NSF Council comprised 'the supreme state power body': the Executive Office simply exercised a delegated authority on behalf of the Council. One vital provision, however, made the

Executive Office effectively unanswerable to the Council's allegedly superior authority. The Executive Office assumed full powers in the intervals between sessions of the Council. Since the Council was rarely convened, the Executive Office continued to exercise power without formal responsibility.

The NSF Executive Office ruled by decree, simply issuing out such instructions as its members deemed expedient and declaring these to be fully legal instruments. The actual business of government and of day-to-day administration was carried out by departments of state, headed by ministers. These were responsible to the Council of the NSF or 'in the interval between sessions' to the Executive Office. The ministers appointed by the NSF enjoyed in the main the same background as the members of the Executive Office, leavened with a few army officers and intellectuals. Like Mazilu and Brucan, a number of the ministerial appointees also had experience in the *securitate*. Nearly all were former communists.

The new Prime Minister, Petre Roman, was so obscure a figure that his career could at first only be learned through background material furnished by the Romanian news agency. He was, according to Agerpres, an engineer by training and a specialist in hydraulics. He was the son of the veteran communist, Valter Roman (formerly Ernest Neulander[5]), who had joined the party in the 1930s and been a Central Committee member at the time of his death in 1983. Gradually, it was learned that, as a scion of the 'red aristocracy', Petre had been educated at the elite *Petru Groza* school in Bucharest and had later been allowed to travel to France to complete his postgraduate studies. Various implausible explanations were given by members of the NSF Executive Office for Roman's selection as the new Prime Minister. He was, at 43, supposedly young, and it was suggested that as the revolution had been waged on the streets of Bucharest by young people, Roman should be considered a representative of Romania's revolutionary youth. This empty justification was later fleshed out with the claim that Roman had been the person who had supplied students with pears to hang on trees in the immediate wake of Ceausescu's last party congress.[6]

Roman's promotion to Prime Minister derived from his close association with the veteran communist leadership. Roman's father had been a close associate of Iliescu and both had belonged in the 1960s to an informal discussion group devoted to planning and management. The organizer of this group was Mihai Draganescu, another colleague of Ion Iliescu, who was subsequently appointed NSF Deputy Prime Minister. Furthermore, Iliescu and Petre Roman enjoyed close links of their own as they shared the same interest in hydraulic engineering. Iliescu's publishing house thus printed several of Roman's books in the mid-1980s. Close personal links with Silviu Brucan may also be demonstrated from the time when Roman was only 'knee-high'. (Unconfirmed reports speak also of an intimate relationship between Petre Roman and Zoia Ceausescu.)[7] The most likely supposition is, therefore, that Roman was appointed Prime Minister because it was thought that he would be a reasonably compliant instrument on behalf of Iliescu and of the older communists.

Other ministers who counted among Iliescu's former colleagues included Sergiu Celac, appointed Foreign Minister on 28 December 1989. A former chairman of the Communist Youth Organization, Celac had also been Ceausescu's personal translator. He was demoted in 1978 probably because he was connected with the defector, Ion Pacepa. Thereafter, he worked as a publisher in the same building as Ion Iliescu, and is reliably reported to have frequently met with the future president.[8] General Militaru, the NSF Minister of National Defence, was also a close confidant of Iliescu. It was Nicolae Militaru who had been primarily responsible for ensuring the support of the generals for Iliescu's new government on 22 December. Captain Mihai Lupoi, who was present at the inaugural meeting of the NSF in the Central Committee Building, and who subsequently attended the Ceausescu's trial, was designated Minister of Tourism.

Other army officers who were rewarded for their support of the revolution included General Mihai Chitac, appointed Minister of Internal Affairs, and General Victor Stanculescu, appointed Minister for the National Economy and later Minister of National Defence. Both Chitac and Stanculescu had joined the revolution on the afternoon of 22 December. However, they were later implicated in the preceding slaughter at Timisoara and their precise behaviour in Bucharest during the period 21–22 December is still open to query. As the officer commanding the 'chemical troops' of the Romanian army, Chitac is likely to have been responsible for giving the order to use teargas on demonstrators in Bucharest. For his part, Stanculescu was linked to the Ceausescus' flight from the Central Committee Building.

Stanculescu responded to these allegations by denying any direct involvement in the Timisoara massacre and by presenting implausible evidence for his immobility on the morning of 22 December. According to his own account, upon being summoned to Bucharest by Ceausescu on 22 December, he had found a compliant doctor who set his leg in plaster. Thus, according to his own account, he had a perfect excuse for being unable 'to participate in Ceausescu's actions against the demonstrators' as well as an impediment to movement sufficient to prevent him lending assistance in the Ceausescus' rooftop escape.[9] Other descriptions of Stanculescu's behaviour on 22 December vary between the allegation that he remained a Ceausescu supporter right up until the time of the president's flight, and the claim that he was an important actor in the 'military conspiracy' which accomplished Ceausescu's downfall.

The majority of other appointments within the new government consisted of technical experts, who were either moved to ministerial rank from academic establishments or, alternatively, were promoted upwards within their ministries. The Minister for Water, Forestry and the Environment, was thus a former university professor and (shades again of Iliescu!) an expert in hydraulics. Stefan Nicolae, NSF Minister of Food and Agriculture, had previously been deputy minister in the same department of state. Likewise, the new Minister of Justice, Teofil Pop, had been a director in the same ministry. 'Experts' made up the lion's share of the 27 ministers and 57 deputy ministers appointed by the NSF in the fortnight following the Christmas revolution.

Although experienced technocrats, the new appointees were almost to a man former Communist Party members. The justification subsequently given that all professional persons of influence in Ceausescu's Romania had automatically to join the party is certainly not invalid. Party membership was, as one Romanian writer was later to explain, rather like a driving license: a necessary qualification for personal mobility. Nevertheless, in many cases the 'experts' were also opportunists whose careers had taken them into the highest reaches of the party and state apparatus. The new Minister of Sport was thus a former deputy editor on the party newspaper. Stefan Nicolae had previously been Romanian ambassador to East Germany and Vice-Chairman of the Romanian-Egyptian Friendly Society, before developing his special interest in food. Stelian Pintilie (Telecommunications), Ion Folea (Geology) and Nicolae Nicolae (Foreign Trade) were all former members of the Central Committee.

As far as it can be ascertained, only two ministers were appointed who did not have a party background.[10] These were Andrei Plesu, Minister of Culture, and Mihai Sora, Minister of Education. Both had had distinguished careers as writers and both had fallen foul of Ceausescu in the late 1980s. Noted intellectual leaders such as Blandiana, Cornea and Dinescu, were not included in the new ministries.

The composition of the NSF Executive Office and the new government reflected the specific circumstances lying behind the formation of the Front. The NSF was created by veteran communists, army and *securitate* leaders, and members of the party *nomenklatura* who came together on the afternoon of 22 December. The new organs of state power created after the revolution were staffed almost entirely by members of these same groups. Likewise, the most influential figure at the meeting on 22 December was Ion Iliescu. In determining the membership of the Executive Office and the new government, Iliescu exercised a decisive influence and it was his protégé who was elevated from obscurity to the position of Prime Minister.

NOTES

1. RFE/REE (8 June 1990).
2. Trond Gilbert, *Nationalism and Communism in Romania. The Rise and Fall of Ceausescu's Personal Dictatorship* (Boulder and London: Westview Press, 1990), pp. 122–3.
3. As a consequence of the 'revelations' about Mazilu's connections with the *securitate*, Mazilu subsequently had the double misfortune to be distrusted both in Romania and in Geneva.
4. Other members of the executive office were Cazimir Ionescu, Bogdan Teodoriu, Vasile Neacsa, Gheorghe Manole and Nicolae Radu.
5. Other sources give Valter Roman's original surname as Katowsky.
6. Anneli Ute Gabanyi, *Sudosteuropa*, vol. 39 (1990), p. 179.
7. *New York Times* (27 December 1989).
8. In 1990 Celac was appointed the Romanian ambassador in London.
9. *Romania Libera* (20 February 1990).
10. It should be pointed out that no list of Communist Party members survives.

13

THE NATIONAL
SALVATION FRONT

Even though it was dominated by former party members, the National
Salvation Front swiftly realized the hopes of the Romanian population.
Starting on 26 December 1989, the NSF began abrogating the most
oppressive and unpopular decrees of the Ceausescu period. No longer
were Romanians obliged to address each other as 'comrade' and
Romania ceased to be a 'Socialist Republic'. In addition, the laws
forbidding abortion were cancelled; the systematization programme
was halted; and passports for foreign travel were promised. In order to
gain the confidence of the population, the *securitate* apparatus was
incorporated within the Ministry of National Defence and made
directly subject to military supervision.

The immediate physical needs of the Romanian people were met by
a series of emergency provisions. The system of rationing was
abolished and a free market in farm produce was permitted. Price
supplements on food sold from shops in the countryside – a measure
used by Ceausescu to force the rural population to 'live off the land' –
were likewise scrapped. The contents of export warehouses were
distributed and meat was made freely available for the first time in
many years. The amount of gas and electricity earmarked for domestic
consumption was doubled and the tariffs for power were reduced.
These measures, announced by Iliescu within days of taking power,
won him immediate and lasting popular acclaim.

In the weeks following the revolution, Romanians were treated to a
series of revelations about the nature and character of the old regime.
The interior of Ceausescu's suburban villa in Bucharest was shown on
television, complete with its gaudy decoration and with Elena's
collection of diamond-studded shoes. Menus listing caviar and other
delicacies were taken from the Ceausescus' kitchen and shown to
viewers. Their correspondence was examined for evidence of the

family's inability to compose grammatically correct sentences. The town houses, hunting lodges and seaside retreats belonging to the presidential family – 84 separate establishments altogether – were similarly opened up to minute and prurient inspection. The press and media circulated extraordinary tales which reinforced the impression conveyed by the television that the Ceausescus had led lives of debauched luxury. One of the Ceausescus' villas at the Black Sea resort of Neptun was thus identified as the location of Nicu's wild parties and night-long orgies. Orchids flown in specially from Thailand were reported as having decorated Elena Ceausescu's tables; and Nicolae was said to have sought rejuvenation by transfusing the blood of babies. Other stories described Elena's promiscuity and told of how rather than being a 'great scientist' she had only completed four years' education.[1] As one commentator later pointed out, in the first days of the revolution the Ceausescu personality cult was rapidly transformed into an equally exaggerated 'anti-cult'. Ceausescu 'the Titan' thus became Ceausescu 'the Satan', the 'living god' became a vampire, and 'Madame Comrade Academician Engineer of World Renown' became a functional illiterate.[2]

The process of collective catharsis and exorcism continued with the trials of Ceausescu's henchmen: Bobu, Dinca, Postelnicu and Manea Manescu. Although the four were only brought to the dock at the end of January, their trial was preceded by press conferences and interviews during the course of which the investigating magistrates announced in advance the guilt of the four men. In their televised courtroom appearances, the four defendants humbled themselves before their accusers. In rehearsed admissions of guilt, they confessed their misdeeds and incriminated both themselves and each other in the charge of 'complicity in genocide'. Manescu thus volunteered the information that Tudor Postelnicu, his co-defendant, was the 'prototype of an innate criminal'. Postelnicu himself confessed to being 'an idiot' and 'vehemently condemned' his past misdeeds. Dinca spent most of his time in the dock in tears, proclaiming his repentance, while Bobu, at the close of the proceedings, thanked the court for its 'extreme patience'.[3] The extraordinary show trial of the four ended predictably enough with sentences of life imprisonment.[4] Over the following months, various other *securitate* officers and former ministers were brought to court. Their trials were conducted amidst evidence of considerable confusion and evasion on the part of the state prosecutor's office.[5]

The Ceausescu anti-cult and the ritualistic humiliation of the former companions of the dead president was accompanied by the first signs of a cult of the new leader. Almost certainly, Ion Iliescu was not responsible for this new development; it emerged spontaneously from a society used to the flattery and adulation of political leaders. Furthermore, Iliescu gave every impression of affability and seemed to exude a genuine warmth and kindness. Unlike the politicians of the preceding half-century, he was actually seen to smile. Thus, his selection as a focus of popular acclaim was not entirely remarkable. As early as 23 December, Iliescu was introduced on the radio as 'the man who sums up the nation's entire confidence,' and who 'has control of the situation and is coordinating the resistance'. Several weeks later, the former party newspaper *Scinteia*, now renamed *Adevarul* (The Truth), published among a string of other pro-Iliescu messages, the following letter from a female reader in Galati: 'I lost my father when I was four; I never knew what paternal affection meant. I regard Mr Iliescu as my father. His smile inspires confidence. We do not have the right to offend him. He is a good man.' Other newspapers used horoscopes and studies in physiognomy as evidence of Iliescu's exceptional qualities and of his character as a 'clean' and honest politician. He was according to one journalist, 'a providential apparition'.[6] At meetings attended by Iliescu the trappings of the old regime were similarly brought out. There were repeated rolls of applause, eulogies along the lines of 'When Iliescu appears, the sun shines', and little girls in white bearing flowers.[7]

The new-found sense of freedom and of material comfort combined with the focus of media interest on the family and accomplices of the former ruler, diverted popular attention away from the actual composition of the new government. At first, it seemed that only a few intellectuals were aware and critical of the inclusion within the NSF and the ministries of large numbers of former party functionaries. It was, therefore, not until the second week of January 1990 that concern began to be more widely voiced about the personnel of the new government. By this time, however, the NSF had consolidated its position sufficiently for Iliescu to be able to claim that any drastic change in the make-up of the government would be 'destabilizing' for Romania.

As early as 26 December, Doina Cornea, the human rights activist in Cluj, had criticized the NSF leadership as consisting only of, 'dubious elements: profiteers, lackeys and liars'.[8] Gradually, over the succeeding fortnight, she was joined in her stand by the leaders of the various new political parties which were being formed at this time, as well as by the increasingly disillusioned band of Romanian intellectuals who formed the Group for Social Dialogue.[9] *Romania Libera*, under the editorship of Octavian Paler, also assumed in the first days of January the character of an 'opposition' newspaper and exposed the past careers of several prominent members of the Front.

The response of the NSF leadership was twofold. Firstly, the presenced of ex-communists in the government was explained by reference to the impossibility of finding experienced personnel who had not at some point been drawn into party membership. On account of this, Cornea herself was upbraided for making 'unfair and irresponsible' comments and for being 'very naive politically'. Secondly, the NSF Executive Office consistently dropped from the government those persons who were revealed as unacceptably compromised. Within a few days of their appointment, therefore, two heavily tainted ex-communists, Constantin Bostina and Paul Niculescu-Mizil, were dismissed from office. Likewise, Dumitru Mazilu resigned from the NSF Executive Office on 25 January following widespread criticism of his previous career in the *securitate*. Other politicians who were denounced in *Romania Libera*, responded by publishing accounts of their heroic actions during the course of the revolution.[10]

During the first week of January, an increasing mood of dissatisfaction grew in the provinces owing to the breakdown in food distribution. As warehouses were emptied of their export consignments, the population found that the supply of consumer goods simply dried up and that conditions returned to much the same as they had been before the revolution. At state shops, which sold scarce goods at subsidised prices, rationing had to be reintroduced. In some areas, monthly supplies of flour and sugar were limited to a kilogram per head, and meat to half a kilo. The 'free market' – in other words the street stalls from which home-grown produce was sold – remained relatively buoyant although its prices were generally much higher than in the state shops. At a time when the average wage was only 2000 lei a month, a kilo of meat cost on the free market roughly 100 lei.[11]

Discontent manifested itself in popular demonstrations against the administrative ineptitude of local officials, to which were increasingly added accusations that the same party functionaries as before the revolution were still in positions of responsibility. In several cities, local

committees of the NSF were purged of ex-communists in an attempt
to put in power new politicians who were both clean and competent. In
Sibiu, demonstrators condemned the municipal authorities for their
'failure to liquidate the old power structure'. In Timisoara, the
revolutionary committee installed to run the city on 20 December was
obliged to resign en masse following widespread accusations that it was
harbouring ex-communists. On 12 January, these protests reached the
capital when a rally addressed by Iliescu and Roman was disrupted by
heckling and violence.

As the spirit of national consensus which accompanied the first days
of the revolution gave way to insults and recriminations, Romanian
politics became increasingly polarized. On the one hand, the NSF
retained substantial popular support and continued to be broadly
perceived as the instrument which had brought down the Ceausescu
government. On the other, there was a vocal body of opposition to the
new government led in the main by students and young people but
including substantial portions of the urban and rural workforce.
Among this group, the prevailing opinion was that the NSF consisted
of no more than a group of communists who had joined together for
their own and not the nation's salvation. The NSF leaders, had, so it
was alleged, conspired to hijack the revolution even while the popular
movement was at its height, and were intent upon leading Romania in
the direction of 'neo-bolshevism'.

In fact, the NSF had no interest in preserving communism which it
perceived to be an ideology so unpopular as to be beyond recall, and
both Iliescu and Roman publicly repudiated their previous
commitment to Marxist beliefs.[12] Nevertheless, the modes of thinking
exhibited by the Front's leaders were rooted in years of lip-service to
the communist ideal. In his speeches and interviews, Iliescu thus
repeated the phrases and slogans inherited from the Ceausescu period.
He frequently described opponents of the Front as 'fascist diversionary
elements' and explained disturbances as the work of 'foreign agencies
and anti-revolutionary circles'. In his speeches, Iliescu appeared to
accept the 'exceptionalist' principle previously espoused by Ceausescu
that there was a separate Romanian road of national development
which not only made the acceptance of western norms of political
behaviour impossible but which also set Romania apart from its
reforming Eastern bloc allies. Most extraordinarily, in several
interviews Iliescu justified his position as president of the NSF with
reference to his life-long commitment to revolutionary communism

which he perceived as identical to patriotic service. As Andrei Plesu was later to observe, Iliescu was a man of little discernment who could 'not avoid having the reflexes of a communist intellectual'.[13]

Iliescu's understanding of democracy and of political pluralism was similarly vitiated by his long exposure to communist ideas. The NSF programme released on 23 December had promised the abandonment 'of the leading role of a single party' and had announced the 'establishment of a democratic multi-party system of government' to be arrived at by the holding of free elections. Within a few weeks, however, Iliescu began to cast doubts on his own commitment to democratic principles. In an interview given on 23 January 1990, Iliescu argued that 'the multi-party system is an obsolete model' and that democracy should not be confused with political pluralism. A few days later, he repeated his conviction that the notion of competing political parties was outdated and no longer relevant. Iliescu's doubts seemed to be shared by Silviu Brucan who in several interviews questioned whether the Romanian population was ready for multi-party politics.

Iliescu's perception of democracy was rooted in the communist principle of 'democratic centralism'. As Iliescu saw it, the Front was the heir of the revolution, which justified its claim to act as the new focus of power in Romania. Additionally, Iliescu perceived the NSF to be a forum which reflected the popular will and which embraced all the motive forces behind the overthrow of the old regime. In his opinion, therefore, the Romanian revolution had, 'conferred legitimacy on the NSF, whose character as a movement has been bestowed upon it by the adherence of whole categories of citizens to its platform'. Nevertheless, although the NSF embodied a wide variety of different views, it sought by methods of consensus 'to rally all creative forces of the country' and 'to unite the broadest interests of all categories of citizens'.[14]

Iliescu's description of the NSF bore striking similarities to Ceausescu's own perception of the role of the Communist Party in the Romanian state. Both Ceausescu and Iliescu saw their respective movements as vested with an authority deriving from the revolutionary actions of the 'broad masses'. Both emphasized the need to embrace a wide spectrum of interests and classes within the framework of a single political organization. Both, moreover, perceived consensus as emerging logically out of the synthesis of contradictory viewpoints and believed that a single party system provided the best forum for 'dialogue' and for 'the exchange of opinions'. As much as his predecessor, therefore, Iliescu failed to make the intellectual commitment to political competition and electoral choice which is the hallmark of parliamentary democracy.

The organization of the NSF at a local level was similarly affected by communist techniques of political centralization. In the days immediately following the revolution, the NSF presented itself as the vehicle of democratic transformation and the instrument through which the popular will was realized. Accordingly it urged the establishment of local committees of the NSF which would speed up the process of political change in the counties and municipalities, and which would act, furthermore, as a means of transmitting opinions to the new government. It was thus stated that the principal function of the lower organs of the NSF was 'to achieve the government's full subordination to the popular interest in line with the principle that it is the government which is in the service of the people, not the people in the service of the government'.[15]

In accordance with this principle, communist-led municipal and county councils were abolished and their power assumed by ad hoc committees of the NSF. In the main, the new units of local government comprised spokesmen who had come to prominence during the revolution and former party functionaries. In a few places, attempts were subsequently made to alter the composition of the new committees by the holding of ballots. However, the Executive Office of the NSF swiftly put an end to such experiments in local democracy reasoning that too rapid a turnover of public officials would hamper administrative efficiency.[16]

NSF committees were established not only in town halls and county seats but also in factories, institutions and enterprises. Some of the new 'enterprise committees' were established at the behest of the workforce; others were imposed unilaterally by municipal committees of the NSF.[17] The enterprise committees usually commenced activity by dismissing unpopular members of the old management team and the most prominent party activists. The rapid turnaround of managers and executives threatened the restoration of normal economic conditions. Accordingly, the Organizational Commission of the NSF Council requested as early as 29 December that enterprise committees should seek to collaborate with the existing structures rather than try to overthrow them. A fortnight later, NSF enterprise committees were furnished with specific guidelines which laid down that they might 'debate and advance proposals' but should not exercise 'political ambitions of management and control over the technical-administrative apparatus'.[18] Accordingly, the party *nomenklatura* which occuped the key positions in the bureaucracy and economy survived the revolution largely intact.

Far from remaining agencies of popular and democratic transformation, the local organs of the NSF were rapidly stripped of power and autonomy, and changed into instruments of the government. Instead of transmitting opinions upwards, they increasingly acted as channels through which government directives were communicated and enforced at a local level. They thus became, as Iliescu himself admitted, 'bodies representing the political power in our state',[19] formally subordinated within a hierarchical framework to the central organs of the National Salvation Front. Their role thus became analogous to that of the local branches and cells of the former Communist Party apparatus. In the same way, the old trade union apparatus of the Ceausescu period was retained. Its officers stayed in place, following instructions given them by the NSF leadership. Only the name of the organization was changed. In disgust at this development, breakaway unions were established, the most important of which became the *Fratia* (Brotherhood), one of the main goals of which was 'the destruction of totalitarian structures and the immediate democratization of labour activity'.[20]

To begin with the NSF leadership claimed that its government was only temporary and that it did not seek to retain power in the long term. As Iliescu explained on 12 January, the NSF did not wish 'to assume power in this state. We are a temporary force which wants to ensure free elections'. Roman, likewise, declared that he had no interest in remaining in politics for more than a few months and expressed his wish to give up the burden of government. Irregularities in the Front's organization and the strong institutional position it had built up on a local level were thus explained away as purely temporary phenomena In regard to the enterprise committees, therefore, Iliescu justified their creation with specific reference to the transitional character of the NSF. 'We are thinking of the moment', he explained, 'when the Front will disappear as a form of political power in the countryside; these organizations can [then] become trade unions in enterprises, based on democratic principles, thus representing the working people's interests at the level of enterprises.'[21] Whether the leaders of the NSF intended from the very first to compete in the elections and judged it best to dissimulate, or whether they decided to participate only later on, must remain a matter of speculation. Surviving accounts suggest that the Executive Office of the Front was divided over this point and was only swung round to its subsequent position by the skilled advocacy oif Silviu Brucan. Nevertheless, after a series of heavy hints in the media, the NSF formally declared on 23 January that it would be running candidates in the forthcoming election.

Announcement of the Front's decision to compete in the election prompted a substantial outcry. Doina Cornea left the NSF Council in protest at the move and over the next week students and leaders of the newly emergent National Liberal and National Peasant parties organized demonstrations in Bucharest. On 28 January a rally of about 20,000 persons invaded the headquarters of the NSF in the Foreign Ministry building, demanding its resignation. Chants heard on the streets five weeks before were shouted again, and posters coupling Iliescu with Ceausescu were held aloft. On the walls of the capital, slogans denouncing Ceausescu's tyranny were repainted, but this time with condemnations of the NSF. The principal objection of the demonstrators was that the government was 'trying to replace the old one-party state with another' and was preparing to contest the election as both 'player' and 'referee'.[22] The biased coverage given to these protests by the Romanian media only deepened suspicions as to the real intentions of the NSF.

The response of the NSF leadership to the new wave of demonstrations aroused further distrust. On 24 January, the Front banned public meetings from the centre of Bucharest and threatened fines and imprisonment for those who defied its injunction. Several days later, draconian penalties were listed for those found guilty of assaulting the forces of law and order in their task of clearing the city centre. When these measures failed to put an end to the demonstrations, the Front embarked on a course of action entirely reminiscent both of the interwar period and of the Ceausescu regime.

During the preceding weeks, members of the government and of the NSF Executive Office had been engaged in touring the country and in rallying support for the Front. A particular target of their activity was the workforce in the large industrial combines and in the mining communities. The fears of these workers that they might face redundancy in the expected shakeout of the economy were allayed. Indeed, the workforce in several vulnerable industries was even expanded. At the same time, substantial wage increases were given, working hours were reduced and holiday benefits were improved. The enthusiasm of 'numerous workers' for the NSF was given as one of the reasons for the Front's decision to enter the electoral contest.

On 28 and 29 January, several tens of thousands of miners from the Jiu valley and Maramures together with other workers loyal to the Front were bussed into the centre of Bucharest. Some of these came apparently of their own volition, others were paid 500 lei, the equivalent of a week's salary, to attend. Their numbers were beefed up by school children who had been given the day off and provided with transport by local NSF enterprise committees. The NSF loyalists stormed the rallies organized by the opposition groups and besieged the headquarters of the rival political parties. In justifying the heavy-handed response of the Front's allies, Iliescu argued that the government had merely been acting in self-defence against a *putsch* organized by the National Peasants Party with the support of the foreign press.

The heavy-handed NSF reaction to protests against its policies led to further defections from its ranks and to a split in its leadership. The distinguished poet and dissident, Ana Blandiana, resigned her membership of the NSF Council on 31 January. Shortly afterwards Silviu Brucan left the Executive Office for reasons which he never fully disclosed. On account of his objections to the bullying tactics of the Front, Captain Mihai Lupoi was sacked as Minister of Tourism in February and a few months later was forced to flee the country. At the same time, substantial international criticism of the NSF threw doubt on the future of the relief economic package then being assembled by the United States, the International Monetary Fund and the World Bank.

Accordingly the NSF leadership began an exercise in damage limitation aimed at salvaging its reputation while still preserving its powers intact. On 1 February, Iliescu announced that the NSF had reached agreement with the other parties on a restructuring of the government. In order to prevent the NSF enjoying an unfair advantage in the election, it was agreed that its Council would be entirely restructured to make it a proper pre-parliament. This would be done by admitting members of the other parties to its deliberations. It was similarly promised that the Executive Office of the Front would be more broadly composed. Thus, the NSF would no longer enjoy any special privileges but would compete in the election on equal terms with the other parties.

Having restored the semblance of order, the NSF began to go back on its earlier commitments. The NSF Council was reformed under the new name of the Provisional Council for National Unity (PCNU) and its membership was increased from 145 to 253. However, representatives of the NSF took almost 50 per cent of the seats on the Council, dividing up the remainder between 50 or so other political organizations and groupings. In order to ensure that the Front retained a majority voice, various phantom parties were established which had separate representation on the Council but which were in fact only the tools and accomplices of the NSF. The Executive Office of the PCNU similarly had a built-in majority of NSF members and its president was Ion Iliescu. On a lower level, the local NSF councils in county seats and workplaces were simply renamed PCNU committees and continued with largely the same membership as before. However, in a number of places, the councillors were sufficiently dissatisfied with the government to assume an increasingly independent position.

The restructuring of the Council and Executive Office failed both to carry conviction among political opponents of the NSF and to staunch the steady trickle of defections from its ranks. Throughout February and March, demonstrators thus returned to the streets of Bucharest. Their protests were countered by rallies of 'pro-government' supporters who were bussed into the centre by local NSF committees. At the same time, the NSF-led Provisional Council sought to defuse criticism by sacking ministers who had been singled out for particular criticism by opposition leaders. In response, thus, to protests from members of the officer corps of the Romanian army, General Militaru was dismissed as Minister of National Defence. His replacement was General Stanculescu, previously Minister for the National Economy and, under Ceausescu, a deputy Minister of Defence.

In the new climate of confusion and violence, there were repeated reports that the NSF had resorted to using the remnants of the *securitate* against its political rivals. To begin with, these allegations were only anecdotal. On 16 February, however, *Romania Libera* published, with the help of a former directorate chief, the names of *securitate* personnel who were still on active service. In order to dispel suspicion, the government arranged special tours of former *securitate* installations and affirmed that all former Ministry of the Interior units had been absorbed within the armed forces. As Deputy Prime Minister, Voican Voiculescu, explained, 'The people who made up the *securitate* are no longer part of any organized structure of the former apparatus. This has disappeared.'[23]

By all appearances, however, the *securitate* service had remained intact despite its absorption within the Ministry of National Defence. According to figures released by the government, less than 5000 personnel had been dismissed. The remaining 15 to 20,000 people continued to be organized separately, with their own officers and training schools. They even continued to ride around in plain clothes in Interior Ministry jeeps. A part of the security service was, however, detached to join the Independent Service of the Judicial Secretariat, the head of which was a former *securitate* major, Vasile Apostol. Eventually in April, the security service was entirely restructured as the Romanian Intelligence Service under the former *securitate* colonel, Virgil Magureanu.

The claim that the Romanian Intelligence Service had been established 'to defend the sovereign right to a free and democratic existence' did not convince those opponents of the government who experienced at first hand its techniques of harassment and intimidation. For this group the reappearance of the *securitate* only confirmed the suspicion that the NSF was less the heir of the revolution and more the heir of the regime it claimed to have replaced.

NOTES

1. Elena's end-of-year school certificates were published in *Cuvantul Romanesc* (January 1990). They demonstrate that she left school at the age of eleven and performed badly in mathematics.
2. Anneli Ute Gabanyi, *Sudosteuropa*, vol. 39 (1990), pp. 195–8.
3. RFE/REE (9 March 1990).
4. An appeal was subsequently lodged on grounds of procedural irregularity. It was rejected.
5. The prosecutions of all former officials and *securitate* chiefs related only to their misdeeds during the actual period of the revolution. Crimes committed prior to the revolution were and have not been made the subject of separate charges. Various politically sinister motives have been imputed to the government for so 'shielding' Ceausescu's accomplices from prosecution. It has to be admitted, however, that were the entirety of the Ceausescu period to be taken into account by the state prosecutor's office, a potentially limitless witch hunt might follow. By confining charges to the short period of the revolution, the courts have encountered substantial difficulty in securing convictions. Thus the only charge that could stick against Marin Neagoe was misappropriation of funds and the

cases against Iulian Vlad and two dozen other leading Ceausescu supporters were only concluded in March 1991 with light gaol sentences. Zoia and Valentin Ceausescu have been freed from gaol, although Nicu and N. Andruta Ceausescu have received sentences of 20 and 15 years respectively.

6. RFE/REE (20 April 1990).
7. *Liberation* (19–20 May, 1990).
8. *Daily Telegraph* (27 December 1989).
9. The Group for Social Dialogue was founded on 31 December 1989 to monitor the new government and to hasten the formation of a civil society in Romania. In January 1990 the GSD began to publish the weekly review *22*.
10. Thus, for instance, Stelian Pintilie, *Romania Libera* (14 January 1990; 19 January 1990).
11. *Heti Vilaggazdasag* (6 April 1990; 19 May 1990).
12. SWB/EE (10 April 1990); *Le Monde* (4 January 1990).
13. *Adevarul* (26 January 1990); SWB/EE (31 January 1990); RFE/REE (24 August 1990).
14. SWB/EE (31 January 1990).
15. SWB/EE (16 January 1990).
16. SWB/EE (29 December 1989; 17 January 1990).
17. SWB/EE (17 January 1990).
18. SWB/EE (16 January 1990).
19. SWB/EE (17 January 1990).
20. RFE/REE (27 July 1990).
21. SWB/EE (17 January 1990).
22. Ibid.
23. SWB/EE (20 February 1990).

14

TIRGU MURES

Under Ceausescu, the Hungarian minority in Transylvania had suffered considerable harassment and discrimination. During the 1980s the government had embarked upon a policy of forcible assimilation and had sought to deprive Hungarians of their sense of cultural and linguistic identity. Hungarian publications thus gradually ceased production and minority-language theatre groups and literary associations were abolished. A persistent shortage of books in Hungarian meant that local libraries in Transylvania consisted almost entirely of Romanian language texts. In the village of Bodoc, for instance, in the ancient land of the Hungarian Szeklers, the local library contained only one book in Hungarian: a text on buffalo breeding.[1] Throughout Transylvania, bilingual signs all but disappeared and in 1988 it was laid down that Hungarian language publications should render place names exclusively in Romanian.

In the drive for conformity, Hungarian educational institutions were progressively closed down so that by the mid-1980s no single Hungarian secondary school survived. In mixed Hungarian and Romanian educational establishments, the number of Hungarian students receiving instruction in their native language was similarly reduced and technical subjects were taught exclusively in Romanian. A further cause of complaint was the forcible merger in 1959 of the Hungarian Bolyai University of Cluj with the Romanian Babes University in the same city. The Bolyai University had been founded in 1872 and counted as the foremost Hungarian institution of higher education in Transylvania. Following its absorption, only literary studies were taught through the medium of the Hungarian language.

The case of the Szentgyorgyi theatre school in Tirgu Mures is also instructive. This was originally a Hungarian foundation, established before the war, and the leading drama college in Transylvania. In the 1980s, however, Romanian students were steadily admitted in preference to Hungarian ones. By the end of the decade Romanians comprised two-thirds of the school's membership and it was found impossible to mount Hungarian language plays.

Hungarians living in Romania greatly resented the loss of their educational facilities. Firstly, they were deprived of many historic institutions which had served their national community over several generations. Secondly, Hungarians anticipated that the loss of teaching in the native language would lead to the erosion of a special Hungarian identity in Romania. Hungarians have always been particularly mindful of their precarious nationhood and have always regarded their language as the mark of their unique national character. The anti-Hungarian campaign, whipped up by Ceausescu in the 1980s, and rapid Romanian immigration to traditionally Hungarian centres, made the minority even more fearful of its prospects for survival.

The revolution in December was greeted with intense joy and relief by the Hungarian community. Firstly, the tyrant was dead and with him went, so it was thought, his discriminatory policies. Secondly, the example of Timisoara, where Romanians had joined in defending a Hungarian pastor against the authorities, seemed to augur a new period of cooperation and tolerance between the majority and minority populations. As one Hungarian poet put it, 'the blood shed for the common cause will be the foundation on which our future will be built'.[2]

Immediately after the revolution, members of the Hungarian community in Transylvania began to revive their previously defunct cultural organs and associations. Theatre groups and literary circles proliferated, each of which sought to give publicity to its activities by printing handbills and journals. The old Hungarian language party newspaper, *Elore* (Forward), was republished as *Romaniai Magyar Szo* (Hungarian Word of Romania). Its editors went out of their way to beg forgiveness for their previous servility and they promised to make the paper the true voice of the national minority. Starting at the end of December, *Romaniai Magyar Szo* began once more referring to places by their Hungarian names. In areas where the Hungarian population predominated, road signs in the minority language were erected. Separate newspapers and clubs were similarly organized by members of the German, Romany and Ukrainian communities.

Hungarians were particularly encouraged by the support they received from the new NSF government. In the NSF communiqué published on 22 December, at the very height of the revolution, Ion

Iliescu undertook, 'to observe the rights and freedoms of national minorities and to ensure their full equality with those of the Romanians'. A fortnight later, the NSF promised that it would seek to implement 'constitutional guarantees for the individual and collective rights of ethnic minorities'. The inclusion of such prominent Hungarians as Laszlo Toekes, Geza Domokos and Karoly Kiraly within the new NSF Council, and the opening up of the media to minority broadcasts, additionally suggested the new government's commitment to equal rights. Thus the radio stations in Bucharest, Cluj, Tirgu Mures and Timisoara each gave over about 12 hours a week to transmissions in Hungarian. Free Romanian Television similarly assigned its early evening viewing on Mondays to programmes in the Hungarian language. Some time was also allocated to transmissions aimed at the German minority in Romania.

These concessions, speedily granted by the NSF, convinced most Hungarians as to the good intentions of the new Romanian government. Thus, most prominent Hungarians took their stand by the NSF platform even after the Front had declared itself a political party. Indeed, in the early months of 1990, the Hungarian Democratic Union of Romania, the umbrella movement of the minority, acted primarily as a vehicle for NSF policy in Transylvania. As Geza Domokos, the Chairman of the HDUR explained, the NSF was 'the guarantor of social peace, of freedom and of the rights of minorities'.

The weeks immediately succeeding the December revolution saw quite considerable chaos in Transylvania. In Harghita county bands took revenge on persons associated with the old regime, killing about half a dozen militiamen and *securitate* officers.[3] Repeated appeals for calm suggest that such reprisal actions were probably quite widespread. At the same time, a large number of young Romanians simply abandoned Transylvania. Many of these had been made to work against their will in the region as part of the scheme of compulsory labour direction for recent graduates (the so called *stagiatura* system). In the weeks immediately following the fall of the Ceausescu government, these young people gave up their rented accommodation and returned to their homes in Wallachia and Moldavia.

The greatest population movement involved, however, neither Hungarians nor Romanians but the ethnic German community in Transylvania. In order to raise hard currency Ceausescu had, during the 1980s, embarked upon 'selling' Germans to the Federal Republic at a price of DM 10,000 a head. Following the revolution, those who had been refused exit visas or who were fed up with waiting, simply left Romania. Possibly as many as 100,000 – a half of the total German community – left for the Federal Republic in the first months of 1990. Most of the remainder gave notice of departure. Whole tracts of the Transylvanian countryside became thus deserted and empty German villages were taken over by Gypsies. In a large number of settlements, only the local German priest remained, ministering to a passing congregation of tourists and conservationists.[4]

Beside the population, the greatest number of changes took place in education. In areas where Hungarians were numerous, local committees of the NSF together with enterprise committees in schools, designated Hungarian as the main language of instruction in many educational institutions. Accordingly, the Romanian children in these schools had to be immediately relocated. This process of transformation affected not just mixed schools but also half a dozen secondary schools where the exclusive vehicle of instruction had previously been Romanian. Amongst these were included two of the most prestigious educational institutions in Transylvania: the lyceums at Cluj and Tirgu Mures. The creation of Hungarian language schools was apparently endorsed by the Ministry of Education, which affirmed the right of members of minorities to receive instruction in their own language.

Higher education was similarly affected. In January 1990, plans were announced by the Deputy Education Minister to reconstitute the Hungarian university in Cluj and to split the Medical University in Tirgu Mures into two separate national sections.[5] Schemes were also put in train to secure Hungarian language teaching at the Szentgyorgyi theatre school in Tirgu Mures, and at the Colleges of Music and of Fine Arts in Cluj. A League of Hungarian Students in Tirgu Mures acted as a pressure group for the reform of higher education in Transylvania along national lines.[6]

The Hungarians of Transylvania proceeded incautiously both in tabling their demands and in precipitately taking over educational establishments. On the whole, they believed that anti-Hungarian feeling was something uniquely created by Ceausescu and that with his death they could immediately achieve a restoration of their rights in an atmosphere of tolerance. Additionally convinced of the justice of their case, they could not conceive that their actions would be taken amiss by either the Romanian population or the new government. In this respect, they did not take into account the way that centuries of suspicion and the more recent drip of nationalist propaganda had poisoned relationships. They quite failed to heed the warning given early on in January by the Transylvanian Hungarian writer, Andras Suto: 'Decades will be needed before the wounds are healed and the nationalism fostered by the dictatorship is buried in the common soil.'[7]

The most obvious concern of the Romanian majority was the speed with which schools had been taken over by Hungarians and designated for exclusive minority use. In Tirgu Mures, Romanian students at the lyceum were forced to seek places for a time in the local technical high school. In Cluj also, Romanian children were hastily moved to the old party training school. Unsurprisingly, they took to the streets in protest along with their parents and teachers. Among Romanian students at Cluj university there were similar protests and a League of Romanian Students was founded to obstruct the reorganization of higher education along national lines.

Misgivings about the pace of change were shared by ministers in the NSF government. Quite clearly, the Deputy Minister of Education, Attila Palfalvi, a Hungarian with a brief for minority affairs, made commitments on the future shape of Hungarian language education without consulting his superiors. As a consequence, he was dismissed at the end of January 'for creating tension in Translyvania'. His successor, Lajos Demeny, worked rather more easily with Minister Mihai Sora and proved altogether more conciliatory. Accordingly, the further conversion of Romanian language schools into Hungarian language institutions was delayed until the start of the new academic year and Romanian children were brought back into the schools from which they had only recently been excluded. Plans for a separate Hungarian university were in the meantime quietly shelved.[8]

The particular fear of the Romanian majority and, indeed, of ministers in the NSF was that separate educational facilities extending through from primary school to university would create a separate Hungarian elite and intellectual class. This was interpreted as quite out of keeping with the traditional unitary character of the Romanian national state and as the prelude to federalization. In the minds of many, cultural pluralism was confused with territorial fragmentation and educational autonomy with political separatism. The misgivings of the majority population were deepened by fears of Hungarian irredentism. Despite continued assurances by both Budapest and the minority leaders in Transylvania that Hungary had no interest in revising its borders, Romanians believed that territorial secession was the ultimate goal of the Hungarian minority. The experiences of the twentieth century combined with Ceausescus's frequent denunciation of Hungarian imperialist ambitions, even convinced educated Romanians of the existence of an international Magyar conspiracy aimed at depriving them of their Transylvanian home.

Events early on in 1990 served to deepen suspicions yet further. The old accusation that Hungarians were crypto-communists was raised yet again on account of the presence within the HDUR of former high-ranking party activists such as Domokos, Suto and Kiraly. Likewise, the murder of the militiamen in Harghita county was widely, and quite erroneously, reported as the work of Hungarian thugs (hence the frequent denunciation in the local Romanian language press: 'Murderers not Revolutionaries'). The Hungarian attempt to set up special schools for themselves was likewise claimed to be typical of their elitist ambitions and a measure of their resurgent pride. Textbooks furnished by the government in Budapest for the use of Hungarian school children in Transylvania were also criticized as containing 'subversive and irredentist' maps and passages. Thus the old stereotype Hungarian was re-created in popular imagination: vain, brutal, politically unreliable and disloyal.

During February 1990, early reports spoke of the re-formation of Iron Guard units in Romania. The Bacau daily, *Desteptarea*, thus carried an advertisement announcing the programme of *The Iron Guard Anti-Communist Army*: 'The Iron Guard will fight against anyone who supports any left-wing ideology,' the manifesto promised. 'We will not give up until we have liquidated all the communists, socialists and dirty lefties ... *Heil Hitler!*'. A few weeks later, a legionary call to arms, entitled 'The Time has Come' was distributed in Tirgu Mures.[9] Although, as it turned out, the alleged reappearance of the Iron Guard provided a useful diversion for political rhetoric, it is altogether unlikely that the legionaries consisted of anything more than just a few old men.[10] In view, however, of the escalating ethnic tension in Transylvania, the establishment of a quite new nationalist organization with an emphatically anti-Hungarian programme, proved altogether rather more alarming.

The *Vatra Romaneasca*, or Romanian Homeland, was established in Romania at the beginning of January 1990, although one informed source claims an earlier origin among exile groups in New York.[11] Other reports speak of the *Vatra* as having received funding from émigrés in Canada, Italy and Spain. In its public statements, the *Vatra* assiduously sought to present itself as a patriotic and cultural organization, which had nothing against minority groups but sought instead constructive dialogue. Its publicity material, as originally reproduced in otherwise highly respected Romanian newspapers, presented the *Vatra* as devoted to 'implementing and continuing the ideals of the December revolution and founded on the wish to establish a real democracy in our country'.[12] By its own estimate the *Vatra* had at the time of its first national conference in May 1990 some five million members, although the true number of its supporters was probably nearer two million.[13] Public occasions to which the press were invited, suggested that flags, families and guitars were the sum of the *Vatra* programme.

Study of the *Vatra*'s membership suggests, however, that it comprised two quite separate elements. On the one side, it attracted a middle class following made up of Romanian professionals who feared competition with Hungarians for the better jobs. The local *Vatra* leadership in Tirgu Mures thus comprised an artist (Radu Ceontea), a secondary school teacher (Nistor Man) and a magistrate (Ioan Sabau). In Cluj, the *Vatra* organizer was a former theologian in the Hungarian Reformed College (Jonel Roman). On the other side, however, the *Vatra* attracted a powerful following among Romanian workers who had, in recent years, been moved into Transylvania from Moldavia. Members of this group were on the whole poorly educated and had been directed to settle in Transylvania precisely because of their low intellectual attainment. They constituted a dangerous rabble element which was easily manipulated by the local politicians who swiftly came to the forefront of the *Vatra* leadership.

Despite the moderate tenor of its publicity material, the *Vatra* acted as a radical nationalist pressure group, which sought to continue Ceausescu's policies of forced assimilation of minorities. It thus relied largely upon the same slogans as the previous regime and presented the Hungarians as intent upon carving out a position of superiority in the Transylvanian Romanian 'homeland'. The Hungarians' pursuit of minority rights was characterized as being typical of their pride and ambition, as displayed over the centuries, and as a threat to the integrity of the Romanian national state. As Radu Ceontea explained:

After almost a thousand years of foreign domination in Transylvania, it is fairly difficult for [the Hungarians] to forget their behaviour as rulers ... They demand rights specific to communities with a federative status, like those in the Swiss Federation, to which they often refer ... Romania is not a multinational state but a national unitary state in which different percentages of minorities live. And no minority is permitted favours just because its ancestors were oppressors for centuries.[14]

Unsurprisingly, this message struck a powerful chord among the less educated groups of Romanians, who enthusiastically embraced the *Vatra*'s propaganda. The following extracts are taken from a recording of speeches delivered during a *Vatra* rally held at Alba Iulia on 4 March 1990:

Our association undertakes to safeguard the territorial unity of Romania! We unequivocally take it as our point of departure that Transylvania is ancestral Romanian land. We demand that the Romanian language be recognized and that in every sphere of life this should be the sole, the official state language ...

Under the pretext of individual and collective human rights, the Magyar lords are coming up with demands for territorial autonomy. Up to now, the lords have not yet said so clearly, but properly speaking what they are trying to do as an ethnic group is to create a federated state within Romania ...

What we reject now is cooperation with the Magyars, who have been the cause of so much mental wickedness ... (chants of 'Romanian language!' 'We'll die but we won't give up Transylvania!' 'Hang Laszlo Toekes!').

At a similar closed meeting held at Reghin, the speakers were constantly interrupted with shouts: 'One country, one language! We are the people! Hungarians are rubbish!', and yet more ominously, 'We want to drink Hungarian blood!'[15]

The *Vatra* organization numbered among its supporters persons of considerable influence. In Tirgu Mures, for example, where in March 1990 the *Vatra* perpetrated its most notorious excesses, the organization enjoyed particularly close links with the local PCNU Council. Thus, the chairman of the Mures County committee (Colonel Judea) and at least one other prominent member (Nistor Man) were both *Vatra* members. The Tirgu Mures branches of the National Peasants Party and of the NSF were again heavily infiltrated by the *Vatra* as were also the local enterprise committees. A large number of unconfirmed reports also tell of the leading echelons of the *Vatra* as comprising former officers of the *securitate*.

On a national level also, the *Vatra* was able to exercise some influence, not least because its large membership made it an important source of votes in the forthcoming election. The Vice Chairman of the national PCNU, Ion Manzatu, is thus known to have had close dealings with the *Vatra*, and the Republican Party, which he headed, operated very much as a front organization for right-wing nationalists. Significantly also, Petre Roman refused on several occasions to condemn the *Vatra*, even though its programme must have been well known to him. According to Roman, the *Vatra* was just a harmless, patriotic movement.[16]

Organs of the press were similarly sympathetic to the *Vatra*. Indeed, the organization boasted its own newspaper, which specialized in running anti-Hungarian stories and which evidently enjoyed quite a high circulation within Transylvania. Other papers such as *Cuvintul Liber* and *Curierul de Vilcea*, maintained a largely sympathetic attitude towards the *Vatra*, publicizing its events and reproducing its propaganda. The infusion of strongly nationalist sentiments within the mainstream of Romanian liberalism meant that reputable national newspapers, such as *Romania Libera*, adopted at first an equivocal position with regard to the *Vatra*, even giving credence to some of the wilder stories put around by some of its members.[17]

During February, outbreaks of intercommunal violence were reported in Transylvania following the vandalism of several national monuments. These, however, were minor affairs which only acquired significance by reason of the laboured demonstrations of Hungarian-Romanian friendship which followed hard upon each desecration. Rather more alarming was an attack mounted by workers armed with iron bars on a Gypsy settlement in Mures county. In the process, six homes were burnt down and the gypsies put to flight across a local cemetery. On 15 March, thousands of Hungarians gathered in town squares to celebrate their national day. In most places, the event passed off peacefully; in a few, however, Hungarian flags and wreaths became objects of dispute, being either raised near Romanian monuments or, alternatively, being torn down by counter-demonstrators. Later on, the government would blame the arrival of tens of thousands of visitors coming from neighbouring Hungary for starting the violence of the next week. In fact, Hungarian border guards reported no great traffic across the Romanian frontier on that day and even local organizers of events admitted that attendance had been generally sparse. At the Petofi monument near Sighisoara, the site of a special shrine, no Hungarian number plates were seen.

The city of Tirgu Mures had for several months acted as a focus for the *Vatra* and, with hindsight, the bloodletting which occurred there was predictable. The city was an old Hungarian centre set in the heart of the Szeklerland. Over the past decades, however, Tirgu Mures had experienced a considerable influx of Romanians who soon accounted for a half of the city's population. An illustration of the ill feeling between the two communities is a fresco in the principal orthodox church there. It emotively depicts Christ being abused by Hungarian soldiers in traditional dress, while Romanian peasants weep. The wall painting was completed only in 1985.

After the revolution, relations became particularly strained in Tirgu Mures on account of the designation of the local lyceum as a Hungarian school and the demands of students at the Medical University for a Hungarian language section. In pursuit of their goal of a separate faculty, Hungarian students in Tirgu Mures went on strike at the beginning of March. For its part, the *Vatra* organized a series of protest rallies aimed against any reorganization of education in the city.

On 16 March, the day following the national celebration, the Hungarian manager of a pharmacy repainted the sign above his shop. Next to the Romanian *farmacie*, he put up the Hungarian equivalent, *gyogyszertar*.[18] The proprietor of a nearby stall, who was a member of the *Vatra*, took exception to the appearance of a Hungarian word and gathered together a crowd of fellow *Vatra* supporters. The pharmacy was ransacked and its Hungarian employees beaten. As a gaggle of onlookers gathered outside the premises, a car driven by a drunken Hungarian ploughed into them, injuring several of their number. Only at this point did the police who had previously gathered near the pharmacy, intervene: to arrest and breathalyze the driver. The supine and partisan way the police force in Tirgu Mures went about its duties was to become ever more apparent in the days which followed.

Shortly afterwards, the *Vatra* planned a major demonstration in Tirgu Mures aimed at forcing Elod Kincses from the Mures PCNU Council. Kincses was a colleague of Toekes and had acted as his personal lawyer during the late 1980s. He was also closely associated with the programme of educational reorganization in Tirgu Mures and his resignation had been high on the list of *Vatra* demands since

February. The *Vatra* decided to take advantage of the tension which had built up over the last few days and to use the demonstration as a major display of its muscle.

Throughout 19 March, committees in nearby factories and villages were asked to muster gangs of Romanians ready for transfer to Tirgu Mures.[19] In the village of Hodac, the local inhabitants were advised by their priest that they should make their way to Tirgu Mures in order 'to stop the Hungarians taking Transylvania away'. In return for participating, Romanian workers and villagers were promised substantial sums of money; others were threatened by local mayors with fines if they did not join in. The groups were issued with weapons and alcohol, and provided with coaches, lorries and police escorts. In the course of the descent on Tirgu Mures, various groups stopped off en route to attack Hungarian villages. The death of at least one ethnic Hungarian was subsequently reported at the village of Ernei.

In the middle of the afternoon a massed convoy of about a dozen coaches led by a police car entered the Square of the Roses in the centre of Tirgu Mures. Axes, pitchforks and sharpened stakes were distributed to the newcomers. These weapons were later described by the government as 'traditional farm implements'. It seems likely, however, that they were taken from caches previously intended for the use of local units of the Patriotic Guard. Having been provided with additional drink by the local orthodox priest, the Romanians flung themselves on a group of Hungarians who were demonstrating in favour of educational reform. Thereafter, bands of Romanians attacked the local offices of the HDUR forcing the Hungarian occupants to seek shelter in the attic. They were subsequently escorted out of the building by the Chairman of the Mures PCNU committee, Colonel Judea, who gave a personal guarantee for their safety. However, once out of the building, the Hungarians were attacked, possibly with Judea's connivance. In the course of the ensuing fracas, successive attempts were made to gouge out the eyes of the distinguished Hungarian writer and local HDUR chairman, Andras Suto.[20]

The next day a Hungarian demonstration against violence took place in Tirgu Mures with members of the crowd waving Romanian flags in a gesture of political loyalty. On this occasion, the Hungarians were joined by a number of Romanians who were anxious to show their disgust at the events of the previous day. Once again, a convoy of Romanians debouched into the city centre and set about the demonstrators, forcing a stampede for safety. A thin cordon of several hundred police and reinforcements of soldiers failed entirely to keep the two sides apart. Indeed, according to several reports, the forces of law and order displayed their partisanship by providing the 'Romanian side' with petrol for firebombs.

The continuing inability of the police to preserve order resulted in Hungarian leaders turning for assistance to their co-nationals in outlying villages. During the afternoon of 20 March, several hundred armed hillsmen from Hungarian Szekler communities along the Niraj River descended in lorries and carts on Tirgu Mures. On the way, they put up road blocks to stop Romanian villagers reaching the city. The Szeklers were joined by Gypsies, who in camp meetings held over the preceding day had voted to throw their weight behind the Hungarians. Once in Tirgu Mures, the newcomers proceeded to ransack the Hotel Grand where they were informed a number of the *Vatra* had taken refuge. In order to combat the Szeklers, the *Vatra* summoned back to Tirgu Mures the peasants it had unleashed the previous day. That evening members of the two national communities fought it out on the streets in full view of foreign cameramen. In one notorious scene, caught on film by an Irish crew, a fallen and motionless Romanian was repeatedly belaboured by unidentified assailants.[21]

The combined bands of Szeklers and Gypsies changed the balance of power in the city. As a consequence, the senior PCNU councillor and *Vatra* organizer, Nistor Man, felt it now necessary to summon full military assistance. Accordingly on the morning of the next day, a convoy of tanks entered Tirgu Mures and army reinforcements took active measures to keep the two sides apart. Although sporadic outbreaks of fighting recurred in the next few days, the worst excesses of violence were now over. The official casualty toll was three dead and 269 injured, which is certainly an underestimate.[22]

The violence in Tirgu Mures clearly had a spill-over effect in local communities, which the NSF government was subsequently at pains to conceal. On 21 March, a Romanian mob in the town of Dumbraveni (Erzsebetvaros) attacked the Catholic Armenian church, which ministered to a largely Hungarian congregation. Rioters captured the local priest, Dr Francisco Diarian, whom they tortured and eventually killed. Having made off with Diarian's car, video recorder and some money, the same group sought out the local Hungarian Reformed Church pastor, the Reverend Ferenc Erosdi. Although the rioters were unable to find him, they smashed up his home.[23]

The response of the NSF government to the bloodshed was determined by electoral considerations. In two months time, Romanians would go to the polls and the NSF was reluctant to criticize the *Vatra* in view of the popular support it retained. Thus, although 'excesses on both sides' were mentioned, and some oblique references made to Iron Guard provocation, Romanians were on the whole absolved from responsibility. Instead, the NSF spokesmen singled out for blame the Hungarian community in Transylvania together with the government in Budapest. The former was accused of having ridden roughshod over local Romanian sentiments; the latter was condemned for having stirred up nationalist feeling. Hungarian radio and television were repeatedly criticized for their biased coverage of events.

In fact, although exhaustive and strident, Hungarian media coverage was on the whole reasonably fair, and the most tendentious reporting came not from Budapest but instead from Bucharest. Romanian television repeatedly gave out that a Hungarian pogrom on the Romanians of Tirgu Mures was underway. Radio stations, likewise, transmitted a steady stream of exaggerated and inflammatory reports throughout the week beginning 15 March. For its part, the Romanian language press portrayed the events in Tirgu Mures as almost exclusively the work of Hungarian extremists. Indeed, local newspaper coverage was so virulent in its content as later to merit special criticism from the Romanian government.

Following the restoration of order in Tirgu Mures, various commissions were appointed to investigate the causes of the recent violence. The local PCNU committee was similarly restructured to include persons enjoying the confidence of both communities. These solutions, however, failed to restore goodwill. The polarization of the two communities was later to be starkly shown in the election returns from Mures county in May 1990. The Hungarians voted almost to a man for the HDUR; Romanians in similarly impressive numbers for the candidates backed by the *Vatra*.[24]

As a consequence of the violence in Tirgu Mures, a mood of uncertainty permeated the region throughout 1990. In Tirgu Mures there were repeated incidents of fighting between Hungarian and Romanian gangs, while in Cluj it was considered inadvisable to converse in Hungarian on the streets. For its part, the *Vatra* continued to organize noisy demonstrations of cultural supremacy. These reached a crescendo in August 1990, at the commemoration of the 50th anniversary of the Hungarian annexation of Transylvania. The

Prime Minister and other government officials attended several of the ceremonies, thus lending credibility to the *Vatra*'s propaganda. In February 1991, the NSF further revealed its sympathy for the *Vatra*. At a regional conference held in Cluj, the party passed a resolution affirming the 'unitary' character of the 'Romanian national state'. Employing a vocabulary entirely reminiscent of the Ceausescu period, the conference officially deplored Hungarian 'chauvinism, irredentism and extremism'.

The pervasive sense of fear and of despair drove many Hungarians to seek refuge in neighbouring Hungary. By May 1990, the exodus was proceeding at the rate of 4000 a month. Nevertheless, among the tightly-knit Hungarian communities of Harghita and Covasna counties, little emigration was reported. Despite the work of the *Vatra*, therefore, Romania is likely to remain a multinational state for the foreseeable future.

NOTES

1. George Schöpflin and Hugh Poulton, *Romania's Ethnic Hungarians. A Minority Rights Group Report* (London: Minority Rights Group, 1990), p. 14; the Szeklers are a Hungarian tribe of hill warriors established in the region during the middle ages.
2. RFE/REE (23 February 1990), citing *Nepszabadsag* (6 January 1990).
3. Murders took place at Odorheiu Secuiesc (where a local militia station was also burnt down), Dealu, Cristuru Secuiesc, and Tirgu Secuiesc. The victims included ethnic Hungarians as well as Romanians.
4. Gypsies also left Romania making for the Federal Republic in particular. In order to restrain the westward flood of Gypsies, the Yugoslav government imposed a compulsory $200 exchange for travellers coming from Romania.
5. SWB/EE (19 January 1990).
6. The manifesto of the League is published in *East European Reporter* (Spring/Summer 1990), pp. 41–2.
7. *Nepszabadsag* (6 January 1990).
8. At the time of writing, it is understood that the Bolyai University may be reconstituted with private funds provided from the Soros Foundation.
9. SWB/EE (23 February 1990); *Nepszabadsag* (21 March 1990), citing an interview with Cazimir Ionescu.
10. An alternative suggestion is that the legionary advertisements and leaflets were distributed clandestinely by the government as part of a bid for political solidarity: SWB/EE (26 February 1990).
11. Mihaly Fulop, a specialist in Transylvanian affairs at the Foreign Ministry in Budapest, cited in *Nepszabadsag* (28 March 1990).

12. *Curierul Romanesc* (15 June 1990).
13. *Mai Nap* (11 April 1990), citing E.M. Barki of the Vienna-based International Committee for Transylvania.
14. *Romania Libera* (17 March 1990); cited by Dennis Deletant, RFE/REE (1 February 1991).
15. *Panorama*, broadcast on Hungarian TV (12 March 1990) and partly reproduced in SWB/EE (17 March 1990). Even more outrageous statements were carried in the Hungarian press in April 1990. These are, however, widely considered to be forgeries. An English language version of one such allegedly fake document is published in the Channel 4 booklet, edited by Derek Jones, *And the Walls Came Tumbling Down* (London: Channel 4 TV, 1990), p. 24.
16. Until the true nature of the *Vatra* became evident to him, the student leader, Marian Munteanu also expressed himself in sympathy with the organization's aims.
17. *Romania Libera* (8 May 1990).
18. There is no evidence, as was commonly reported in western press reports, that the shopkeeper put up a sign saying 'No Romanians served here'. He was in fact following an instruction from the local directorate of pharmacies.
19. The following villages provided recruits: Hodac, Toaca, Ibanesti, Rusii, Munti, Zau de Cimpie.
20. Suto was taken to hospital in Tirgu Mures, sightless and with several broken ribs. He was subsequently transferred to clinics in Budapest and Boston, Mass. He lost most of the sight in his left eye.
21. The Romanian victim of this outrage was Mihaila Cofariu, an inhabitant of Ibanesti. He was not, as Hungarian television repeatedly reported, a Hungarian. The identity of his assailants is uncertain. A British eyewitness has reported that, judging from the angle of the attack, the assailants might well have been ethnic Romanians. According to the same reporter the fighting was so confused that persons were frequently attacked by members of their own community.
22. Julius Strauss in *East European Reporter* (Spring/Summer 1990), p. 41.
23. I owe this information to a senior source in Dumbraveni. Diarian was born in Constantinople, studied in Rome, and had a Paris doctorate. The Armenian community in the town numbered 37 a few years ago. Most of the worship in the Catholic Armenian church is conducted in the Hungarian language.
24. In Mures county 11 per cent of the vote went to the HDUR; 34 per cent to the *Vatra*-backed AUR.

15

THE ELECTION

The NSF came to power committed to holding free elections and the electoral law published on 14 March was a textbook illustration of democratic procedures. The law recorded that in Romania all power 'belongs to the people' and that it should be exercised 'in accordance with the principles of democracy, liberty and the human dignity'. The electoral process in the new Romania was to be 'universal, equal, direct, secret and freely expressed'. In accordance with these principles, all adult citizens were allowed the right to vote, including those charged but not convicted of criminal offences. Thus even members of the Ceausescu family, in prison and awaiting trial, were entitled to participate in the ballot.

The electoral law specified that the Romanian people would be choosing not so much a parliament as a constituent assembly. The principal function of the new body was to devise a constitution while at the same time enacting such laws as were thought to be necessary in the interval before a properly appointed legislature could be assembled. Thus, the relationship of the various organs of government one to another and their respective powers were left deliberately vague. It was the function of the new constituent to settle these constitutional issues and the Electoral Law did not seek to pre-empt or to influence its decisions. Confusingly, however, the Electoral Law always referred to the new constituent body as a parliament.

The Romanian parliament would consist, so the Electoral Law pronounced, of two houses: an Assembly of Deputies and a Senate. The former was to comprise 387 members, the latter 119. Apart from size, there was little apparent difference between the two bodies and the precise formulation of their respective powers was reserved for discussion at a later date. Members of the two houses were to be chosen by a system of proportional representation based upon county constituencies and party lists. Thus, Covasna, the smallest county in Romania, would send four deputies and two senators to the parliament; the city of Bucharest would have 39 and 14 representatives respectively.[1]

The Electoral Law provided for the simultaneous election of a national president, whose powers were given in some detail although the length of his incumbency awaited future discussion. Candidates for the presidency were obliged to gather 100,000 signatures each as evidence of their popular support before they could be entered on the ballot. This provision ensured that of the nine persons who originally declared themselves to be presidential candidates, only three ended up in the lists. The Electoral Law obliged the President to choose a Prime Minister from among the ranks of the majority party or coalition and specified that, once elected, the President should give up his former party-political affiliation.

The main task of the new parliament was to draw up the details of the constitution and it was laid down that it had only 18 months in which to fulfil this duty. If the parliament failed to agree on a constitution after this period, then it would be automatically dissolved and new elections held. Even before the 18 months had elapsed, if the President felt the parliament was making insufficient progress on the constitution then he might dissolve it regardless. Once a constitution had been approved, fresh elections had to be held within the next 12 months. Thus, the new parliament could remain in session for an absolute maximum of only two-and-a-half years.

By the time the election was held, there were in existence over 80 political parties. Of these, however, only four proved to be of any significance: the National Salvation Front, the Hungarian Democratic Union of Romania, the National Liberal Party and the National Peasants Party. Altogether these four parties accounted for 333 seats in the Assembly and for all but five places in the Senate. Romania's two 'historical' parties, the Liberals and the Peasants, were always regarded as the main rivals to the NSF. Both were formed within days of the revolution and they rapidly established a patchy network of branches and party offices across the country. The parties were led by veterans of the pre-communist era and both made a conscious appeal to the principles and programmes which had served them so well in the interwar years. As it turned out, however, the commitment of the two parties to their 'historical' leadership and ideas made them appear irrelevant and outmoded in the eyes of the electorate.

The National Liberal Party was reconstituted on 31 December by veterans of the party's former student organization, all of whom were now of course quite elderly. The party adopted as its secretary Radu Campeanu, once the leader of the Liberal Youth organization, who had spent many years in gaol and had subsequently emigrated to France. The Liberals defined their goal as 'to disseminate the ideas of political and economic liberalism, to which all peoples that have been oppressed by totalitarianism aspire today'.[2] The party enthusiastically embraced Romania's 'return to Europe' and advocated the rapid introduction of western norms of social, political and economic organization. More specifically, the Liberals laid firm stress on the rule of law, on the codification of individual rights and on the need to impose constraints on the power of the state. In several pronouncements, the party appeared to hint that it favoured the restoration of a constitutional monarchy. The economic policy of the NLP was, however, overwhelmingly pragmatic. It advocated a slow privatization of industry, the rapid dismantling of the state service and retail sector, and (in contrast to the National Liberal ideology of the 1920s) the encouragement of massive western investment. The NLP directed its appeal overwhelmingly towards the more sophisticated urban intelligentsia, which it perceived as the electoral constituency most fully in tune with its liberal and intellectual philosophy.

The National Peasant Party was reconstituted at almost exactly the same time as the NLP by former leaders of its pre-communist organization. Corneliu Coposu, a Transylvanian lawyer in his mid-seventies, who had once been the secretary-general of the NPP, was appointed its president. Coposu's deputy, Ion Puiu, had many decades before been the chairman of the Peasant Youth movement. Both men were, however, rapidly eclipsed by Ion Ratiu, a 72-year-old émigré who had not set foot in Romania since 1940. A multimillionaire property developer and shipping magnate, Ratiu was also the head of the London-based World Union of Free Romanians. Ratiu was appointed to the committee of the NPP in January 1990 and several months later was appointed the party's presidential candidate. With a natural confidence and authority, and impeccable academic (Cluj and Cambridge) and business pedigrees, Ratiu seemed to the NPP leadership a fine illustration of its party's commitment to material prosperity and success.

The programme of the National Peasants Party was rooted in its appeal to traditional Romanian values. The moral and spiritual backbone of the Romanian nation was perceived to be the rural peasantry and the NPP sought to rebuild this constituency. The NPP advocated, therefore, the rapid dismantling of state and collective farms, and the return of the land to the rural workforce. At the same time, the NPP espoused a strongly Christian identity and called for the reintroduction of orthodox values to Romanian public and private life. Early on, therefore, the NPP went into coalition with Christian political movements similarly wedded to 'the nation's moral recovery' and to the promotion of 'Christian ethics'.

The NPP's economic policy was predicated on rapid privatization and the conversion of all state industries into joint stock companies. However, industry took second place in the NPP programme to agriculture and its manifesto specifically advocated the transfer of investment from the towns to the countryside. Thus from the very first, the NPP distanced itself from the more numerous urban workforce and lined itself up with a peasant constituency which did not as yet really exist.

The National Salvation Front, which entered the electoral contest at the end of January, was distracted neither by ideology nor by a historical legacy. From the very first, it espoused a strictly pragmatic viewpoint which was well in keeping with the 'survivalist' strategy of its ex-communist leadership. At the same time, the NSF proved remarkably flexible and accommodating, and quite happily stole the clothes of its rivals. By claiming to represent a 'consensus' of interests, the NSF was able quite plausibly to offer something for everybody. The heart of the NSF electoral strategy was to win over the urban workforce while simultaneously making enough promises with regard to agriculture as to ensure itself the rural vote. Thus, on the one hand, the NSF committed itself to an industrial policy which would not lead by privatization to unemployment; on the other, it met the interest of potential entrepreneurs by promising support for new businesses. It allowed, furthermore, land to be distributed in small parcels to the rural workforce while preserving the infrastructure of the collective farms. Where local pressure for the dismantling of collectives was greatest, it simply authorized the local PCNU councils to go ahead and satisfy popular demand. By the time the election was held, one-third of all Romania's arable land had been given over to private use, thus effectively pre-empting much of the NPP programme.[3]

The Hungarian Democratic Union of Romania joined the electoral contest relatively late. Although the Union had been formed at the end of December 1989, it was for the first few months happy to associate itself with the NSF. Its leaders, most notably Karoly Kiraly, Geza

Domokos and Andras Suto, were all former party activists with career patterns similar to those of the NSF leadership. Kiraly had in the 1970s been party secretary of Covasna county before he fell out with Ceausescu. For his part, Domokos was the former editor of the Hungarian language party newspaper, *Elore*, and head of the *Kriterion* publishing house in Bucharest. Suto was a former deputy in the Grand National Assembly and a candidate member of the Central Committee. Kiraly and Domokos also had close links with the core of dissident veterans which gathered round Brucan and Birladeanu.

Following the violence at Tirgu Mures, the HDUR began to distance itself from the NSF which it perceived as being partly responsible for the violence. At its party conference in April 1990, the HDUR resolved to contest the elections as a separate force in support of a programme of guaranteed rights for national minorities. In order to broaden its electoral appeal among Hungarian Romanians Laszlo Toekes, recently elected Bishop of Oradea, was appointed the party's Honorary Chairman. Throughout the election campaign, the HDUR conspicuously sought to avoid giving offence and eschewed polemic. It even invited members of the *Vatra* to attend certain of its functions.

The NSF built up its commanding lead over the other parties by stressing two vital points: that it was the heir of the Christmas revolution and that it represented the broad national consensus. Consistently, therefore, the NSF leaders reminded the voters of the key role that they had played in the events of December 1989 and that they had all in their various ways defied the Ceausescu regime. As Ion Iliescu stressed, on 8 April, the Front was 'the emanation of the revolution' and embodied the popular movement which had overthrown the dictatorship.[4] By contrast, the other parties were latecomers to the revolutionary stage and were led by persons who had not even been in Romania at the time of the revolution. At the same time, the NSF established its credentials as a broad, national force of democratic renewal. To begin with, it set itself firmly against an economic sell-out to foreign enterprises, promising that the country's resources would remain in the hands of the nation. Roman and Iliescu thus spoke disparagingly of those who would 'subjugate' Romania to 'foreign wealth' and promised to maintain 'national control' over the economy. As Iliescu put it, 'We do not want to alienate our national wealth, and we do not want our enterprises to be transferred into the hands of foreign capital.'[5] In this way, the Front drew on the long tradition of protectionism and economic sovereignty espoused both by Ceausescu and the interwar governments.

Having established its popular reputation as the party of national economic control, the NSF was free to trim its policies. By the time elections were held, the NSF admitted that it was ready to allow 100 per cent foreign ownership of enterprises as well as the repatriation of all foreign currency profits. This concession, which was far greater than anything promised by the rival parties, won over the financially astute without apparently alarming those who had already swallowed the Front's talk of economic sovereignty. By the eve of the election, Silviu Brucan was offering the electorate the prospect of Romania being the new South Korea of Europe with a standard of living comparable to Austria's.

Just as it pandered to traditional prejudices in regard to the national economy, so the Front whipped up the class sentiments deriving from the communist period. The free market policies espoused in particular by the NPP would, so it was claimed, lead to extremes of wealth and poverty as the rich got richer and the workforce was made redundant. Thus, from the very first, the NSF leaders promised that the economy would be transformed without recourse to unemployment and that the state would continue to prop up vulnerable industries. Brucan thus spoke of how the revolution should not lead to the return 'from the historical past of a rich class ready to share profits with its western employers', and he warned Romanians about the lessons of British and American capitalism.[6] In similar vein, Iliescu promised that only the NSF social programme 'would alleviate the effects of a market economy, which fatally polarizes wealth and poverty, leading to discrepancies between the privileged and the masses'.[7] The Front's repudiation of specifically western forms of economic and social organization owed much to traditional Romanian ambivalence towards Europe and to the continuing fashionability of the 'exceptionalist' doctrine.

Rather than moderate its commitment to a free market and attend to the concerns of the industrial population, the NPP continued to promote an unabashedly capitalist philosophy. Indeed, Ratiu played right into the hands of the NSF. He promised that he had special contacts in the West who would sort out aspects of the Romanian economy and he stressed his powerful business connections abroad. Most extra-ordinarily, his election posters portrayed him wearing a bow tie and looking every bit the capitalist of Romanian and communist legend. Less than a fortnight before the election, he announced details of a package of unemployment benefit. As for the NLP, it advocated exactly the same gradualist approach towards the economy as the NSF, but without the attraction of a popular nationalist vocabulary. Thus its programme seemed both imitative and pale.

A particular criticism of the opposition parties was that the NSF consisted almost entirely of ex-communists and that its leaders were no more than 'wolves in charge of sheep'. This accusation was most strongly put by the leaders of the various student and intellectual movements which were 'monitoring' the Front although not formally participating in the campaign as electoral rivals. According to the representatives of such groups as 21 December, December 16–22 Association and the Group for Social Dialogue, the NSF was intent on salvaging the communist system and on introducing a version of *perestroika* or of neo-bolshevism. Members of these groups often overstated their case by presenting it as an established fact that Ceausescu had been overthrown by a *putsch*, that he had been executed to stop him implicating the NSF in his crimes, that casualty figures had been deliberately exaggerated for diversionary purposes, and that the fighting in Bucharest had been surreptitiously prolonged so as to give the Front time to establish itself in power.

Starting on 22 April, a permanent anti-communist demonstration took place in Bucharest's University Square, which was subsequently proclaimed a 'communist-free zone'. Although numbering only a hard core of several hundred, the demonstrators were able to rally substantial support. On 17 May, a crowd independently estimated at 100,000 mustered to show solidarity. The principal demand of the protesters was that former party activists should be disallowed from both the new parliament and the presidency: a prohibition which would have disqualified most of the Front's candidates. The protesters took as their platform a petition drawn up in Timisoara during March 1990 which sought to put the record straight about the nature of the December revolution and which additionally demanded the resignation from high office of all former party functionaries and *securitate* personnel.[8] According to the organizers of the petition they had by the time of the election gathered some six million signatures, although more realistic estimates put the true figure at 150,000.[9]

These criticisms of the NSF failed to carry conviction among the vast bulk of the population. The programme of the Front seemed an explicit rejection of communism, and the names of Iliescu and Roman were indelibly linked in the popular imagination with the overthrow of the old regime. Criticism of the Front as an instrument of 'communist salvation' seemed quite unjustified given that the NSF had within days of taking power abrogated all the most unpopular measures associated with communist rule. Additionally, the hardships and injustices experienced over the last decades were largely attributed more to the Ceausescus and their clique than to ideology and the *nomenklatura*. Thus not only did accusations of neo-bolshevism appear implausible but they missed their mark altogether as a term of abuse.

Criticism of the NSF as a vehicle of ex-communists may even have helped the Front. Under the Ceausescus, moral compromise had been a way of life for the majority of Romanians. One-third of the adult population had been explicitly drawn into party membership; the remainder had been involved in a web of silent collaboration. The personal dilemmas which had impelled men like Iliescu into serving the Ceausescus were known and understood by the electorate, which had no interest in raking over complicity. The NSF offered the easy alternative to confrontation with the past. It simply declared the Communist Party and system to be dead and so buried the issue completely. In contrast, the appeals from young people to expose and punish collaborators seemed not only a measure of their own previous insulation from the responsibilities of adulthood but also the prelude to a potentially limitless witch-hunt.

From the very first, the NSF led in the opinion polls by a margin of over 50 per cent. Its party membership of almost a million far exceeded that of its rivals: the NPP claimed 400,000; the NLP half this figure. Furthermore, the NSF evidently had enormous funds at its disposal, allegedly contributed by its supporters but which were most probably taken from the coffers of the now defunct Romanian Communist Party. It was able to pay its managers 7000 lei a month and in early April the party mounted a glossy and expensive conference. NSF local headquarters also acquired stacks of cheap pornography and football magazines which were distributed to the party's importunate supporters.

The NSF took advantage of the machinery of state to help its campaign and to create a sense of popular well being. The network of PCNU local and enterprise committees provided an extensive national framework for the dissemination of the Front's policies. They acted as the centres for the distribution of campaign literature and for the presentation of easily understood slogans. In the run-up to the election, the NSF interspersed television coverage of the campaign with pop videos and rushed alcohol and meat to city centres. This was at a time when the NSF government was claiming that there was insufficient money available for the state to purchase basic medical supplies.

In contrast to the NSF, the other parties had to rely largely on the small government grant of 40,000 lei to subsidize their activities and on voluntary help. Regulations designed to prohibit the bankrolling of elections prevented the Ratiu millions reaching the NPP's coffers. The opposition campaign literature almost entirely consisted of hand-typed and poorly produced xeroxes. National Liberal propaganda was thus printed on the reverse of discarded posters sent from the Netherlands. The local organization of the opposition parties was additionally poor and failed to touch substantial areas of the countryside. Quite incredibly, the HDUR failed to establish contact with the Hungarian *csango* community in Moldavia, with the result that the *csango* vote went in the end largely to the NSF.

Nevertheless, the NSF was sufficiently concerned about its electoral prospects as to resort to various underhand devices, although at what level these malpractices were sanctioned is hard to establish. Early on the NSF used a myriad of phantom parties to confuse the electorate. When environmental issues began, therefore, to come to prominence, the NSF encouraged its 'green wing', the Ecological Movement, to stand in the election against the independent Romanian Ecological Party. A further bloc of parties, distinguished in the main by the adjective 'democratic', were formed in alliance with the NSF to undermine the strength of emergent regional groups. Others adopted in their publicity material the slogans and emblems of the NPP and the NLP. The Front's use of phantom parties bears a strong resemblance to the techniques employed by the communists in the period 1944–7.

The NSF was additionally unscrupulous in using the state media against its competitors. Romanian television thus typically combined its news coverage of the Front with stirring anthems and clever graphics. By contrast, its cameras homed in unfairly on opposition rallies, identifying such unsavoury elements in their ranks as barefooted Gypsies. News broadcasts covering NPP meetings repeatedly fixed on elderly faces in the audience to convey the impression that this was the party of 'old men'. Likewise, while the NSF received considerable space allotted to its activities the other parties were given short shrift. Newscasters and presenters frequently pulled faces whenever their names were mentioned. The television also added to the campaign of rumours and slander, even suggesting on one occasion that Ratiu had previously been married to Doina Cornea.

While the opposition press was deprived of newsprint by the state authorities, copies of the NSF press, most notably the dailies *Adevarul, Azi* and *Libertatea*, were widely distributed. *Adevarul*, in particular, was able to take full advantage of $3 million worth of new printing equipment. The NSF press contributed to mischief by publishing a gamut of false reports variously claiming that Cornea was clinically insane and that Ion Ratiu was of Hungarian background. On 6 May, *Azi* published an absurd story claiming that Campeanu had formerly worked for the *securitate*. The use of slander and of anonymously written articles was entirely reminiscent of the campaigns of denunciation waged with such effect during the Ceausescu years. As Ana Blandiana and the student leader, Marian Munteanu, explained, 'Disinformation, intrigues and calumnies are part and parcel of the specific strategy of communist regimes.'[10]

Other branches of the administration which worked against the opposition parties included the Bucharest municipal authority, which was slow to allocate offices to the NPP and NLP, and the judicial service. In what were widely suspected to have been politically motivated decisions, the courts disqualified from the electoral lists three prominent members of the HDUR on technical grounds. Most alarmingly, however, the relevant authorities failed to take decisive action to stop the violence which increasingly disfigured the Romanian election campaign.

Starting at the end of January, the opposition parties experienced the considerable disruption of their campaign activities by supporters of the NSF. Responsibility for several of the attacks on the personnel and offices of the NLP and NPP may be apportioned indirectly to the NSF leadership. The rallies of workers which the Front mustered in Bucharest on 28 January and 19 February 'in order to defend the revolution', were so inflamed by alcohol and rabble-rousing speeches that violence was bound to ensue. However, the vast majority of incidents either occurred spontaneously or were the work of local committees of the NSF and there is no evidence linking them to a coordinated plan of intimidation.[11] Furthermore, the murder of at least one prominent campaign manager seems to have been inspired more by personal than by political grievances.[12]

Intimidation was directed in the main at the political leaders of the opposition parties. Campeanu was attacked on 5 May at Braila by a mob armed with clubs and broken bottles. A week later a meeting addressed by the Liberal leader in Brasov was broken up by NSF supporters, one of whom threatened Campeanu with a revolver. For his part, Ratiu was forced when addressing a meeting at Buzau to take shelter from a mob in the local police station. His wife, visiting a psychiatric hospital in Bucharest, was chased by a crowd of patients led by a nurse. In other incidents, party managers and officials were attacked, allegedly with the connivance of the police. On 16 May, NPP Chairman, Corneliu Coposu, said on Romanian television that over the preceding months two of his party members had been killed and a further 113 injured. On 19 May on French television, Campeanu similarly complained that the election campaign had been 'riddled with incidents and violence and conducted in a climate of insecurity'.[13]

Although the opposition parties exploited the campaign violence in an attempt to discredit the NSF, making some wild and unfounded allegations, the scale of intimidation was such that the United States felt it necessary to recall its ambassador for consultations. In order to pre-empt criticism, the Ministry of the Interior announced the results of its own enquiry into the campaign. In a communiqué published on 5 May, a spokesman for the ministry stated that there had been altogether 105 recorded incidents of violence: a figure which apparently included damage to posters. 70 persons had been convicted in regard to these offences, of whom seven had received custodial sentences. In short, according to the ministry, the election campaign had 'taken place in a democratic atmosphere of calm, without unusual incidents'.[14]

The ballot opened on 20 May and was conducted at 13,000 polling stations in the presence of just under 500 international observers. Since the electoral roll was over a decade old, many voters had to be registered on the spot and have their personal identity cards duly stamped.[15] The large number of parties standing for election meant that the ballot paper took the form of a booklet. In Bucharest, it contained no less than 37 pages. The registration of voters and the need to read through the extensive rubric and list of candidates led to long queues forming outside the polling stations. Often, voters waited several hours to receive their booklets and then gaggled together in the polling booths trying to understand their contents. Electoral fraud was particularly common in rural locations, which most international observers failed to reach. In Kelata, a group of soldiers occupied the polling station and spent the whole day voting; elsewhere, clerks inspected the completed booklets. In remote areas, the ballot was counted on the spot by NSF officials and the result telephoned through to Bucharest. Observers in several places also reported finding ballot booklets which had already been filled in.

The election was certainly flawed. The most striking evidence for this lies not, however, in listing irregularities, most of which cannot now be proved, but in simply analysing the number of votes cast. According to the Central Electoral Bureau in Bucharest, 17.3 million persons were eligible to vote, of which 82 per cent or just over 14.8 million chose to exercise this right. The population of Romania is less than 23 million of which it is unlikely that more than 70 per cent are over the age of 18. As one Austrian observer of the Romanian election implied, this would suggest that at least a million spurious electors and votes were added at some point into the process.[16] Quite how this was achieved is uncertain.

The final result of the election was delayed until 25 May, when the Central Electoral Bureau published the following returns:

Presidential Election

Candidate	No. of votes cast	Per cent of poll
Ion Iliescu (NSF)	12,232,498	85.07
Radu Campeanu (NLP)	1,529,188	10.16
Ion Ratiu (NPP)	617,007	4.29
(invalid votes: 447,923)		

Chamber of Deputies and Senate

Name of Party	Per cent of votes cast for Chamber	No. of seats obtained in Chamber	Per cent of votes cast for Senate	No of seats obtained in Senate
NSF	66.3	263	6.7	92
NPP	2.6	12	2.5	1
NLP	6.4	29	7.1	9
HDUR	7.2	29	7.2	12
Rom. Ecological Movement	2.6	12	2.45	1

Examination of these figures suggests a clear consistency in patterns of voting, with the NSF emerging as the clear winner by a massive margin in presidential, Chamber and Senate elections. Furthermore, these figures closely coincide with opinion polls taken before the election and with an exit poll projection made in conjunction with the West German INFAS organization.[17] Despite all the evidence of electoral irregularity and fraud, therefore, there can be little doubt that the NSF was the party which enjoyed the support of the overwhelming majority of Romanians.

Critics of the NSF were fast to point out that its share of the vote, and in particular the tremendous support shown for Ion Iliescu, were reminiscent of election results in the communist period, when the party would characteristically recieve 97.8 per cent of the vote.[18] The analogy is as unjust as it is misleading. The election of 1990 has its closest parallels not in the Ceausescu years but in the interwar period. In the 1920s and 1930s, the government party 'made' the elections, employing the full resources of the state to influence the poll in its favour. The NSF did much the same. Its campaign was well resourced and received considerable, almost exclusive coverage in the state-run media. The opposition parties were consistently misrepresented and deprived of the means of putting across their point of view. The NSF took advantage of its nationwide network of councils and committees to harass the opposition campaign, and local supporters of the NSF did not baulk at violence. Nevertheless, the opposition parties must bear some of the blame for their defeat. In their concern to uphold the historic traditions of their parties, the NLP and NPP failed to present attractive policies to the electorate. Judging by election results throughout much of Eastern Europe in 1990, the NPP should have stormed to victory in Romania as a populist party rooted in the flexible traditions of Christian Democracy. Instead, the NPP took an ideological stand by 'fast marketization', even at the cost of widespread unemployment.

In contrast to the 'historic' parties, the NSF speedily appreciated popular anxieties about the pace of economic change and made undertakings specifically designed to allay the electorate's worries. At the same time, it spoke in the language and jargon which the Romanian population could best understand, and did not hesitate to use a nationalist and class vocabulary, which had its roots in the prejudices of the preceding decades. By giving out that it had no interest in raking over past misdeeds, the NSF effectively closed the book on the Ceausescu period, while at the same time emphasizing the role which its leaders had played in consolidating the revolution. Ironically therefore, despite all the accusations of crypto-communism and of neo-bolshevism that were levelled against it, the NSF was the only party to run on a pragmatic, non-ideological ticket, tailored for the moment. This, in combination with its control of the apparatus of state, ensured its decisive victory at the polls.

NOTES

1. RFE/REE (4 May 1990).
2. RFE/REE (16 February 1990).
3. Economist Intelligence Unit, *Country Report: Romania*, no. 2, (London: EIU, 1990), p. 19.
4. SWB/EE (10 April 1990).
5. SWB/EE (31 January 1990).
6. *Romanian Libera* (18 July 1990).
7. SWB/EE (20 April 1990).
8. An English language version of the Timisoara petition is given in the *East European Reporter* (Spring/Summer, 1990, pp. 32–5).
9. George Fodor in *The World Today*, vol. 46, (July 1990), p. 126.
10. RFE/REE (25 May 1990; 8 June 1990).
11. *Cuvantul Romanesc* (May 1990).
12. The much publicized case of Vasile Valescu; see *The Independent* (9 May 1990).
13. Reported SWB/EE (22 May 1990).
14. SWB/EE (8 May 1990).
15. This circumstance explains why more people voted in the election than were originally on the register.
16. Professor Andreas Kohl, deputy of the Austrian Peoples Party, speaking on 21 May 1990. Kohl cited the figure of 60 per cent eligibility; however, Romanian census returns for 1985 suggest 70 per cent to be more likely.
17. SWB/EE (22 May 1990).
18. 1985 election result. Voting under the communists was conducted, of course, under an open ballot.

16

POLITICS AND VIOLENCE IN POST-REVOLUTIONARY ROMANIA

Police and Army

The electoral victory of the National Salvation Front conveyed the impression that it enjoyed a monopoly of power in the new Romania. The opposition parties had been routed and control of both the government and the legislature was now firmly vested in the Front. The Front's previous use of extra-legal methods of 'persuasion' and its drive towards political hegemony had apparently received the approval of the electorate. With its popular backing thus ensured, the Front could further intimidate its critics and assume the authoritarian mantle of the Ceausescu regime. As miners and security men patrolled the streets of Bucharest in June 1990, and NSF membership soared to an apparent four million, it did indeed seem that Romania had returned to the condition of a one-party state and that parliamentary democracy had been superseded by dictatorship.

These impressions were, however, for a large part illusory. From the very first, the awesome reputation of the National Salvation Front far exceeded its actual influence. As Ion Iliescu lamented in January 1990, 'Everyone suspects that we have some very strong structures and that we are holding all the reins of power ... The truth is that the Front's structures are a little bit fragile ...'.[1] The lightning shifts in policy, the hasty deceptions practised to accommodate the opposition, and the inability of the government to maintain order, all suggest the accuracy of Iliescu's complaint.

The victory of the NSF at the polls four months later did little to consolidate the actual authority of the new leadership. Firstly, evidence of electoral fraud further undermined the legitimacy of the government in intellectual circles and provided ammunition for the Front's opponents. The vulnerability of the government to the charge that its authority was 'illegitimate' expressed itself most obviously in its repeated refusal to allow the 'legitimate' sovereign to return to Romania.[2] Secondly, since parliament had been reduced to a cipher of the ruling party, the opposition was increasingly tempted to employ extra-parliamentary means as a way of making itself heard. The government was thus faced with the prospect of disorder on the streets which it was unable to control by ordinary methods of policing.

An important factor hindering the Front in the accumulation of power was the unreliability of the forces of law enforcement. Following the revolution, the militia was renamed as the police and was comprehensively purged. Several thousand senior officers are believed to have been dismissed or to have resigned in the weeks immediately following the revolution. The remainder consisted largely of young, inexperienced staff. With a few exceptions, these showed a marked reluctance not only to take on the regime's political opponents but also to confront those openly engaged in criminal activity. Since there were plenty of old scores left to settle, and a threatened policeman would usually give up rather than discharge his handgun, it was thought expedient to occupy the police with routine tasks. In country areas, therefore, they were largely confined to the safety of their stations, and only ventured out to cadge drinks from villagers. In towns, they were principally employed in guarding installations, in providing support for the army, and in pestering tourists for baksheesh. Under these circumstances, it is hardly surprising that criminal violence in Romania reached an unprecedentedly high level, giving rise to Europe's worst murder rate. In a single month, July 1990, the country witnessed no less than 367 murders, 182 attempted murders and 93 homicides. There were additionally 259 serious assaults and 390 instances of rape.[3]

The police had played only a minor and equivocal role in the revolution. The army, by contrast, had proved crucial to the success of the popular uprising. From the very first, therefore, both officers and men perceived themselves as guardians of the revolutionary legacy and as the country's first line of defence against a communist restoration. Many of their number thus shared the concern felt by many civilians at the persistence of former high-ranking communists in positions of influence. While civilian protesters directed their criticism at former communists in the government, their military counterparts singled out those officers who had compromised themselves during the revolution. The junior ranks received unexpected support from their senior commanders. Considerable resentment was felt among the General Staff at the recall to active service of retired officers who were former associates of Ion Iliescu and whose function appeared to be almost entirely political.

As early as 28 December 1989, there was a demonstration in the Brasov garrison over the promotion of officers who had been implicated in the recent shooting of civilians. Over the next few weeks, these complaints became widespread and resulted in servicemen and cadets holding rallies in Bucharest. The demands of the military protesters were coordinated by a 'Committee for Action to Democratize the Army', which published on 12 February 1990 the text of an appeal to the President. The Democratization Committee called for the removal of all officers who had compromised themselves under the Ceausescu government, for the retirement of army personnel recently brought back into service by the National Salvation Front, and for the resignation of Generals Militaru and Chitac, who were respectively the Ministers of National Defence and of the Interior. Mihai Chitac was clearly too implicated in the bloodshed of 21 December to enjoy the confidence of the army, and Nicolae Militaru was widely believed to be pro-communist in his sympathies.

The initial response to the NSF was to try to defuse criticism by raising officers' pay and by threatening supporters of the Committee with courts martial. However, neither the carrot nor the stick worked. When both the President and the Minister of National Defence refused to see members of the Committee to discuss their grievances, demonstrations involving several thousand officers and men were held in Timisoara and Bucharest. These meetings took place with the support of the General Staff which even threatened to organize its own rallies unless the recently reactivated officers were dismissed.

Eventually, the NSF government gave way. On 14 February, representatives of the Democratization Committee were invited to discuss their petition with Petre Roman, and the Prime Minister immediately capitulated to several of their demands. Two days later, General Militaru was dismissed. At the end of the month, 14 of the 20 senior officers recalled to service after the revolution were placed on reserve.

Militaru was succeeded as army minister by General Victor

Stanculescu, whose own account of his actions during the revolution was widely disbelieved. A commission appointed to investigate Stanculescu's behaviour between 17 and 21 December refused to absolve him from the accusation that he had participated in the murder of civilian demonstrators. Nevertheless, by posturing as a democrat and by playing up his family's military record, Stanculescu was able to manipulate the Committee for his own purposes. He used it to conduct a purge of officers known to be personally hostile to him, and he deflected most of the Committee's attention on to General Chitac, whom he perceived as a rival influence. The Democratization Committee secured Chitac's dismissal on 14 June and, having served its purpose, was abolished the same day.

The extent of the Committee's support within all three branches of the armed services was plainly considerable. It was thus able to muster on to the streets of Timisoara and of Bucharest several thousand supporters at any one time. Its delegation to the Prime Minister consisted of 58 officers, up to the rank of colonel, from 33 separate units. Attempts by the government to discomfort the Committee by arranging 'demonstrations of loyalty to the Minister of Defence' were seldom successful. At a meeting held at the Constanta Institute for Naval Forces, 64 out of 70 officers present voted against a government appeal to express their allegiance to the minister. The airforce garrison in Timisoara gave a similarly firm endorsement to the Committee's programme. The Committee categorically rejected the idea that the armed forces might be employed 'to resolve differences among the various political groups and parties' and emphasized instead the army's role as a 'national force', which was above politics. In accordance with these principles, the army consistently revealed its unreliability as an instrument of political coercion. On two occasions, therefore, 12 January and 18 February, the army failed to prevent demonstrators invading government buildings in Bucharest; it similarly arrived late in Tirgu Mures in March and then only after an urgent request to attend delivered by the local *Vatra* leader. Whenever confronted by angry demonstrators, both soldiers and officers tended to relive the experiences of December 1989, refusing to disperse the crowds and frequently fraternizing with the protesters. The army justified its reluctance to use force with the slogan, 'We will never fight the people.' In his frustration, Ion Iliescu accused the troops of having been misled by the Democratization Committee's talk of a 'passive' military role, and Petre Roman spoke of Romanian soldiers having been rendered psychologically incapable of violence.[4]

The inability of the police and of the armed forces to maintain order was strikingly revealed in the government's confrontation with demonstrators in Bucharest. On 22 April, a prolonged anti-communist protest began on University Square in the centre of the capital. The participants demanded that all former communist activists be deprived of public office for the next ten years and that the television be freed from government control. As part of the campaign, over a hundred demonstrators began a hunger strike which, as their condition worsened, attracted considerable international publicity. A hard core of several hundred protesters camped out in the square on a plot of weeds in front of the Intercontinental Hotel. Their number was frequently augmented during the daylight hours by several thousand sympathizers and onlookers.

The permanent demonstration in University Square or, as it was renamed, the Anti-communist Zone, was led by several groups and supported by a number of noted intellectuals. The principal organizations involved were the 21 December Group, the People's Alliance, the 16–21 December Group, and the League of Students. These groups, although not aligned to any one specific party, were broadly in favour of 'a second revolution' aimed at replacing the 'survivalist' regime of former communists with a government which was genuinely committed to political pluralism. In the main, they took their stand by the Timisoara Declaration and its demand for the resignation of all 'neo-communists' from public office.

The demonstrators consisted in the main of young people and students. Their main spokesman was the 28-year-old Marian Munteanu, chairman of the 4000-strong Bucharest University Students' League. In an interview with Radio Free Europe, on 5 May, Munteanu defined the character and aims of his organization as follows:

The Students League is a body somewhat like a trade union. It is a non-political organization; this does not mean, however, that we do not have political opinions. It means that we support the principles of democracy, pluralism and dialogue, and not a specific political party ...

In subsequent discussions, Munteanu held fast by the principle of passive resistance and denounced the 'hidden violence' perpetrated by the Iliescu government.[5] In token of their good democratic credentials, Munteanu and his fellow demonstrators enjoyed the personal support of Doina Cornea, who joined the hunger strike for a short period, the poetess Ana Blandiana, and Octavian Paler, the editor of *Romania Libera*. Backing was also given by the powerful and independent *Fratia* trade union under the leadership of the outspoken Miron Mitrea.

Although the protesters sought to keep their demonstration a peaceful one, the Anti-communist Zone invariably attracted a number of disreputable elements. Since the police were reluctant to enter the Zone, some criminal activity clearly did take place. It is most unlikely, though, that this included 'the profiteering, prostitution, gambling, theft, violence and drugs' which the government later claimed.[6] Additionally, the spill of demonstrators impeded traffic on one of Bucharest's principal highways and was in contravention of various municipal regulations. These aspects of the protest prompted Ion Iliescu to label the demonstrators 'hooligans' (*golani*).[7]

The authorities proved, however, entirely incapable of removing the protesters. On 24 April, police moved into the square and set about some young people with truncheons. The number of police was inadequate for the task of clearing the Zone and they were soon forced to give up the attempt. During May, several more assaults on University Square were planned but were subsequently called off in view of the large number of protesters present. It was only on 13 June that the Zone was eventually cleared with the assistance of worker paramilitaries. Even so, once the 'forces of order' had retired, the square was promptly reoccupied by demonstrators.

The Fragmentation of Power

In view of the government's inability to enforce its will in the capital, it is hardly surprising that its writ in parts of the countryside should have virtually ceased to run. Throughout the spring and summer of 1990, political power was taken in the provinces by a number of separate groups over which the Salvation Front exercised little control. In Oradea, influence was retained by a coterie of Ceausescu appointees led by Doru Draghici, a former Communist Party county secretary. They fixed local contracts and engaged in lucrative black market operations across the Hungarian border. Draghici also had available his own private army of ruffians which he later lent the government to help put down the protests in Bucharest.[8] In the Jiu valley, power was retained by the same network of former party apparatchiks, managers and trade union leaders as had been active during the Ceausescu period.[9]

Elsewhere the local NSF/PCNU councils established by the Front in the wake of the revolution, proved increasingly reluctant to follow the government's bidding. Many assumed an independent posture, negotiating with government representatives as equals and failing to enforce disagreeable instructions. Others, as in Brasov, proceeded to plunder the region for the personal benefit of their members. It is a telling illustration of the weakness of the government that it was obliged in August 1990 to accommodate many local 'bosses' by appointing them to office in the newly-established prefectures and county councils.

Throughout large parts of Transylvania the influence of the *Vatra* organization was such that the NSF could rarely proceed to the implementation of its policies without having gained in advance the consent of its local officers. By the summer of 1990, the *Vatra* had moved into a position of opposition to the NSF, which it regarded as corrupt and 'neo-communist'. The *Vatra* however, established contacts with local branches of the security service, and its leaders were privy to telephone and postal interceptions.[10] As a petition drawn up in Cluj noted, 'in Transylvania, power is not in the hands of the councils and the forces of order, but in the hands of the *Vatra Romaneasca* Association'.

The fragmentation of political power extended to the workplace. Most factories continued to be run by workers' committees, the membership of which was frequently divided by rival trade union loyalties. At best, the workers councils shared power with managers, jointly deciding on priorities and promotions. At worst, they organized the theft of machinery and supplies. On collective farms, the local management retained substantial discretionary powers. As in the region around Baia Mare, it frequently impeded the return of land to the peasantry. Even the modest agricultural reforms proposed by the government foundered on the inherited traditions of rural graft.

The resolve of the government to overcome these obstacles was weakened by serious internal divisions. These rifts only became fully apparent once the election campaign was over and there was no longer any need to present a united front to the voters. Although the principal source of contention was economic policy, this issue was overlaid by personal differences and rivalries.

The Economy

By the summer of 1990, industry and agriculture were in a virtual state of collapse. According to a government statement issued on 1 September, over 800 large enterprises had reported losses so far that year, totalling in all some 25 billion lei. Owing to an absence of raw materials and to distribution difficulties, many factories were working well below capacity. One previously profitable small plant in Brasov county which made spare parts for cars, reported a loss of 35 million lei in just three months on account of delivery schedules to the factory not being met. The production of Dacia cars accordingly came to a virtual standstill. Whereas in 1989 Romania had exported 35,000 models to Hungary, it managed to deliver only a hundred in the first three months of 1990.[11] The workforce elsewhere, newly liberated from the tyranny of party-appointed managers, simply failed to turn up for work. In an instance which was far from unique, one Transylvanian coal mine only fulfilled 12 per cent of its plan in the period January to June 1990 on account of staff absenteeism. According to a local resident, the mine's personnel devoted most of their working hours to drinking.

This situation was not relieved by the initial refusal of the government to allow unemployment. Those without work were retained on the factory payroll and given a reduced wage. There was thus no incentive for them to hunt out employment elsewhere. Only at the beginning of 1991 was a national scheme of unemployment benefit introduced with relief administered as a proportion of the average wage. At this time, the real number of jobless was estimated to be between 150,000 and 800,000, and growing rapidly. By the middle of the year, unemployment had semi-officially topped one million.

Although the majority of collectives reported profits in 1990, the condition of rural agriculture was evidently desperate. Meat remained in short supply and peasant plots, not collectives, provided the bulk of the domestic supply of fruit and vegetables. Despite the handing over of a large portion of agricultural land to personal use, the terms of ownership were sufficiently uncertain to discourage the investment of time and resources. Most of the new proprietors did not have a proper title to their land, their property deeds being neither signed nor stamped. This nebulous legal situation persisted even after the land reform undertaken at the beginning of 1991, since the ownership of land was made conditional upon its proper cultivation.[12] Compulsory state procurement of privately grown produce acted as a similar disincentive to small farmers. Nevertheless, the direst warning for agriculture was provided not by the undersupply of any single commodity but by a collapse of grain prices in the west of the country. This was caused by ethnic Germans reaping their final harvest before emigration to the Federal Republic. Prior to departure, they sold off what in the past would have been their next year's seed, thus flooding the local markets with wheat. Even so, the provision of bread remained uncertain. In Bucharest, what few loaves were on sale in September 1990 were over a week old.

Although the government managed to survive 1990 without recourse to power cuts, nearly all commodities with the exception of jam and newspapers were in short supply. In some country districts, drastic rationing had to be introduced which allowed local residents only one kilogram of meat, sugar and flour per month. Razors, matches and cigarettes were unobtainable for long periods and petrol stations were usually closed. 'Price liberalizations' introduced in November 1990 and April 1991 pushed up the cost of foodstuffs and of other essential goods by between 100 and 300 per cent, thus putting what little was available in the shops beyond the pocket of the average Romanian.[13]

In the face of such deprivation, many villagers resorted to a primitive subsistence economy, living off home-grown vegetables, free-range hens and private stills. Although supplies were generally more plentiful in the towns, the inhabitants lacked the opportunity for private cultivation and were frequently forced to beg food from their relatives in the country. Under these circumstances, transactions in barter became sufficiently commonplace for at least one county committee to request the payment of business taxes in kind.

A telling indication of the scale of hardship under the NSF government was the rise of prostitution in the capital. The number of women working the streets of Bucharest is estimated to have grown by roughly a hundred a week during 1990. Many of the newcomers consisted of educated ladies who sought to use their linguistic accomplishments in pursuit of the dwindling supply of western visitors. Among menfolk, resentment occasionally spilled over into nostalgic demonstrations during the course of which the name of Nicolae Ceausescu was applauded and his various achievements were fondly recalled.[14]

Within the Salvation Front government, there were broadly two responses to the economic crisis. A radical group gathered round

Adrian Severin, the Minister for Privatization, advocated the shock treatment of the economy. Severin recommended that half the country's bureaucrats be dismissed and all unprofitable factories be closed down. He also suggested a devaluation of the lei within three months and swingeing price increases which would reduce the need for state subsidies and also mop up the monetary overhang in the economy.[15] A more moderate version of the Severin programme was submitted in the form of the 'Postolache paper' (named after the secretary of state for the National Economy) to Prime Minister Roman shortly before the election and was thought at the time to have met with his approval. Certainly, in his inaugural address following reappointment as Prime Minister, Roman indicated that he was in favour of privatization, of slimming down the state bureaucracy, and of a transition to a market economy. During 1991, however, Roman began to distance himself from the radicals and to adopt a more cautious 'social democracy'.

The most substantial opposition to radical reform came from the ranks of the communist 'old guard'. Ion Iliescu repeatedly denounced privatization on the grounds that it would make some people very wealthy and would add to social injustice. Iliescu's fears were shared by the president of the Senate, Alexandru Birladeanu, who argued that a market economy was a luxury which should only be permitted once the shops were full! Since the Iliescu-Birladeanu wing of the NSF dominated the upper house, it was able to impose substantial constraints on the reform process. Entrepreneurs continued to be liable to 40 per cent taxation on all profits, and they are additionally forbidden to sell goods at more than 10 per cent above the official state market price. No grants or special tax concessions were allowed for new businesses; instead a whole series of petty regulations were enforced which strangled enterprise in red tape. Likewise, although foreign investment was officially welcomed, continued over-regulation and a lack of cooperation from managers and bureaucrats discouraged western entrepreneurs. In addition, foreign companies were only allowed to repatriate 15 per cent of their hard currency profits.

The conservative wing of the NSF also managed to impede the progress of privatization. Although 'shares' in state firms were distributed to staff, these were made non-negotiable instruments. Nor did share ownership permit the workforce to determine the future direction of the business. All state enterprises remained bound to the national plan which was determined centrally. Even though the plan

introduced in 1990 was substantially shorter than its predecessor, the
scope of its regulation was certainly as broad as that devised in
communist Hungary during the late 1960s. Altogether 400 different
products were included on the 1990 plan, each of which had 14
separate 'target indicators'.[16] As a consequence both of resistance by
NSF conservatives and of a continued belief that economic growth
could be 'regulation-led', the marketization of the Romanian economy
remained incomplete.

The conflict between radicals and conservatives derived in part from
ideology. The new government appointed by Prime Minister Roman
on 28 June 1990 consisted overwhelmingly of youngish 'technocrats'.
Most were in their forties and their reputation as genuine experts in
their field was extolled by Petre Roman. Despite in many cases a
background in the communist bureuacracy, their approach was
overwhelmingly pragmatic and shaped by an awareness of how other
East European countries were making the transition from a state to a
market economy. By contrast, the Iliescu-Birladeanu wing comprised
former party activists whose thinking continued to be rooted in
communist ideology. This group was opposed to radical change and
bore a deep distrust of all forms of capitalist enterprise.

Political Clientage and the Romanian Intelligence Service

Iliescu's opposition to radical economic change derived, however, from
more than just ideological considerations. During 1990 he had been
steadily accumulating a powerful personal following among the
industrial working class. This was the section of Romanian society
whose employment was most obviously threatened by an economic
shake-out. During the election campaign, Iliescu had delivered his
strongest appeal to the workers and had guaranteed them their jobs.
He had also cultivated close personal links with the National
Confederation of Romanian Free Trade Unions, the successor
organization of the communist labour front. The NCRFTU had in the
summer of 1990 about two million members and its leader was Ion
Calinescu, who had previously been Ceausescu's Deputy Minister of
Labour. NCRFTU branches in mining communities and at the
Republica works in Bucharest provided Iliescu's points of contact with
the groups that he would subsequently deploy as his own private
army.[17] Iliescu similarly enjoyed support amongst the *nomenklatura*,
which continued to occupy key administrative positions both in the
civil service and the economic bureaucracy. Roman's frequent

criticism of this group for 'inertia' and the threat of redundancy pushed the *nomenklatura* on to the side of the conservatives and into Iliescu's lap.

Iliescu's interest in client-building extended also to the secret police. In the spring of 1990, he began to regroup the *securitate* personnel who had previously been placed under the overall supervision of the Ministry of National Defence. These were reorganized as the Romanian Intelligence Service and placed under the command of Professor Virgil Magureanu. One purpose behind Iliescu's formation of the RIS is likely to have been his fear that the army was becoming too powerful and that he needed a counterweight with which to balance the influence of the new Minister of National Defence.[18]

The organization of the RIS, in terms of its personnel, duties, departmental structure and record keeping, bore close similarities to the old *securitate*. The top ranks of the RIS were filled by former *securitate* colleagues of Magureanu. Local branches of the RIS were staffed by officers previously employed in Ceausescu's secret police.[19] Altogether the RIS is thought in its first year of operation to have included at least several thousand former *securitate* personnel and to have reactivated the old informer networks of the Ceausescu period. Records made public in May 1991 suggest, furthermore, that the RIS had acquired the former *securitate* archive and was continuing to keep extensive surveillance records.[20] It appears also that some of these records had been made available to staff working for the extreme nationalist newspaper, *Romania Mare*, which specialized in denouncing critics of the government.[21]

A further deployment of ex-*securitate* personnel was announced in July 1990. In that month, former members of the *securitate* Fifth directorate were merged with army units to make up a gendarmerie service, which was organized within the Ministry of the Interior. The communiqué announcing the formation of this new group reassured Romanians that the gendarmerie officers were graduates of Ministry of the Interior training schools, thus indirectly confirming their previous employment in the *securitate* service. The function of the gendarmerie was explained as the defence of public buildings and of prominent personnel.[22]

In January 1991, the powers of the secret police were expanded significantly with the excuse that there was an Iraqi threat to Romanian security. The border was placed under the direct control of the RIS and gendarmerie, and Romanian citizens were 'reminded' that they should register foreign visitors with the police. This ominous development, which revived the practices of the Ceausescu period, was entirely missed by the Commission of the European Community and the Group of 24. Having instead noted 'the positive efforts of the government' and 'the progress of the reform process in Romania', both organizations voted to extend fresh economic assistance to the country.[23]

The Miners

The importance of the paramilitary detachments of workers and *securitate* was strikingly apparent on the occasion of the miners' notorious descent upon Bucharest in June 1990. Despite the publication of the report of the parliamentary commission investigating the disturbances, the precise circumstances attending this episode remain uncertain. Nevertheless, Iliescu was clearly implicated in the outrage and the forces which he unleashed on the capital consisted in the main of his own private armies. The readiness of the President to resort to vigilante violence is striking evidence of the disintegration of Romanian politics into a purely physical contest.

At dawn on 13 June, units of the police and army cleared the Anti-communist Zone in central Bucharest and established a cordon around University Square. During the afternoon of that day, attacks by unidentified groups took place on the guard. Petrol bombs were thrown and coaches were set on fire. It is uncertain who was responsible for this attack. The student leader, Marian Munteanu had previously called on his supporters not to use violence. Eyewitness accounts suggest that the attack was most likely the work of *provocateurs*. Certainly, the police failed to take action even though the number of trouble-makers was at first small and they may even have encouraged firebomb attacks on their own vehicles.

Over the next few hours, gangs of youths attacked the Ministry of the Interior, the offices of the Romanian Intelligence Service, the television station and various government buildings. The police continued to refrain from intervention and the only units of the army in attendance consisted of blue-bereted paratroops. A subsequent government statement condemned the police for having displayed on 13 June, 'frailty in decision-making and a lack of firmness', and disingenuously pointed to a 'failure of communication' between the Ministries of the Interior and of National Defence. The president of

Romanian Television, who is not otherwise known as a critic of the government, was later to claim that the attack on his station was led by former *securitate* officers in disguise.[24]

At 6.00 that evening, Ion Iliescu broadcast an appeal 'to all conscious and responsible forces'. He requested civilian loyalists to rally in the centre of Bucharest in order to defend the government and democracy. Later on, he spoke of an attempted coup perpetrated by legionaries presumptuous enough even to have dressed in the uniform of the Iron Guard. Curiously, however, even before Iliescu had delivered his first appeal for help, 10,000 miners from the Jiu Valley had already boarded railway trains and were on their way to the capital. Given the state of the Romanian railway service, it is extraordinary that they found sufficient transport for their journey.[25] The entry of the miners into Bucharest was preceded by the arrival of workers bussed in from nearby factories. A formidable contingent was provided by the *Republica* works and was led by Mircea Dulgheru, an official of the local NCRFTU branch. The speed with which miners and other workers assembled in the capital suggests that the rioting on 13 June was either cleverly anticipated or craftily prearranged by members of the government.

Upon their arrival at the Gara de Nord railway station, the miners were met by former *securitate* personnel. They were issued with maps of the city and with lists of persons who should be detained. One group which subsequently perpetrated considerable violence was led by a former *securitate* major, Nicolae Camarasescu, who had been arrested at the end of December for shooting civilians. While several thousand miners attended a rally where they were addressed by Ion Iliescu, the remainder toured Bucharest. Fulfilling their allotted tasks, they variously arrested government opponents and beat up members of the public whose dress, attitude and age they found disagreeable. In this phase of the 'pacification', which lasted until 15 June, the miners were supported by members of the police and army. The violence meted out on young people was frequently accompanied by applause from passers-by who had swallowed Iliescu's talk of a foiled legionary coup. In a final demonstration of their prejudices, the miners set upon a Gypsy encampment in the suburbs, where they engaged in looting and casual brutality.

'Hooligans' and gypsies arrested by the miners were on the direct instructions of Virgil Magureanu handed over to the police.[26] They were subsequently interned in the former *securitate* prisons at

Magurele and Baneasa, where many of them were maltreated and beaten.[27] Among those so detained was Marian Munteanu who was kept in solitary confinement for almost two months.

The miners did not stop, however, at clearing the streets. Detachments broke into the offices of anti-NSF newspapers, where they smashed up printing equipment. Others raided the homes of opposition MPs and other critics of the government. Attacks on *Romania Libera* and on the home of Dumitru Mazilu were led by former *securitate* staff who were recognized by their victims. Yet another group of miners burnt down part of the Peasants Party offices, but not before they had engaged in a curious course of action. Since the strange affair of the NPP headquarters has not been widely reported even in Romania, it merits some elaboration.

The main office of the Peasants Party in Bucharest is located at 34 Bulevardul Republicii. Its premises were formerly occupied by the National Water Council of which Ion Iliescu was director between 1979 and 1984. Iliescu's office was located on the first floor. The Peasants Party encountered considerable opposition from the municipal authorities when it tried to take over the building at the beginning of 1990. At the time, however, it attributed this obstruction to political ill will. On 14 June, the staff working in the headquarters building were violently ejected by miners who had in their possession oxyacetylene cutting equipment. The miners proceeded to hack into the wall of a room which had previously served as Iliescu's office. Hidden behind the brickwork was revealed an iron safe. This was duly burnt open by the miners and the contents of the safe, believed to consist of papers, were removed.

Having received formal thanks from President Iliescu the miners and other workers departed from Bucharest on 15 June. Behind them, they left perhaps as many as 21 dead and 650 injured. Quite what they had otherwise achieved is uncertain. The opposition parties and press speedily recovered from the battery of the preceding days and vigorously renewed their criticism of the government. The liberal Minister of Education, Mihai Sora, resigned in protest at the invasion of teaching institutions and various foreign aid packages to Romania were halted. All that had been proved was that Iliescu had a private army which came at his beck and that he had succeeded in reforming the *securitate*. Most probably, that was simply all which was intended: a display of paramilitary power in the capital for the benefit of other politicians. Just as the case of the safe in the wall smells of knavery in high places, so the entire sequence of events between 13–15 June has the same rancorous hint of a conspiracy at the top. As Laszlo Toekes put it, using the language of Biblical mystery:

> I venture to say that Iliescu is struggling in a dark power system ... The military, the *securitate*, the old *nomenklatura* and power relations, as well as dark hidden secrets, indicated perhaps that he had to make a compromise ... Either from weakness or from so-called political rationale, he chose to conform.[28]

Toekes's assessment was typically obscure and characteristically shrewd. Romanian politics had moved outside the bounds of legality, of constitutional practice, and of proper judicial enforcement. It had become reduced instead to a contest for raw power, fought out on the streets by client groups in the pursuit of shadowy political goals. In this respect, there is a close analogy to the interwar period when the collapse of parliamentary government gave way to repeated disorder and to demonstrations of political muscle on the streets of the capital. Seen in this light, Iliescu's assertion that the violence of June was the work of Iron Guard legionaries was not entirely inappropriate.

NOTES

1. SWB/EE (25 January 1990).
2. King Michael was denied the right to enter Romania on 12 April 1990. He was subsequently given a Romanian visa in December 1990, but was ejected 12 hours after his arrival on Christmas Day.
3. Statement of Ministry of the Interior, given in SWB/EE (17 August 1990).
4. SWB/EE (5 April 1990; 16 June 1990).
5. RFE/REE (20 July 1990).
6. At least, following the dispersal of the demonstration in June 1990 there were no prosecutions of persons for these offences: Helsinki Watch, *Romania. Aftermath to the June Violence in Bucharest* (New York and Washington, DC: Helsinki Watch, 1 May 1991), p. 15.
7. Iliescu later apologized for this remark.
8. *Baricada* (7 August 1990). Possibly, some of Draghici's troops were recruited in Hungary.
9. *22* (16 November 1990).
10. I owe this information to a senior councillor appointed by Petre Roman.
11. The Dacia is based on the old Renault 9 design and is one of the few mass production vehicles capable of coping with Romanian roads.

12. *East Europe and USSR Agriculture and Food Monthly* (March 1991), pp. 15–16.
13. The first round of price increases affected non-essential goods; the second, deferred from January 1991, affected foodstuffs.
14. Such demonstrations occurred in the summer of 1990 at Turnu Severin and at Sfintu Gheorghe. On the reappearance of the Ceausescu cult, RFE/REE (31 May 1991).
15. A widespread problem in all of Eastern Europe is the extent of private savings, which is a legacy of the period when private purchasing power outstripped availability of goods. If these savings are released too rapidly into the economy, they will precipitate both inflation and a balance of payments crisis.
16. *Kapu* (July– August 1990), p. 18.
17. Iliescu was later to complain that not all NCRFTU branches had responded to his call for help on 13 June.
18. Victor Stanculescu was eventually moved in April 1991 to the Ministry of Industry.
19. The head of the RIS in Tirgu Mures, Alexandru Puscas, is thus allegedly a former employee of the *securitate*.
20. *Romania Libera* (25–26 May 1990).
21. In a style reminiscent of the Ceausescu years, *Romania Mare* frequently slandered opponents of the government and corroborated its attacks with detailed material coming from highly informed but unattributed sources.
22. SWB/EE (28 July 1990).
23. Letter of Head of Unit, Directorate General External Relations, Commission of the European Community (5 February 1991). Aid had been cut off by the EC on 14 June 1990 and its restoration had been made conditional on significant steps being taken towards political pluralism.
24. *Romania Libera* (30 November 1990).
25. The charter of trains normally requires at least three days notice in Romania, unless (as appears to have happened on 13 June) direct instructions are received from the Transport Ministry.
26. *Dreptatea* (27 September 1990).
27. United Nations, Economic and Social Council, *Rapport sur la situation des droits de l'homme en Roumanie* (E/CN.4/1991/30), p. 13.
28. Budapest TV (17 June 1990), cited in RFE/REE (6 July 1990). A justification of the miners' assault on Bucharest was published in the *Sunday Times* (1 July 1990) by the Labour MP, George Galloway. His article was subsequently reprinted in the NSF daily, *Azi* (8 August 1990). An equally intelligent assessment along much the same lines is given in the Spartacist *Workers Vanguard* (29 June 1990).

17

'A HOPELESS TURMOIL'

No country is a slave to its past, condemned as in some Nietzschean nightmare always to re-live previous episodes in its national history. It would thus be mistaken to believe that Romania is bound ineluctably to return to the cycle of violence and dictatorship which has distinguished its political experiences over the last century. Nevertheless, the revolution of 1989 did not suddenly give Romania a clean sheet upon which to draw a new future. Older traditions, as well as older politicians, rapidly reappeared to haunt the political round and to impel the country away from the bright vision of a modern, liberal democracy. Thus, almost uniquely in Eastern Europe, Romania failed to make the transition from totalitarianism to parliamentary rule.

The initial failure of democracy to take root in Romania owes much to its ingrained political culture. Historically, politics has been the preserve of an elite: either a few thousand landowners as in the last century, or the coterie of politicians round the king as in the interwar period. The educated classes have tended to defer to their political masters, accepting preferment as the reward for compliance. Any hopes that this situation might change in the post-war years were rapidly dispelled by the unique tyranny of the Ceausescu government. Among the bourgeoisie and intelligentsia, the prevailing trend was disengagement and a retreat into the private world. Politics was perceived by this section of society as the preserve of a small body of party functionaries, who were remote from influence but whom one had ritually to applaud. Thus there never developed within Romania an 'alternative society' of dissidents, independent trade unions leaders and sophisticated *samizdat* readers.

When Ceausescu fell, therefore, the only group sufficiently well organized to take power were the disaffected party veterans. Although in order to bolster their own image, these politicans subsequently gave out that they had for long plotted Ceausescu's downfall, the revolution of 1989 was entirely spontaneous and popular. It originated in Transylvania and was carried by a tide of resentment to the streets of the capital. Nevertheless, the greater experience of the old party bosses and their close links to the army and *securitate* allowed them to take power in the political vacuum which succeeded Ceausescu's flight. The 'survivalist' regime of ex-communists, inaugurated in the Central Committee Building on the afternoon of 22 December, became the government of the National Salvation Front.

The National Salvation Front consolidated its position by relying upon techniques inherited both from the Ceausescu period and from the interwar years. In the first months after the revolution, the NSF established a hierarchical cell structure of councils as a way of building its authority in the localities. Reviving the old traditions of bureaucratic patronage, it sought also to retain its supporters both within the government and the regional administration. At the same time, the Front increasingly relied upon its own bands of loyalists to intimidate the opposition, and it used force rather than arguments to convince its critics. Political debate thus took second place to a contest for power on the streets, reminiscent both of the 1930s and of the immediate post-war period. The resort to these crude methods had resulted by the summer of 1990 in a degree of violence sufficient to consume its own practitioners.

The election campaign witnessed the widespread use of methods inherited from the interwar period: ballot-rigging; the harassment of opposition politicians; and manipulation of the media. As it turned out, the NSF had no need to rely on these techniques. It presented superficially attractive policies, while simultaneously delivering its appeal to Romanian exceptionalism. The Front's repudiation of western-style programmes proved of decisive interest to an electorate which was deeply impressed by its own uniqueness as a nation and still fearful of European capitalism. By arguing that Romania should not adopt western norms of economic organization, but should try to follow an easier 'Romanian way', the NSF exploited the fears and prejudices of an immature electorate.

The danger of Romanian exceptionialism is that it may easily degenerate into the type of crude nationalism which distinguished interwar Romanian politics. This sort of shift was evident even as early as March 1990 in the city of Tirgu Mures. It was also unmistakeably apparent in the pages of the weekly *Romania Mare*, which espoused openly anti-Hungarian, anti-Gypsy and anti-Semitic programmes. *Romania Mare* enjoyed from its inception in June 1990 a circulation of half a million copies. Its editorial team was led by Eugen Barbu and Corneliu Tudor, two of the most notorious anti-Semites of the Ceausescu period. Almost certainly, *Romania Mare* may be held responsible for a recrudescence of synagogue burning and of graveyard desecration. Equally alarming was the continued influence of the quasi-legionary *Vatra*, and the consistent failure of the government either to curb or to condemn its extremist rhetoric.

Owing to the essential weakness of the NSF government, to its internal rivalries, and to its limited control over large areas of the country, Romania might go in two directions: either towards anarchy compounded by xenophobic violence; or into a 'second revolution'. The latter is now more likely than the former. Firstly, Romania has in the 1990s what it lacked in 1989: an 'alternative society' of dissident intellectuals and democratic trade union leaders, and an articulate opposition press. There are over 900 journals and daily newspapers in Romania, and only a few of these are uncritically pro-government. Although the opposition press still largely substitutes polemic for investigative writing, it has contributed to a sophistication both of popular perceptions and of the vocabulary of politics. Secondly, the burgeoning opposition groups are assuming an increasingly defiant stance and know, after the incident with the miners, that they hold the moral high ground of politics. They enjoy the backing of a large section of the army, particularly among the substantial group which previously backed the Military Democratization Committee. The formation in autumn 1990 of new umbrella groups such as the Democratic Anti-totalitarian Forum (subsequently renamed the National Convention for the Establishment of Democracy) and the Civic Alliance, also suggests a new sense of purpose on the part of the hitherto fragmented opposition. When popular frustrations build up, as they surely will given the poor prospects for economic recovery, the various dissident and opposition groups can expect a groundswell of support in their favour.

It remains to be seen, however, whether the scale of hardship will be sufficient to overcome the traditional distrust of workers for intellectuals and students, and of the labouring classes for the urban bourgeoisie. The evidence suggests, however, that it may. The rapid growth of the *Fratia* trade union, which claims a membership of three million, and the emergence of a second powerful democratic federation of labour, the *Alfa*, certainly suggests that the NSF cannot hope to rely on the loyalty of the Romanian working class. Even the miners may no longer be reckoned the docile instruments of the government. At a remarkable meeting held in Brasov in September 1990 under the auspices of the Group for Social Dialogue, Miron Cosma, the leader of the Jiu Valley miners' union, embraced the student leader, Marian Munteanu, who a few months before had almost been killed by miners in Bucharest. Cosma explained that the miners had been 'the first victims' of the events in June, having 'fallen into the trap' laid by the government.[1] By bringing the miners into the streets of Bucharest in June 1990, and employing them for political purposes of his own, Ion Iliescu may well have alienated one of his most important groups of supporters.

The 'second revolution' could be bloody. Romanian revolutions, be they in 1907 or 1989, usually have been. The country's politics has traditionally lacked mechanisms for achieving peaceful change and for resolving conflict in an orderly fashion. For most of the nineteenth and twentieth centuries, therefore, Romania laboured under a false constitutionalism which prevented popular frustrations being mollified through democratic renewal or a change of government. Thus, resentment was bottled up until it burst out altogether in a flood of bloodletting.

The NSF has not noticeably departed from the traditions of its predecessors. Romania is still a facade democracy where the possibility of effecting change by peaceful constitutional means is remote. The danger is that post-revolutionary Romania seems to have missed out the 'nineteenth century' phase, when control was exercised by a strong, arbitrating monarch. Instead, it is already in a dangerous 'Carolist phase', where the head of state is tainted by partiality, where the political leadership is divided, and where power on a local level has already reached a high degree of fragmentation. The day of reckoning may not be far off. Either the government will have to restructure itself to accommodate leaders of the opposition, or it will have to resort to increasingly brutal, and futile, methods of political coercion.

It is to the shame of the National Salvation Front that it has retained the worst traditions and techniques of the pre-communist period. It has thus reinvented the 'politics of illusion', while proclaiming its commitment to democracy and to freedom. Romania now has a parliament, elections, and an independent judiciary. Its leaders earnestly discuss the shape of the new constitution.[2] Reality, however, keeps on breaking through the thin veneer of parliamentary democracy, just as it did in the last century and between the wars. Conspicuously rigged elections, the retention of a secret police, the intimidation of opposition leaders and newspapers, the resort to private paramilitaries, the reappearance of xenophobic nationalism, and a relentless campaign of disinformation conducted by ministers and the state-run media alike, all give the lie to the democratic facade erected by the new regime.

In his searing criticism of the Romanian National Liberal government, Constantin Radulescu-Motru wrote in 1924 that it had adopted 'glorious urban institutions' and 'liberal, democratic techniques'. Yet, as he pointed out, this was all sham; behind the facade the 'habits of the past' persisted in the form of ballot-stuffing, clientage, anti-Semitism, and corruption. As a result, the political life of Romania had been reduced to 'a hopeless turmoil'. Almost 70 years later, precisely the same charges may be laid on the government of the National Salvation Front and the same consequence observed.

NOTES

1. RFE/REE (14 December 1991).
2. A constitution providing for a liberal democracy, although with strong powers retained by the President, was approved by parliament in November 1991 and endorsed in a referendum held on 8 December with 76 per cent support.

EPILOGUE:
ROMANIA IN 1991–92

Romanians experienced in 1991–2 a steadily worsening economic situation. In the first six months of 1991, the price of consumer goods grew at an annual rate of over 100 per cent. Although there was a fall in the rate of inflation after the round of price increases in April 1991, the cost of living continued to rise both uncontrollably and far in excess of salary increases. The average monthly wage at the end of 1991, 10,000 lei, was only enough to buy three pairs of shoes or a winter coat. One kilo of pork cost 400 lei, a loaf of bread 25 lei, and eggs 14 lei apiece.[1] Unemployment likewise grew sharply, and is thought to have more than doubled during the calendar year to an official figure of 300,000.[2] Industrial production continued to fall. Figures released at the end of 1991 indicated that output had declined by about a third over the previous year. As a consequence of falling production, many factories were put on short-time working with a corresponding reduction in the wage paid to employees.

In the countryside, the uncertainties attending the government's privatization of agriculture resulted in similar decline. In the autumn of 1991, the export of farm produce had to be prohibited for fear that the cities would otherwise starve, and food and fuel were once again rationed. For the first time since the Second World War, Romania had to import cereals. The admission in January 1992 by the Minister of Agriculture that over half the country's eight million hectares of cornfields had not been ploughed for spring sowing, suggested that further falls in agricultural production might be expected.[3]

Romania's continued economic misfortune drove many of its inhabitants to seek refuge abroad. Figures released by the General Passport Directorate in the last months of 1991 indicated that as many as half a million Romanian passport-holders had already left the country. In addition, many thousands of Gypsies are believed to have crossed into neighbouring Hungary and Czechoslovakia without proper papers. Throughout Central Europe, both railway terminals and police stations bore witness to the flood of Romanians seeking work abroad as illegal migrants.

Despite the hopelessness felt by most Romanians, the National Salvation Front retained its position as the leading political force within the country. Opinion polls conducted during the summer of 1991 recorded the large support still enjoyed by the NSF. In the local elections held in February 1992, NSF candidates secured an overall 57.8 per cent of the poll: only a few percentage points below the landslide election result in May 1990. By contrast, the opposition umbrella group, the Democratic Convention, obtained a paltry 8.2 per cent. There can be no doubt that in the parliamentary elections likely to be held in mid-1992 the NSF will once again form the party of government.

The continued success of the NSF in retaining a popular mandate may be partly explained by the lack of a convincing opposition. In order to combat the perceived hegemony of the NSF, the opposition groups and parties combined forces in such organizations as the Antitotalitarian Forum (established August 1990) and, more importantly, the National Convention for the Establishment of Democracy. The NCED or Democratic Convention was formed in December 1990 and was composed of the NLP, NPP, HDUR and various smaller party-political groups. It was later joined by the Civic Alliance, a loose grouping of intellectuals, students, journalists and trade union leaders, which had hitherto operated as an unaffiliated pressure-group for democratic reform. The parties belonging to the Democratic Convention contested the February 1992 local elections on a joint list and under a common symbol.

Despite their success at coalition-building, the opposition parties failed to present the electorate with a credible alternative to the NSF. They were united not by any distinctive and shared policies but only by their determination to unseat the incumbent government. The vast weight of their propaganda was therefore devoted to 'exposing' the past careers of the NSF's leaders and to carping at 'neo-communism'. Additionally, the parties of the Democratic Convention revealed themselves to be both irresolute and easily manipulated. Thus the parliamentary group of the HDUR obtained no support from its coalition partners when criticising the clauses on minority rights in the new Romanian constitution. For its part, the National Liberal Party allowed itself to be compromised by agreeing in September 1991 to join an NSF-led cabinet. At the time, the defection of the NLP put the very survival of the Democratic Convention in doubt. In its eagerness to win for itself a place in the government, the National Peasants Party subsequently toned down its own criticism of the NSF.

Throughout 1991 the principal purpose of the NSF's leaders remained as it had been from the time of the Front's inception: to retain a position of power and influence for themselves and for their supporters in the old communist *nomenklatura*. The determination of the Front to hold on to power at any price meant that it refused to adopt a narrow political position, preferring instead to trim its policies so as to meet the needs of the moment. Flexibility and ambiguity remained, therefore, hallmarks of the NSF's political trade. Thus, on the one hand, the NSF presented itself as a moderate party of reform which alone possessed the political experience and technical expertise to steer the country. (The appointment of new ministers was customarily accompanied by statements alluding to their solidly democratic and liberal credentials.) On the other, the parliamentary caucus of the NSF, which was dominated by Alexandru Birladeanu and Dan Martian, inveighed against the human cost of rapid marketization and advocated a very gradual economic reform. For their part, other NSF leaders frequently espoused the same xenophobic and crudely nationalist positions as those championed by the *Vatra* and *Romania Mare*. The Hungarian minority in Transylvania was singled out for special condemnation by NSF leaders who frequently referred to plots aimed at carving out an autonomous Hungarian district in the region. In a manner entirely reminiscent of Ceausescu, at the very height of the disorder in Bucharest during September 1991 Prime Minister Roman called attention to the threat of Hungarian irredentism and announced the 'discovery' of a Hungarian-Transylvanian government-in-exile.

During 1991, the first steps were announced to refound the Romanian economy on the basis of a free market. In February and August respectively, programmes were announced to reform landholding and to privatize industry. Both schemes were, however, flawed by the continued interest of the NSF both to remain in overall control of the national economy and to embed its own supporters in the nascent private sector. The government's plans for privatization thus envisaged the sale of only 53 per cent of state enterprises. The commanding heights of the economy – transport, communications, energy, munitions and mining – were to remain in state ownership. Shares in businesses scheduled for privatization were to be divided unequally between Private Ownership Funds (POFs), which received 30 per cent of the allocation, and State Ownership Funds (SOFs), which held the remaining 70 per cent. It was proposed that when businesses were privatized, their shares would be distributed by the POFs to the population at large, and that these shares might then be freely traded on a new Stock Exchange. The 70 per cent of shares retained by the SOFs would be sold off piecemeal over a span of seven years.

A rapid breakthrough to privatization was thus neither anticipated nor planned. The state would instead retain such 'strategic control' of the economy that even Alexandru Birladeanu warned of the risk of étatism.[4] Moreover, it seemed unlikely that the government would meet the unambitious timetable set for the sale of shares by the SOFs. As late as December 1991, only six firms out of a possible 6000 had been identified as suitable for privatization. It was thought at the time that the slow sell-off of shares was designed to ensure that industry passed into the hands of the wealthier part of the population rather than to foreign or institutional investors (though West European firms were understandably reluctant to invest in Romania). Thus, the true outcome may be that by the time the process of privatization is completed, the Romanian economy will be owned by those who prospered under communism.

A similar interest in retaining economic control impeded plans for land reform. The land law passed in February 1991 established that Romanians might hold no more than ten hectares of private agricultural land.[5] Even then, ownership was conditional upon the land's proper cultivation and strict limits were imposed on the sale of properties. Nor did the land law envisage the dismemberment of collectives and state farms. These were instead to be refounded as cooperative associations and their existing management structures were to be retained. Strong informal pressure was applied on peasants who attempted to leave cooperatives and to set up as independent farmers. But for a change of name the older structure of economic relationships in the countryside thus survived largely intact.

The success of the NSF in retaining both popular support and a high degree of control over the economic infrastructure was vitiated by factional fighting inside the government. Within the NSF leadership an open split developed between President Iliescu and Prime Minister Roman. The conflict was not, as was frequently reported, over the pace of economic change. By the middle of 1991 Iliescu had clearly accepted the inevitability of market reforms, and the successor he eventually chose to replace Roman had a reputation as an economic liberal. It seems more likely that Iliescu perceived Roman as a personal rival with a strong body of independent support in the administration and as a potential candidate for the office of President. Iliescu's misgivings were shared by Alexandru Birladeanu, who accused Roman of attempting to make himself a 'dictator'.[6]

The conflict between Iliescu and Roman certainly influenced the outcome of the 'miners' rebellion' in September 1991. It may even have been the cause of this new outbreak of collective violence. Whether, however, the miners were on this occasion being manipulated by factions within the government, or whether their descent on the capital was entirely spontaneous, must for the time being remain uncertain.

During the first half of September there had been lengthy talks between union leaders and government representatives over wages and conditions in the Jiu Valley. On 17 September, a broad measure of agreement was reached by the two sides. However, a week later, on 23 September, a general strike was called in the Jiu Valley with the aim of forcing a parliamentary delegation to inspect the region. On the evening of the next day, between five and ten thousand miners stormed Petrosani railway station. Having hijacked two trains, the miners made their way to Bucharest. At this stage, the expressed aim of the miners' leader, Miron Cosma, was simply to force the dismissal of Roman as Prime Minister. Cosma is known to have close personal contacts with Iliescu and to have acted on Iliescu's behalf during the miners' previous descent on the capital in June 1990. Unconfirmed reports claim that Cosma was also being blackmailed for having killed a woman in a car accident several months previously.[7]

Having arrived in Bucharest on the afternoon of 25 September, the miners made several attacks on government buildings, on the headquarters of Romanian television, and on the parliament. They were repelled by units of the gendarmerie and by tear-gas. In contrast to the events of June 1990, the miners were on this occasion joined by students and were actually welcomed into University Square by Marian Munteanu. Munteanu went so far as to put on a miner's helmet and to greet Cosma as his 'brother'.

As the fighting in the capital worsened, the rioters began to couple Iliescu's name to Roman's and to demand the resignation of both. On 27 September, a crowd of several thousand attempted to storm the

Cotroceni Palace, which is the President's official residence. As a supporter of Iliescu, Cosma endeavoured to deflect anger away from the President. He announced that he was negotiating with Iliescu and that valuable concessions had already been won. Following the announcement of Roman's resignation on 26 September, Cosma advised the miners to return home since their aims had now been accomplished. It was only on the evening of 27 September, however, that the miners left Bucharest. The three days of fighting had left at least three people dead and almost five hundred injured. In order to forestall any further outbreak of disorder, a price freeze was introduced on basic foods.

Despite the calls for his own resignation, Iliescu skilfully exploited the disorder in the capital and was able to force Roman from power. On 26 September, several communiqués emanating from the President's office announced that the Prime Minister and cabinet had resigned in order 'to facilitate a political solution to the crisis'.[8] Later that day, however, Roman denied that he had resigned and claimed instead that he intended to remain in office 'as long as law and order were not restored'. He also described the miners' action as 'a movement that turned into a coup d'etat, a kind of communist putsch coming from the bottom'. Other ministers told of how they had learned of the cabinet's resignation from the radio.[9]

In a communiqué published on 26 September, the President promised to establish a government of 'broad national opening'. Over the next week, Iliescu held meetings with leaders of the NSF and the opposition parties over the composition of the new government. On 1 October, Iliescu announced that he had asked Theodor Stolojan to form a government. A fortnight later, Stolojan presented his new cabinet to parliament. An important omission from the new government was General Victor Stanculescu, which at the time suggested that the influence of the army in Romanian politics was in decline.[10]

Although the new cabinet contained three members of the National Liberal Party, it was emphatically not the government of 'broad national opening' promised by Iliescu. The team of 21 ministers contained nine representatives of the NSF and seven 'independents', most of whom had previously been closely associated with the NSF. The Ecological Movement of Romania and the Democratic Agrarian Party, which had one minister apiece in the new government, were also satellite parties of the NSF. The new Prime Minister, Theodor

Stolojan, had himself been Minister of Finance under Roman until April 1991 after which he had become head of the National Privatization Agency. Although Stolojan claimed never to have been a member of the NSF, Roman subsequently disclosed that he was 'our man'.[11]

The new Prime Minister (born 1943) certainly enjoyed a reputation as an economic liberal and as an enthusiastic advocate of rapid marketization. His background during the communist period is less certain. Nevertheless, it does seem that Stolojan had enjoyed a spectacular career under Ceausescu. As Deputy Director of the Currency Convertibility Department of the Ministry of Finance in the early 1980s, he had been involved in Ceausescu's programme to repay all Romania's foreign debt. In 1987 he had been appointed Director of the International Relations Department and of the Foreign Exchange Department of the Ministry of Finance. He had also been a principal organizer for the party in the same ministry. Although these aspects of Stolojan's career tell us little about his present commitment to democratic reform, they do suggest that he may share along with the leadership of the NSF a strongly survivalist instinct.

February 1992

NOTES

1. *Insight: East European Business Report,* January 1992.
2. Government figures for unemployment are notoriously unreliable since they only include those who are jobless, without pay, and actively seeking work. A large number of the unemployed are, however, retained on the payroll of their former workplace and given a very reduced salary. Thus, they do not appear on official statistics.
3. RFE/Radio Liberty Daily Report, no 5, 9 January 1992, citing Petre Marculescu in *Dimineata,* 3 January 1992.
4. *Romania Libera,* 17 July 1991.
5. A future ceiling of 100 hectares was promised.
6. *Adevarul* 30 March 1991, cited RFE *Research Report* 3 January 1992.
7. RFE/REE 18 October 1991.
8. The communiqués were based on decisions allegedly taken by the Supreme Defence Council, a security organ under the chairmanship of the President and of which the Prime Minister is also an *ex officio* member.
9. RFE/REE 18 October 1991; Eastern Europe Newsletter 7 October 1991.
10. As Stanculescu had been courting the NLP for a number of months and had established personal links with the exiled King Michael, he had already become a frequent target of abuse in the NSF press.
11. RFE/REE 8 November 1991.

POLAND

USSR

HUNGARY

BUKOVINA

MOLDAVIA

BESSARABIA

Iasi •

TRANSYLVANIA

WALLACHIA

• Bucharest

BLACK SEA

YUGOSLAVIA

SOUTHERN DOBRUDJA

BULGARIA

**Romania after the
First World War**

Area acquired 1918-1920

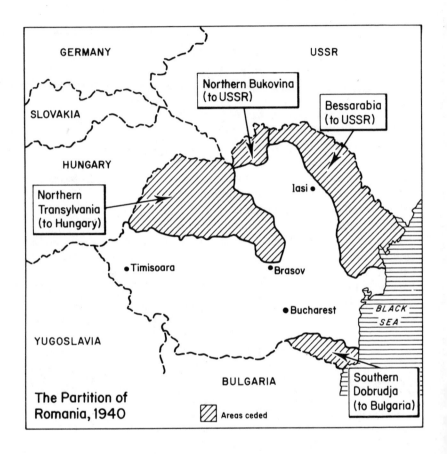

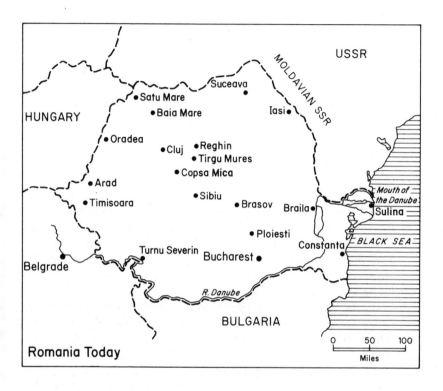

Romania Today

ADVICE AND
FURTHER READING

Romania has the worst historical literature of any East European country. Its own writers were grievously affected by a blind nationalism in the interwar years, and by a slavish conformity to ideology in the communist period. In addition, few western historians have turned their attention to Romania's past. Incredibly therefore, the fullest account of the history of Romania is still R.W. Seton Watson's *History of the Roumanians*, first published by Cambridge University Press in 1934. The reader may, however, profit from D. Chirot's *Social Change in a Peripheral Society: The Creation of a Balkan Colony* (New York: Academic Press, 1976), which is more readable than its title suggests, from Georges Castellan's *A History of the Romanians* (Boulder and New York: East European Monographs, 1989), which relies too heavily on older Romanian works and also lacks an index, and from Vlad Georgescu's *The Romanians: A History* (London: I.B. Tauris, 1991).

On the whole, any English language work published in Romania before 1990 is not worth reading since it will consist mainly of the achievements and antecedents of the Communist Party. A notable exception is Dinu Giurescu's *Illustrated History of the Romanian People* (Bucharest: Editura Sport-Turism, 1982), providing one is prepared to scour between the lines. *A Concise History of Romania*, written by Andrei Otetea (London: Robert Hale, 1985), has an interesting commentary by Andrew MacKenzie which includes the memorable line, 'It is obvious to me, as a visitor to Romania for 17 years, that conditions have greatly improved there and the regime is more relaxed than it was.' MacKenzie also demonstrates Ceausescu's popularity by reference to the 'sustained applause' which he receives at conferences. One is reminded of Robert Maxwell's question to Ceausescu in 1983, 'What has – in your opinion – made you so popular with the Romanians?'

Specific twentieth-century developments are better served. David Mitrany, *The Land and the Peasant in Rumania* (London: Oxford University Press, 1930) is exhaustive and exhausting; far more tractable is its successor volume by Henry Roberts, *Rumania. Political Problems of an Agrarian State* (New Haven: Yale University Press, 1951), which encompasses the politics of the interwar years. C.A. Macartney, *Hungary and Her Successors 1919–1937* (London: Oxford University Press, 1937) provides useful material on Transylvania, although from a strongly 'magyarophile' position.

There is little English language literature on the Iron Guard and the interested reader is best referred to general studies on interwar fascism, most notably Eugen Weber and Hans Rogger, *The European Right: A Historical Profile* (Berkeley: University of California Press, 1965) and Peter Sugar, *Native Fascism in the Successor States 1918–1945* (Santa Barbara: ABC Clio, 1971). There is useful material also in Hugh Seton Watson's *Eastern Europe Between the Wars 1918–1941* (Cambridge: Cambridge University Press, 1945). The legionary movement in exile in Spain, Latin American and the United States has supported the publication of a number of legionary works, including C.Z. Codreanu's *For My Legionaries* (Madrid: Editura Libertatea, 1976). Incredibly, Alexander E. Ronnett's *Romanian Nationalism: The Legionary Movement*, which is a vindication of the Iron Guard, was published by Loyola University Press of Chicago in 1974.

For the communist and Ceausescu periods, the reader is referred to Kenneth Jowitt, *Revolutionary Breakthroughs and National Development: The Case of Romania* (Berkeley and Los Angeles: University of California Press, 1971); Michael Shafir, *Romania, Politics, Economics and Society* (London: Frances Pinter, 1985); Robert R. King, *History of the Romanian Communist Party* (Stanford: Hoover Institution Press, 1980); Dinu Giurescu, *The Razing of Romania's Past* (New York: World Monuments Fund, 1989); and Trond Gilberg, *Nationalism and Communism in Romania* (Boulder and Oxford: Westview Press, 1990). The communist takeover is ably discussed by Ghita Ionescu, *Communism in Rumania 1944–1962* (London: Oxford University Press, 1964). Due credit should also be paid to Julian Hale, *Ceausescu's Romania* (London: 1971), who shrewdly determined the unpleasant side of Ceausescu when others were busy lauding him, to Mark Almond's incisive *Decline Without Fall: Romania under Ceausescu* (London: Institute for European Defence and Strategic Studies, 1988) and to David Turnock's pioneering studies on the Romanian economy.

The most revealing personal accounts of the Ceausescu years are Ion Mihai Pacepa, *Red Horizons. The Extraordinary Memoirs of a*

Communist Spy Chief (London: Heinemann, 1988); Chief Rabbi Rosen
of Romania's *Dangers, Tests and Miracles* (London: Weidenfeld &
Nicolson, 1990), and David Funderburk, *Pinstripes and Reds*
(Washington, DC: Selous Foundation, 1987). The last is the
reminiscence of a former US ambassador to Bucharest. Study of this
work provides some important clues as to the curious contents of
Pacepa's own autobiography. Laszlo Toekes's autobiography, *With
God, For the People* (London: Hodder & Stoughton, 1990) deals largely
with his own experiences during the Ceausescu period.

Most existing biographies of Ceausescu are the works of
fellow-travellers. Anything written in particular by Hamelet, Newens
or Govender, or published by Pergamon, is to be rejected. The only
English language biographies worth reading are: Mary Ellen Fischer,
Nicolae Ceausescu. A Study in Political Leadership (Boulder & London:
Lynn Rienner Publishers, 1989); Edward Behr, *Kiss the Hand You
Cannot Bite. The Rise and Fall of the Ceausescus* (London: Hamish
Hamilton, 1991); and John Sweeney, *The Life and Evil Times of Nicolae
Ceausescu* (London: Hutchinson, 1991). The first of these is a
heavyweight academic text; the other two are racy but well researched
accounts. For those confident enough to tackle Flemish, Julien
Weverbergh's *Nacht in Roemanie* (Antwerp, 1989) is a mine of
information. Mark Almond's *The Rise and Fall of the Nicolae and Elena
Ceausescu* (London: Chapmans, 1992) and Nestor Ratesh's *Romania:
The Entangled Revolution* (New York: Washington Papers no 152,
Praeger, 1991) both appeared too late for any of their conclusions to be
included in this account.

The most recent developments in Romanian politics have an uneven
literature. The best source for current trends is the weekly Radio Free
Europe/Report on Eastern Europe which replaces the Background
Reports and Situation Reports current until the end of 1989. Radio
Free Europe has a highly informed group of researchers and I am
particularly indebted to material written by Paul Gafton, Dan Ionescu,
Marvin Jackson, Judith Pataki, Carmen Pompey, Michael Shafir,
Vladimir Socor, Crisula Stefanescu, and Mihai Sturdza. Additional
'digested' material is most readily available in the *Eastern Europe
Newsletter*.

A number of books have appeared dealing specifically with the
Christmas Revolution. Most of these are straightforward blow-by-
blow accounts, although for the quality of its photos *Libertate. De
Roemeense Revolutie* (Amsterdam: Tweede Wereld Centrum, 1990)

deserves mention. The first analytical account of the revolution was provided by Anneli Ute Gabanyi, *Die unvollendete Revolution. Rumanien zwischen Diktatur und Demokratie* (Munich, 1990), extracts from which have also been published in the journal *Sudosteuropa*. Gabanyi's account was composed hastily however, and has thus a reputation for inaccuracy. The 'instant-analysis' given by Michel Castex, *Un mensonge gros comme le siecle. Histoire d'une manipulation* (Paris, 1990), which presents the revolution as a KGB plot, is also unreliable.

Romanian accounts of the revolution which I have seen are poor and superficial: *Dosare ale Revolutiei* (Cluj: Revista Tribuna, 1990); *Cronica Insingerata a Bucurestiului in Revolutie* (Bucharest: Tineretul Liber, 1990); and *Romania December 1989–December 1990*, published by the Romanian newsagency Rompres. Perhaps there are other Romanian works available, but given the present standards of distribution it is hard to know what books have been published. The only Hungarian work on this period with which I am familiar is *A Conducator Vegnapjai* (Budapest: MTI Newsagency, 1990) which contains a pastiche of indiscriminately assembled press items. George Galloway and Bob Wylie's paperback, *Downfall. The Ceausescus and the Romanian Revolution* (London: Futura 1991), is unintentionally a conduit for NSF disinformation. Very little of it can be believed.

Before moving on to sources for current affairs, I would like to add a few cautionary words. Firstly, after decades in which they were subject to extreme political manipulation, many Romanians are now convinced that nothing ever happens by accident. Random events are thus conjoined to develop elaborate conspiracy theories which are immediately believed. This results in the most extraordinary explanations for events and assurances that the explanations are absolutely true. The plots in time will find their way into the Romanian media and thence into the western press. Secondly, Romania is full of rumours which are all largely believed by the population, and which are sharpened by a tendency towards exaggeration. Many Romanians have friends who know girls raped by Nicu Ceausescu; others have close information that Gypsies steal children and that Hungarian restaurants serve up babies. The visitor to Romania is strongly recommended before departure to read Steven Sampson, 'Rumours in Socialist Romania', *Survey*, vol. 28, no. 4 (1984) pp. 142-64. Finally, the present Romanian government has chosen to exploit the tendency towards conspiracy theory and rumour-mongering by making up myths of its own, which it is highly adept at disseminating. The

disinformation emanating out of Bucharest is intended to sow
confusion and slander at home and abroad, and to buttress the
authority of the NSF government. Michael Shafirs 'Preparing for the
Future by Revising the Past' in RFE/REE, 12 October 1990, indicates
the broad purpose behind much of the present government's
manipulation of the media.

With these cautionary words, the reader is directed to the BBC
Summary of World Broadcasts, which provides an English-language
resumé of the most important news items transmitted out of Romania,
to the daily survey published by Radio Free Europe, and to the
quarterly *East European Reporter*, which includes a wide selection of
sources and interviews with reliable commentaries.

In the making of this book, I have relied extensively on *Romania
Libera* and on such other of the 900 Romanian newspapers and
weeklies as I have been able to obtain since the revolution. The
Transylvanian Hungarian press, most notably *Nepujsag* and *Haromszek*,
has also proved of particular value. Typically though, much of my
information is provided by private sources, with all the limitations
which this implies.

Abbreviations Used in the Notes

RFE	*Radio Free Europe*
RFE/BR	*RFE Background Report*
RFE/REE	*RFE Report on Eastern Europe*
RFE/SR	*RFE Situation Report*
SWB/EE	*BBC Summary of World Broadcasts (Eastern Europe)*

Index

abortion, 44, 45, 81, 132
Adevarul, 134, 169
Afghanistan
agriculture, 9, 10, 47, 20, 33, 62, 62, 63, 66-71, 162, 163, 180-84, 196, 199
agro-industrial complexes – *see* systematization
AIDS, 80-2
Alba Iulia, 16, 152
Alfa, 194
Amphitheatre, 41
Anti-Communist Zone, 166, 178-9, 186
Antitotalitarian Forum – *see* Democratic Antitotalitarian Forum
Antonescu, Marshal Ion, 26, 27, 29, 31, 32, 46, 50
Apostol, Gheorghe, 39, 40, 75
Apostol, Vasile, 143
Arad, 99, 103, 110
Ardeleanu, General Vasile, 84, 105, 107, 109
Armenians, 10, 156, 159
army, 53, 62, 92, 93, 95-97, 102-11, 116, 123, 126, 131, 137, 156, 174-8, 186, 187, 192, 201
Association of Former Political Prisoners, 31
Averescu, General Alexander, 19

Baia Mare, 78, 180
Baneasa, 56, 125, 188
Barbu, Eugen, 193
BBC, 87
Bessarabia, 3-5, 14, 15, 17, 22, 35, 47
Blrladeanu, Alexandru, 75, 107, 108, 164, 164, 183, 184, 198-200
black market, 58, 65
Blandiana, Ana, 57, 58, 108, 111, 126, 131, 141, 169, 179
Bobu, Emil, 105, 114, 115, 133
Bolyai University, 145, 148, 158
Bostina, Constantin, 135

bourgeoisie, 11, 13, 59, 191
Braila, 85, 169
Brasov, 54, 73, 83, 89, 97, 103, 110, 125, 170, 176, 180, 181, 194
Bratianu family, 12
Brezhnev, Leonid, 41
Brucan, Silviu, 75, 76, 77, 108, 112, 113, 115, 116, 119, 120, 125-9, 137, 140, 141, 164, 165
Bucharest, 5, 6, 11, 19, 28, 30, 37, 38, 50, 53, 66, 67, 74, 75, 79, 80, 89, 92, 95, 96, 99-11, 116, 118, 119, 122, 125, 128, 130, 132, 140, 141, 147, 161, 166, 169, 170, 175-82, 186-8, 194, 200, 201; rebuilding of, 66, 67
Budapest, 66, 73, 149, 150, 157
Bukovina, 3, 4, 15, 22, 26
Bulgaria, 80, 91, 92, 99

Calinescu, Ion, 184
Camaresescu, Nicolae, 187
Campeanu, Radu, 162, 169, 170
Canada, 79, 88, 151
Caramitru, Ion, 127
Carol I, King (1881-1914), 2, 12, 21
Carol II, King (1930-40), 14, 20-2, 25, 26
Ceausescu, Elena, 38, 50-3, 56, 60, 94, 95, 102, 105, 114-20, 124, 132, 133, 143
Ceausescu, Ilie, 45, 46, 103, 115
Ceausescu, Marin, 38
Ceausescu, N. Andruta, 38, 143
Ceausescu, Nicolai: background and rise to power, 37-9; popularity, 40-2; political beliefs, 44, 46, 63, 91, 92, 137; foreign policy, 35, 39, 41, 43, 47, 63, 64, 70; use of history, 45, 46, 49; personality cult, 45, 46, 49, 50, 66, 100; presidency, 49; knighthood, 47, 73; and nationalism, 35, 42, 45-8, 64, 71, 72; conspiracies against,